VICTORIAN WOMEN, UNWED MOTHERS AND THE LONDON FOUNDLING HOSPITAL

Victorian Women, Unwed Mothers and the London Foundling Hospital

Jessica A. Sheetz-Nguyen

continuum

Continuum International Publishing Group
The Tower Building
11 York Road
London SE1 7NX

80 Maiden Lane
Suite 704
New York, NY 10038

www.continuumbooks.com

First published 2012

British Library Cataloguing-in-Publication Data
A catalogue record for this book is available from the British Library.

ISBN: HB: 978-1-4411-1092-3
PB: 978-1-4411-4112-5

Library of Congress Cataloging-in-Publication Data
A catalog record for this book is available from the Library of Congress.

Typeset by Fakenham Prepress Solutions, Fakenham, Norfolk NR21 8NN
Printed and bound in Great Britain

For my parents
Mary Helen Reich Sheetz and Gerald Roy Sheetz

Contents

Acknowledgements

This book was born from the lives of Victorian women, mothers, sisters, daughters, aunts and friends. It seeks to give voice to the voiceless in their times of need. Its provenance, however, stems from a summer spent in the archives of Marquette University processing the extensive correspondence of Dorothy Day, foundress of the Catholic Workers Movement. Reading and re-reading about her affection and consideration for the poor created a new sensitivity that I had not before held. Her voice instilled a desire to uncover the lives of those who could not write for themselves. Considerable support from Marquette University's Department of History and Graduate School nurtured the seed of this insight. Their patient guidance and funding enabled me to carry on research in London.

There, I received expert guidance from a young archivist at the Greater London Record Office, Tim Harris, now Head of Access and Buildings at the London Metropolitan Archives, formerly the GLRO. Tim Harris directed me to approach Colin Masters at the Thomas Coram Foundation for access to the Foundling Hospital files dating after (around) 1870, then held in a large steel safe in the basement of the building now housing the Foundling Museum on Brunswick Square. I went for an interview with Mr Masters on a cold and damp January day in 1993. Upon reflection, Mr Masters wanted to know whether the information about to be revealed would be in safe hands. I hope I have lived up to that promise I made on that day. I wish to acknowledge and thank the Coram Foundation for the privileged access I received that year and each year thereafter.

This book comprises about one-third of a larger manuscript, my dissertation entitled '"Just Deserts": Public and Private Institutional Responses to Poverty in Victorian London: Space, Gender, and Agency'. It has taken almost two decades of reflection, teaching and conference papers to come to grips with the Foundling Hospital materials. Inspiration came from my first publication on the subject, in an article entitled: 'Calculus of Respectability: Defining the World of Foundling Hospital Women and Children in Victorian London' published by *Annales de Démographié Historique* in 2007. A portion of this article appears in this book.

Encouragement to submit a proposal and to see it through to publication originated with Lars Tharp, serving at the time as curator at the London Foundling Museum. A summer afternoon brainstorming session with Lars pushed me to take the next step. Further contacts with Caro Howell, now director, at the Foundling Museum added considerable support.

Men and women from the academic community of British Studies in the United States and United Kingdom pushed me along the way as well. These include Anthony Brundage, who shared his focus on the poor laws with me, and Sonya Rose, who first commented on a conference paper at the Midwest Conference on British Studies. I also appreciate the coveted support of Laura Tabili and Lynn Mackay, sisters-in-arms, who sympathized with the plight of an over-worked professor.

Time spent in London, teaching and working with graduate and undergraduate students from the University of Central Oklahoma at the British Library in the summer of 2011 helped me wrestle with the manuscript as I started to prepare it for submission to Continuum Books. I tasked many, including Justin Burch and Stephanie Diaz with reading chapters and identifying places where a lack of clarity appeared. Significantly, Mary Margaret Vick, a student in one of my first women's history classes, contributed over the long run. Mary provided a treasured can-do spirit and many improvements to the text. Several others aided in editing this book, including: Dennis Savill, Michael Greenwood, and Kim Storry. I am grateful to them for their special contributions.

Finally, over the course of 20 years, I received unconditional love and considerable financial support from my parents, sisters and brothers, and my husband Kenneth Minh Nguyen. Without their loyalty, I would not have finished this project.

List of Tables

List of Archival Collections Consulted

London Guildhall Library and Archives
London Metropolitan Archives
Royal London Hospital Archives
Thomas Coram Foundation Archives
Westminster Diocesan Archives

Introduction

In 1859, Secretary of the London Foundling Hospital, John Brownlow, received a letter from a mother of five children requesting acceptance of her illegitimate infant. Barbara F. was 32 years of age and married to William F., Trumpet Major of Her Majesty's 3rd Dragoon Guards then stationed in India.[1] Since she was married with children, she was automatically disqualified as a potential petitioner according to the rules of the institution. Nonetheless, her account is telling, because it portrays a model of everything the successful petitioner was not. The woman had been living with her brother-in-law and his wife at 15 Beaumont Row, Mile End (East of the Tower of London). She was more or less an abandoned wife, because she had not heard from her husband in a long time, causing great anxiety. She left her brother-in-law's house to go to lodgings at 36 George Street, Langham Place, situated just to the west of the British Museum. One night in December, after putting her children to bed at 7 p.m., leaving them unattended, she went to Mile End to find out whether a letter awaited her. She returned about 10.30 p.m. She did not have enough money to take a bus to Tottenham Court Road. Thus, she walked to Farringdon Road where she could catch a ride with the fare money in her pocket. On return to her neighbourhood, she met fellow lodger, Louisa K., whose male companion poured her something to drink. The beverage, whatever it was, got her drunk, and she reported she got 'quite stupid'.[2] The man took her home in a cab. 'Then she found herself pregnant.'[3] She delivered the infant at St Pancras Workhouse. As the mother of a newborn, she was quite miserable; worse, she never saw the man before or after. Not knowing where to turn, she looked to the Foundling Hospital for benefits of training and education for her child.[4] She was, however, ineligible. In the first place, Barbara F. was already married with children. Therefore, if she had gone through the application process, she would need to tell the committee that she could not accept a promise to marry before giving consent to 'c.c.' or criminal conversation. Since she delivered her infant in a workhouse, it was clear she was unemployed. Moreover, she tried to circumvent the rules of the hospital by writing directly to the secretary. Instead, she should have gone to the Guilford Street gate, picked up the application and started the long and tedious process of petitioning for admission of her infant to the most respectable and prestigious charity in the metropolis.

The treatment of and care for indigent women and children in all societies raises a myriad of problems. These issues also stir many debates; consider the recent furore over public health care in the United States. This book, *Victorian Women, Unwed Mothers and the London Foundling Hospital*, tells the story of single mothers who applied to the London Foundling Hospital for admission of their infants. It takes four basic historical and social research questions as its undergirding: (i) What did Victorian London charity workers say poor mothers deserved? (ii) How did wealthy benefactors ration and control their benefits? (iii) How did the concept of 'respectability' influence the benefactors in their selection process for the deserving? (iv) How and under what circumstances did the unwed mothers, who petitioned the London Foundling Hospital for relief of their illegitimate infants, achieve their objectives? These conversations, then as now, challenged social obligations and responsibilities because the question that remains is who will pay and under what circumstances.

The nineteenth-century Foundling Hospital modelled English values and its beneficiaries reflected the same. The institution served as a crucible in which ideas forged together through practice. The large estate located on Brunswick Square provided Victorians with an icon of 'respectability'. Its name was a misnomer. Neither a hospital, nor a poor law workhouse, it did not receive foundlings. It accepted infants from respectable domestics who gave West and North London addresses as their domiciles. The well-funded and privately operated institution presented its public duty as the preservation of infant life; its more clandestine endeavour preserved reputations of women who bore out-of-wedlock infants. Admission of the baby could only occur after the governors of this establishment carefully assessed the mother's reputation by moral measures to see if she met community standards for an impeccable reputation, with the exception of this one fall from grace.

The research and analysis presented in this text departs from the traditional studies of the Foundling Hospital by placing the spotlight squarely on the lives and voices of the lone mothers who the law held solely responsible for their out-of-wedlock infants in the nineteenth century. It sets their lives in place, by situating them on the streets of the metropolis and serving in the homes of the wealthy. It takes their perspective by telling the stories they never had a chance to tell because they were working. It documents their accounts through their petitions to the hospital for assistance. From the packet, the application form, the oral transcripts and letters of recommendation, the tattered lives of exceptionally strong women emerge. The choices they made under the constraints of the Poor Laws and the moral imperatives of society clearly indicate agency and action. By taking a point-by-point account from the mother's perspective, this study compiles data from the decision-making process and analyzes the rationale for abandonment of her infant to this charity. The analysis takes direction from Louis B. Namier, who constructed a sequence of essays based on data profiling the social class and political persuasion of members of the House of Commons in the mid-eighteenth century. Instead of looking at the profiles of powerful individuals, this account creates a collective snapshot of respectable young working-class women, who had been abandoned by the fathers of their infants.[5]

Historiography

The framework for this study departs from earlier scholarship analyzing the eighteenth and nineteenth century Thomas Coram archives that focused on infants and children, developed institutional histories, or explored the lives of women without extrapolated–quantitative data from the petitions. New claims drawn from qualitative and quantitative assessments reveal fresh information about the identities of the mothers and their choices. This collective approach to historical research takes cues from British social history, which offers a rich field of monographs published in the latter half of the twentieth century. Consider E.P. Thompson's *The Making of the English Working Class* (Vintage, 1963), in which he explores the historical agency of printers and publishers as they reshaped political landscapes.

Just under a decade later, Gareth Stedman Jones' *Outcast London: A Study in the Relationship between Classes in Victorian Society* (Oxford, 1971) inspired researchers to start thinking about the question of class and society, taking London as its backdrop. The magisterial history by Lawrence Stone, *The Family, Sex, and Marriage in England, 1500 to 1800* (Harper & Row, 1977), guides scholars in search of the historical and hidden aspects of private lives by incorporating demographic analysis. Stone addresses the issue of pre-nuptial pregnancies, and his understanding of traditional marriages informs the interpretation of data provided by the Foundling Hospital collection. A young man who had promised marriage, cleared the way for pre-marital intercourse. When the betrothed learned she was pregnant, she normally pressed for marriage, but in many instances, the father first abandoned the mother before she gave up her babe to the Foundling Hospital. Here at this nexus we see the mother's strain, pressure and desire to remain 'respectable' in the eyes of society. To be sure, one could not be a part of the middling classes and raise a child as a lone mother.

Two studies are particularly useful for understanding the role social stratification played in creating the middling classes. Leonore Davidoff and Catherine Hall's research, *Family Fortunes* (Chicago, 1987), examines rising middle-class values and gender roles for women; the lady organized the household and men managed civil society. A good supplement for understanding the middle classes is F. M. L. Thompson's *Rise of Respectable Society* (Harvard, 1988), which elaborates on and describes the ideals of the middle classes. Both accounts portray the ideals of the men who judged the women coming to the Foundling Hospital for assistance. By contrast, Judith Walkowitz adds the dimension of gender to the issue of working-class women on the streets of London in *City of Dreadful Delight* (Virago, 1992), wherein she examines 'representations' of the destitute in the era of Jack the Ripper. Most recently, Seth Koven's essential addition to the nexus between charity workers and the poor, *Slumming Sexual and Social Politics in Victorian London* (Princeton, 2004, 2006), takes the perspective of middle-class social explorers in East London. These distinguished scholarly contributions move us closer to understanding the mentality of those who identified the street-bound poor as worthy of reform. Gertrude Himmelfarb's *Poverty and Compassion: The Moral Imagination of the Late Victorians* (Knopf, 1991) provides an intellectual history of the wealthy who worked as change agents in the age of Victoria as she cleverly articulates the theoretical groundwork for understanding the self-help mentality as espoused by Samuel Smiles.

Victorian Women places the world of unwed mothers under the overarching legal construct of the New Poor Laws, passed in 1834, and atop the geo-political and socio-economic landscape of Victorian London. Experts in Victorian poor law studies include Anthony Brundage, Ursula Henriques and Pat Thane. Brundage delivers the most clearly articulated and easy to understand overview of the passage of the New Poor Law amendments in *The Making of the New Poor Laws: The Politics of Inquiry, Enactment, and Implementation, 1832–1839* (Rutgers University Press, 1978). Ursula Henriques' article 'Bastardy and the New Poor Law' in *Past and Present* and *Before the Welfare State: Social Administration in Early Industrial Britain* (Longman, 1979) addresses salient issues relating directly to the problem of unwed motherhood and the law. Pat Thane contributes significantly to understanding the Poor Law as a social institution, arguing the legislation embodied the concept of the 'stable two-parent family primarily dependent on the father's wage, and overlooked the poverty of women and children'. See 'Women and the Poor Law in Victorian and Edwardian England' in *History Workshop Journal* and *The Foundations of the Welfare State* (Longman, 1993).[6]

A recent study by Gillian Pugh, *London's Forgotten Children: Thomas Coram and The Foundling Hospital* (The History Press, 2007) provides historical research that covers more than two centuries from the perspective of founder Thomas Coram, the children, his immediate beneficiaries, the contributions of Dickens, institutional relocation from London in the twentieth century, and institutional effects on its children and grandchildren.[7] This valuable reference offers a backdrop for eighteenth-and nineteenth-century studies. Scholars have yet to surpass the magnum opus on the narrative of the eighteenth-century Foundling Hospital, *Coram's Children,* by Ruth McClure (Yale, 1980). Alysa Levene's *Childcare, Health, and Mortality at the London Foundling Hospital* (Manchester University Press, 2007) compliments McClure's work. A most useful article by Adrian Wilson, 'Illegitimacy and Its Implications in Mid-Eighteenth-Century London: The Evidence of the Foundling Hospital', published in *Continuity and Change* in 1988 extrapolates data on out-of-wedlock births using historical demography as a method of analysis.[8] The most recent survey of the nineteenth-century London Foundling Hospital, *Love in the Time of Victoria* by Françoise Barret-Ducrocq, published in French in 1989 and translated into English by John Howe (Verso, 1991; Penguin, 1992) relies on petitions submitted between 1850 and 1880. While she provides an examination of the nineteenth-century institution and the petitioners, her account overlooked the prevailing code of honor that this study coins as the 'calculus of respectability', or the process by which the committee decided to accept or reject an application for admission. The binary interpretation of the Foundling Hospital women as either 'prostitutes' or hapless victims, in *Love in the Time of Victoria*, pays little heed to the middle-class preoccupations of mothers who hoped to preserve their principled reputation and retain their jobs. While Barret-Ducrocq suggests that Victorians had a difficult time distinguishing domestic service from prostitution, John Gillis challenges this claim, arguing the Foundling Hospital petitioners were of the respectable sort.[9] See John Gillis' article, 'Servants, Sexual Relations, and the Risks of Illegitimacy in London, 1801-1900', in *Feminist Studies*, which provides a statistical overview of the occupation and class of Foundling Hospital petitioners and their partners between 1801–1900. See as well Anna Clark's book, *Women's Silence, Men's Violence: Sexual Assault in England, 1770–1845* (Pandora, 1987), which incorporates the Foundling Hospital petitions to 1845. For a thorough demographic overview of the interconnection between fertility and illegitimacy, see Simon Szreter's *Fertility Class, and Gender in Britain, 1860* (Cambridge, 1996).[10] For a literary review of the Foundling Hospital, see Jenny Bourne Taylor, 'Received a Blank Child': John Brownlow, Charles Dickens, and the London Foundling Hospital – Archives and Fictions' in *Nineteenth Century Literature.*[11] Stepping beyond these studies allows for new ways of understanding the mothers' choices; this analysis takes into account statistical samples of discrete pieces of information found in the petitions in order to create a biographical overview of these women.

Methodology

Scholars have long taken an interest in the history of poverty and its wide-ranging and adverse consequences for society. What sets this book apart from others are four analytical frames: (i) history, the study of change over time, especially as it relates to regulations governing the delivery of social welfare; (ii) space, analysis of locale, interior sectors of buildings, or outer shells, that carry meaning about the owners of the building, streets, parliamentary and poor law registration districts, and cities wherein human activities take place; (iii) gender, the framework for analysis of human behaviour based on perceived sexual differences and exercise of power through the poor laws and the criteria for admission at the Foundling Hospital of an infant born out-of-wedlock; and (iv) agency, the ability of individuals to act, to choose one thing and not another, in historical and unique ways. These intertwined elements, emphasized repeatedly, unfold as the narratives of women's choices in relation to their children.

Space

Where did these working-class women live? In Victorian London, social space reflected values or community norms; the place where someone lived said as much about who they were as a person as the church they attended or school in which they were educated.[12] In *The Production of Space*, Henri Lefebvre discusses the vital role spatial environment plays in defining and contextualizing human experience.[13] 'Lived space', in Lefebvre's words, includes housing, neighbourhoods, and public venues such as monuments, museums, parks and government buildings. Many sites have, or had, long historical pasts, which people associated with images and symbols laden with sacred and political messages relating to the wealth and grandeur of empire. The neighbourhoods or locales act as 'kernels of affective or emotional elements', capable of conjuring up the roots of English history and associated feelings of power, pride or inferiority depending on one's perspective.[14] Institutions such as hospitals, orphanages, shelters and workhouses carried both representational and practical functions affecting the quality of life and defining how individuals and groups who relied on these places for assistance saw themselves and others. Such is the case of the Foundling Hospital.[15]

Home to about one-tenth of the British populace, by the end of the nineteenth century, London's teeming streets constructed spatial identities not only for London and the United Kingdom, but also for the British empire.[16] In Victorian London, social spaces such as the Houses of Parliament, Tower of London, Westminster Abbey, Saint Paul's Cathedral, poor law workhouses, the Foundling Hospital, and wharves and docks along the River Thames manifested and reinforced political, spiritual, and economic power. Permission or access to these sites corresponded to written and unwritten rules embedded in public policy, gender roles, class and ethnic stereotypes.[17] Likewise, private spaces such as the mansions and townhouses lining fashionable West End thoroughfares, compare favourably with and hold broad appeal for the historically minded, those who wish to know about life in the past, especially when juxtaposed against the hovels typifying the environmentally degraded East End of the metropolis. Charles Booth's classic study *Life and Labour in London*, which coded London street by street according to the density of poverty and the moral character of inhabitants, dramatically affirms the social significance of such locales.[18] Booth's analytical frame, coding and evaluating wealth and poverty by his systematic list of terms, lettered A to Z, provides an example of Edward Soja's concept of 'cognitive mapping'.[19] In *Postmodern Geographies: The Reassertion of Space in Critical Social Theory*, historical geographer Soja encourages historians to include 'mapping and acting' to reconstruct the past. British social historian Adrian Wilson concurs with Soja and suggests historians frame social action within spatial and geopolitical contexts. As this study will demonstrate, social and spatial practices in Victorian London reflected visions of 'respectability' that held serious consequences for poor women.[20]

The discipline of historical geography is instructive to understanding of the social landscape of London and its environs. Inspiration for this analytical tool originated with trying to find answers in the activities of daily life. Where did the mothers live, and how might the location have affected the success or failure of their petitions? Those who study the social history of London from the eighteenth to the twenty-first centuries acknowledge that the metropolis comprises many different towns unified around the 'high street' where one can find the goods and services necessary for everyday life. They will also be quick to acknowledge that class-based divisions were as pronounced in the nineteenth century as they are today. To account for this social phenomenon, this research first took account of the history of the salubrious location and the magnificence of the Foundling Hospital estate, located near Russell Square, well known to locals and travellers to London alike. The second component of analysis drills down to the particulars of each case and tabulates addresses of the mothers, fathers and recommenders. Each petition provides a street address. Next, using the *London County Council Lists of the Streets and Places within the Administrative County of London* it became possible to identify the Parliamentary Registration District.[21] The great value of this resource is that it records historical changes over time, so if the street had been re-districted, it also allows us to keep track of the alterations. To group the districts and to apply Soja's 'cognitive mapping' strategy, this study relies on David R. Green's metropolitan divisions in *From Artisans to Paupers: Economic Change and Poverty in London, 1790–1870* (Scolar Press, 1995). Without this organizational tool, the findings would lack precision and clarity.[22]

Gender

What social rules and legislated bills shaped everyday life for the lone mother in ways markedly different from those of the father of her child? Surprisingly, in discussing the construction of 'lived space'. Henri Lefebvre says little about gender. For this analytical frame, the study turns to Joan Wallach Scott who focuses on gender as a historical construct or lens through which we arrive at a more nuanced understanding of the past.[23] Her definition of gender rests on two propositions: 'Gender is a constitutive element of social relationships based on perceived differences between the sexes, and gender is a primary way of signifying relationships of power.' Scott advocates the use of 'gender as an analytic category that can explain persistent inequality'.[24] She urges feminist historians to raise questions about social activities, to pursue and examine the personal experience in relation to a larger social framework, and to ask where human agency rests. In 'Gender as a Personal and Cultural Construction', Nancy J. Chodorow warns against reducing gender to a single defining issue.[25] Chodorow contends that a gendered word derives meaning from a multitude of psychological characteristics peculiar to individuals. She suggests one's sense of gender is fused with personal meanings set amid cultural constructions and social activities. More specifically, gender is constructed through kinship, private networks, charities, the economy and the polity or laws.[26]

As this study will demonstrate, gendered constructions of power significantly shaped the poor laws and admission policies at the London Foundling Hospital. From the Reformation onward, men organized, raised funds for, and administered a range of charities including those dedicated to assisting orphans, unwed mothers, foundlings and prostitutes. Importantly, however, rules regarding appropriate female behaviour determined the extent to which women and children received assistance. Gendered rules led to stereotyping of women at the workhouse gate, constraints on courtship, marriage, and more importantly, after passage of the New Poor Laws, the financial responsibility for an out-of-wedlock child in cases where the mother had been abandoned by the father.

Agency

What was a lone mother to do? In 1994 Louise Tilly, then President of the American Historical Association, called historians to pay greater attention to the role of the subject or actor's 'agency'.[27] She invoked the scholarship of the godfather of British social history, E. P. Thompson, who envisioned history in the following way: 'If we observe men [women and children] over an extended period of time we observe patterns in relationships, ideas, and institutions in which individuals live their own history.'[28] F. M. L. Thompson not only concurs, but in a seminal article, 'Social Control in Victorian Britain' in *The Economic History Review*, he eloquently argues that the labouring poor established their own values and accepted middle-class values where it proved advantageous to their needs.[29]

The critical social theorist, Anthony Giddens, illustrates how space and values are intertwined by incorporating E. P. Thompson's concepts of 'class' into his interpretation and analysis of social structures. Then he enfolds the analytical categories of time and space into the definition of 'historical agency'. Giddens defines social activities as networks of actions and interrelationships. He suggests that most activities are repeated and individuals can explain what, why and how they perform the daily activities within the same space, time after time. Building on Karl Marx and Thompson, Giddens reiterates Thompson's thesis argues individuals make history under conditions, not of their own choosing, and defines the relationship between the actor and act as 'agency'. For Giddens, agency is the capacity to choose a course of action, to operate under certain circumstances while having the option to have done differently. Since social interactions occur within locales or social spaces such as a room in a house, a street corner, the shop floor of a factory, towns and cities, or nation-states, and since these occur repeatedly in a particular space, historians should try to explain the ways in which a community appropriates and designates spaces to perform a specific purpose. Giddens contends histories of everyday life should incorporate the spatial aspects of social life by placing actors within the context of institutional histories such as those of the workhouse, lying-in homes, the employer's residence or the Foundling Hospital estate.[30] These examples provide an understanding of the shared values of a community and illustrate how humans create and order social life not only across time but also across space.[31]

To answer questions about the historical agency of women, poor women in particular, the following accounts focus on unwed mothers who faced dire choices and consequences as they struggled with the stigma of illegitimacy and the legal and social burdens of motherhood. It explores the degree to which social and personal constraints shaped their choices. A woman based her actions, regarding pregnancy and childcare, on internal emotional limits, her value system, and external opportunities. Some met with severe constraints, including a lack of material resources such as money, food, clothing and shelter. Further, an unwed mother had become an outcast amongst Victorians, who believed a woman's character and integrity were reflected in her condition and whether she chose a private or public institution for assistance. Historical agency is revealed by examining private events in everyday life through case studies situated within formal and spatial frameworks against the backdrop of Victorian London.[32] Historical agency, then, is illustrated by tracing the ways in which women made choices under the social constraints of their era.

Sources

In addition to the Foundling Hospital collection, significant primary sources and detailed information on the content of the Poor Laws contributed to this study. These include the House of Commons Sessions Papers, known as the *British Parliamentary Papers, Hansard Parliamentary Debates* (referred to here as *Parliamentary Debates*), and *The Mirror of Parliament*, with accounts specifically transcribed by Charles Dickens. A competitor cropped up under William Cobbett's leadership as the publisher Hansard began to record and publish the parliamentary debates in 1803, hence, *Hansard Parliamentary Debates*. Both *Hansard* and *The Mirror of Parliament* reported the debates surrounding passage of the poor relief bill. Defense of the 1834 amendments and the Royal Commission on the Poor Laws occurred within years of passage. Nassau Senior's *Remarks on the Opposition to the Poor Law Amendment Bill by a Guardian* is but one example of protests against further changes. Passage of the landmark bill continued to receive reviews throughout the century, including Major Craigie's assessment of the impact on ratepayers in 'The English Poor Rate and Recent Statistics of its Administration and Pressure, Read before the Royal Statistical Society', and a lengthy report on metropolitan poor law administration by Henry Longley, *Report to the Local Government Board on Poor Law Administration in London; With Special Reference to the Disposal by Boards of Guardians of Applications for Relief*. Thomas Fowle closes the Victorian Era with his treatise on the Poor Laws dated 1892–3.[33]

The following assessment bases its data collection and analysis on the extensive Foundling Hospital collection held at the London Metropolitan Archives. Upon in-depth review, the findings and documentation for *Victorian Women, Unwed Mothers and the London Foundling Hospital* suggest it is time for a reappraisal of the institutional mission and its beneficiaries. Victorians, informed by Thomas Malthus and Jeremy Bentham and concerned with saving ratepayers' money, introduced draconian measures such as the New Poor Laws and workhouses. Witnesses, such as Dickens, watched the dramatic growth of an imperial city where conspicuous consumption was only matched by the number of rooms in a home, and servants in employment. The Foundling Hospital nestled into this landscape, measuring the worthiness of a petitioner by a calculus of respectability. Each year, scores of women applied for relief of their infant. After her hearing, the Foundling Hospital secretary bundled the petitions year by year with a red or white ribbon; these documents form the archival core of the analysis. Mothers' letters to the secretary also prove fruitful as artifacts giving insight to values and emotions attached to her infant. Arriving on pieces of pale blue and beige paper and occasionally paper scraps, the sooty and dirty letters remained stuck together, as they had been placed on a spindle and not examined by scholars since the day they were received and filed at the Foundling Hospital. Admissions registers, forms and instructions to doctors and nurses help to contextualize the life of the foundling and day-to-day operations of the institution.

This study assesses a set of accepted and rejected petitions dated between 1842 and 1859, accepted petitions dated 1860 to 1892, and several accepted petitions dating from 1841. It aims to represent fairly the mothers who attended their hearings when applying for assistance. Methodologically, the following account departs from traditional historical research by necessity. After acknowledging the poor did not write for themselves or others, we are faced with the question of how to read and evaluate their personal accounts. By analyzing transcripts of oral testimonies enfolded in the Foundling Hospital petitions and by tracking the choices women made, we can derive a deeper understanding of the strains and stresses of the Victorian age. In short, most historians concur that writing about the working poor is challenging, because their research depends on texts from the past. Scullery maids and delivery boys did not write about their lives, they were busy trying to make ends meet. This research integrates and connects agency and voice as they appear in the rich archival collections.

During the Poor Law debates, MPs pointed to the institution on Guilford Street as a model for all charities and even for the workhouses. The New Poor Laws rejected the Elizabethan and Georgian statutes requiring fathers of children born of out wedlock to provide for them, thus making Victorian mothers even more vulnerable than before. Thus, in order to distinguish the woman who applied for assistance at the Foundling from the women who 'fell' on the poor laws, governors actually defined, defended, and indeed demanded a high level of respectability for its 'hidden' beneficiaries, lone mothers. The cross-fertilization of poor law policy with Foundling Hospital standards yields meaningful connections that directly affected the lives of Victorian women.

Over the course of the years from 1741 to 1907, the Foundling Hospital admitted 22,594 infants. Numbers fluctuated according to the admissions policy. On average, the Foundling Hospital received 200 petitions per year. Between 1887 and 1907, applications declined. Only two years, between 1891 and 1901, recorded more than 100 applications. The last year, in which the institution admitted children, was 1953.[34] When the research for this study began in 1992, petitions dated after 1892 remained closed; the Thomas Coram Foundation granted permission to use the Foundling Hospital petitions dated between 1880 and 1892. Today, the Coram Foundation retains the 110-year confidentiality rule. The petition packet consists of three standard sections, the application form, the oral deposition transcript and letters from recommenders. The major categories drawn for the form include the mother's age, address, occupation, place of confinement, or the site where she delivered her baby and the father's address and occupation. The second set of artifacts analyzed for this study is the oral transcripts. The secretary transcribed the accounts from the young woman's testimony before committee men. The documents contain details such as length of acquaintance, whether or not she had received a promise to marry and if she had given consent to sexual relations. Ancillary information includes the Foundling Hospital investigator's notes and letters from the petitioner, the family, or the father of the infant, all used as evidence to support the petition. The stewards of this collection release new petitions each year, for example, the rejected petitions dating between 1856 and 1899 appeared after the bulk of the research for this project was completed.[35]

This study assessed the Foundling Hospital petitions both qualitatively and quantitatively, yielding two separate surveys. The first examines accepted petitions from the decennial years 1851, 1861, 1871, 1881 and 1891. The second is a 50-year statistical survey of petitions dated between 1842 and 1892. The total accepted petitions available for the statistical survey numbered 2,279, from which 10 per cent or 227 were randomly selected by year. The total set of rejected petitions was about four times larger than the accepted. The study used the statistical rule of significance for this group, and selected a data set comprising 5 per cent of the total or 129 for the years when rejected petitions were available. In addition, randomly selected petitions, not included in the statistical survey or among the decennial survey years, are individually cited.[36] To maintain confidentiality, all petitioners are identified by their first name and last initial, applying the practice used in discussing medical records. Quotations from letters and transcripts appear with their original punctuation, sentence structure and spelling. The petition dialogues and narratives have been arranged by questions asked of the petitioner.

This project reveals new discoveries about the identities of the often misrepresented mothers who rang the Guilford Street bell in pursuit of an application form. In *Victorian Women, Unwed Mothers and the London Foundling Hospital*, the convergence of government treatment of the poor with Foundling Hospital admissions are examined in Chapter 1 'There Can Be No Reason for Giving to Vice Privileges Which We Deny Misfortune'. Chapter

2 'Ornament of the Metropolis: Victorian Representation and Reality' draws on the history of the Foundling Hospital to create a broad overview of the petitioning process. It relies on Foundling Hospital papers, testimony before Parliament, a sermon by James Augustus Hessey and journalistic and literary accounts from Charles Dickens. Moving from accounts provided by texts relating to the actual content of the petition packet, Chapter 3 'Circumventing Social Geography: The Unwed Mother's Search for Respectability' profiles the mothers by address and takes steps towards defining the meaning of respectability by explaining how social geography played a role in securing access to the institution for the infant. The contours of the mother's image deepens in Chapter 4 'When First Acquainted with Father I Was' by drawing data from the petition form and creating analytical frameworks to extrapolate information regarding her life choices. For example, some things, such as the age of the candidate, were not within the mother's purview, but her occupational status could be controlled, at least partially. The data from the form also included information about the father, his occupation, place to which he 'absconded', thus contributing to a fuller picture of the petitioners' lives.

Sheer desperation moved women to the Guilford Street gate for a petition. To gain admission for her infant, however, Foundling Hospital rules required not only completion of a form, but also a hearing. Chapter 5 'Is My Own Name Really Required, for on that Everything Depends' details the petitioner's experience as she stood before a panel of several men, who asked her to reveal intimate details relating to the conception of her baby. A string of questions helped to frame the respectability of her character: Where were you working when you first met the father? How long had you known him before you first stepped out together? Did he offer a promise to marry before you gave consent to sexual intercourse? This chapter explores the answers to the questions through data and textual analysis to demonstrate the respectability of the mothers, who willingly put themselves through this test for the survival of their babies. Those who came to the assistance of the mothers operated within a web of connections and proved of utmost importance to the success of her request. Chapter 6 'If You Will Kindly Take Her from Me, You Will Save My Character' analyzes the respectability of institutions where mothers delivered their infants, the rank of supporting recommendation letters, and an account of a recommendation that fell apart. For example, Charles Dickens, a friend of the Foundling Hospital, could not secure admission for a young woman named Susan Mayne when the hospital enquirer uncovered unsavory aspects of her private life. Significantly, we did not hear Mayne's voice, what she wanted or why, throughout the discussion her case. As the mid-century mark passed, literacy among women increased. Chapter 7 'Dear Mr Brownlow Will You Please Tell Me… ' analyzes important expressions of working-class mothers' sentiments through countless letters, which express a sense of relief, loss, grief and ongoing concerns for the infant. The public image of the Foundling Hospital, however, focused on its successes with infants and children. The second part of this chapter explores changes over time in the care for and treatment of the inhabitants of this large institution. Progressive in nature, Thomas Coram's vision bore fruit by nurturing and teaching countless children, who were born of London's most respectable domestics, and then bringing them into adulthood.

1

'There Can Be No Reason for Giving to Vice Privileges Which We Deny Misfortune': Legal Constraints for Victorian Mothers

> With respect to the Mother, there can be no reason for giving to vice privileges which we deny to misfortune.[1]

> The natural inequality of the two powers of population and of production in the earth and the great law of our nature which must constantly keep their effects equal form the great difficulty that to me appears insurmountable in the way to the perfectibility of society.[2]

> Those who framed the act of Elizabeth were not aware of that principle as to population, with regard to which Malthus had since enlightened mankind. Those who framed the act which commenced the foundation of a system that separated labour from its rewards, seeing no doubt what would be the effect of such a system, laid an obligation on the child to support his aged parent. If we look to the consequences of this on the property of the country, they were to the full as melancholy as any other of the ill effects flowing from the mal-administration of the poor laws.[3]

The recommendations for the New Poor Law Bill went into committee on 26 May 1834 where the majority of debate continued.[4] Returning to the floor of the House of Commons for day speeches, MP Poulette Scrope, the first speaker on the agenda, stated he would have liked to address settlement and bastardy issues, but chose to abstain until a later session. Instead, he confined his comments to poor law administration. Scrope posited: 'For more than two centuries it [the poor relief system] had been the blessing and boast of England – the guarantee of her internal tranquility – the security for the lives of the poor – and for the property and peace of the rich.'[5] In other words, the poor deserved the safety and security of state aid. The poor laws provided the wealthy with assurances the poor would be cared for and therefore disinclined to foment revolution because of an uneven distribution of wealth, a crucial consideration. These laws deserved the title of the great charter of the 'English' poor.[6] Scrope continued: 'In spite of the abuses by which it had been of late years perverted, [the poor relief system] had been throughout, one of the most pregnant and copious sources of the wealth, the strength, and the prosperity of this country.' In order to reduce the ruinous strain on ratepayers posed by outdoor relief, or the distribution of material support such as bread, coals, rent and clothing, proposed changes were required.[7]

During the Poor Law debates in the House of Lords, Chancellor Brougham claimed the poor laws militated against the 'work ethic'.[8] They 'sinned upon every instance, on every count, by day and by night, during winter and good weather, in famine and in plenty, in peace and in war' by benefiting those who did not work.[9] This brought him to another sensitive issue. He did not believe charity should pick up where the poor laws left off. Charities for the aged, infirm, foundlings and unwed mothers were against all sound principle. The only sorts of charities he approved of included hospitals and dispensaries, which provided aid to individuals who were ill through no fault of their own. Brougham regarded these institutions as 'safe charities, not susceptible to abuse'.[10] He specifically identified one organization with which he was most familiar, the Foundling Hospital on Guilford Street in London. Using the phrase, 'ornament of the metropolis' to recognize success, Coram's foundation abandoned its open and unconditional admission standards over 70 years earlier in favour of a more selective policy measuring the respectability of the mother's character for access. 'Not a single foundling could be admitted there now', he said.[11] The institution operated as a model social welfare agency, and he believed it would behoove poor law administrators to take lessons from the Foundling Hospital by making wise financial investments and developing a highly selective entrance policy for future workhouses.[12] He hoped the poor laws would serve as some sort of 'preventive measure' against improvidence, and then there would be no need for the Foundling Hospital.[13] Such measures, in the minds of other parliamentarians, related directly to women. Further, in the opinion of some Victorians, there would be no need for the Foundling Hospital or the poor laws, if women held their fertility in check, if poor women preserved their chastity until marriage, if families kept their children from the streets, and if the Irish had the good sense to emigrate some place other than London.[14] These issues framed parliamentary debates regarding the poor laws from the turn of the nineteenth century. The intertwined questions of rising population, increasing poverty, the uncontrollable fertility of poor women and costs to the ratepayer played out in the halls of Parliament and held serious consequences for the destitute.

Thomas Malthus, a prominent eighteenth-century political economist, who published *Essay on Population,* started the conversation. In response to fears he raised regarding the geometrical growth of population and the strains it potentially had for the government, Parliament ordered the first census in 1801. According to Thomas Lacqueur, 'Malthus made the seemingly irrepressible power of sexual desire the central axiom of his work on population'.[15] He argued improvidence, meaning failing to plan for the future, early marriages, pre-nuptial pregnancies and unwed motherhood typified social behaviour among the labouring poor.[16] Legislation, Malthus believed, should be liberated from moral philosophy, or sentiments protecting the weak. Laws governing the distribution of scarce resources to the poor should follow 'natural economics'. The principles of a well-balanced economy followed natural laws, therefore, parishes should not spend on food and shelter for infants, children, mothers, the aged and disabled because this increased survival rates and a culture of dependency.[17] Malthusianism directly influenced opinions of men in Parliament. In short, this economic theory laid the conceptual framework for a new social regime articulated in the 1832 Royal Commission on the Poor Laws, which in turn created serious legal constraints for women facing the problem of birthing an infant *sans* the sanctions of the church and/or state.

Malthusianism underpinned a penchant to count people, not just to enumerate, but also to discover where individuals resided, under what circumstances, and in which type of employment they worked. This data confirmed Parliament's worst fears, a growing class of out-of-wedlock children. Thirty years after Malthus published his famous *Essay on the Principle of Population*, the Population Act required Parliament to take decennial counts. The 1831 national census first measured occupations and ages within parliamentary registration districts. The compiler noted difficulties in deciding whether women, children and servants should be classified as members of a family, under the occupation of the adult male, or without an occupation altogether. Later counts included tabs for family relationships, family size, age, sex, occupation, birthplace, religion (1851) and fertility, or live births per thousand women of child-bearing age (1911).[18] The 1837 Civil Registration Act required the registration of births, deaths and marriages.[19] This information proved highly valuable to government officials, because they could estimate the direct costs of 'improvidence'. These parameters, which measured every angle of social life, inspired Foundling Hospital governors to re-evaluate admission policies with more care.

Significantly, from 1750 to 1850, which includes years covered by this study, the crude birth rate rose, while the crude death rate fell across the country, and between 1801 and 1825, the overall fertility rate stood at its highest between 1551 and 1975.[20] Out-of-wedlock births rose to 6.5 per cent by 1850, increasing the ire of ratepayers.[21] The first national returns on poor rates, or taxes levied on property owners to pay for the needs of the destitute, estimated 11 per cent of the population received assistance in 1801.

A decade later, 12 per cent were on relief, but children had been omitted from the estimate; therefore, the figure was probably higher. In 1821, roughly, 7.2 per cent received aid, and by 1828, approximately 7.7 per cent depended on support from local poor law authorities.[22] By 1828, MP Robert Slaney questioned, who should pay for the poor?

A Committee Is Formed to Craft A Bill

To address rising poor law rates and ratepayer concerns, Parliament formed a committee. On 17 March 1832, William IV appointed Lord Chancellor Henry Brougham as head of the Poor Law Commission and selected William Nassau Senior as chair.[23] In addition, several others contributed their efforts: Bishop of London Charles James Blomfield, Bishop of Chester John Bird Sumner, W. Sturges-Bourne, Henry Bishop, Henry Gawler, Walter Coulson and James Traill.[24] Nassau Senior recruited John Sumner, Bishop of Chester and professor of political economy at Oxford and Nassau Senior's tutor at Eton. Reverend Henry Bishop, a political economist, served at Oriel College, Oxford. Walter Coulson, a newspaper reporter and lawyer, worked with Jeremy Bentham as his personal secretary. W. Sturges-Bourne's reputation as a poor law reformer preceded him. Sturges-Bourne had presided over a select committee investigation of parish vestries in 1817–18, which resulted in the creation of the Sturges-Bourne Act that stipulated vestrymen would be elected and paid for their services by the rates. The Bishop of London and the Bishop of Chester represented the House of Lords on the commission. The Bishop of London, a conservative, spoke out vociferously during the Poor Law debates in the House of Lords; the Lords heard less from the Bishop of Chester. Nassau Senior also called Edwin Chadwick to join the commission, another man who had worked for Bentham as secretary. Contemporaries and scholars agreed with the way in which Nassau Senior and Chadwick and others reviewed the poor laws. Moreover, they implemented an international survey of systems to aid the poor, sending questionnaires to European countries and specific states in the United States.[25] These men formed the most influential members of the Poor Law Commission. Nassau Senior organized the administrative details while Chadwick outlined remedial measures.[26] With their help, Chadwick drafted the Report of the Royal Commission, published lengthy surveys and accounts, wrote, proposed and submitted recommendations to Parliament.[27]

Radical MPs found the Commission and their recommendations disconcerting and raised strident protests during debates. In the House of Commons, William Cobbett explained how Malthus directly influenced members of the House of Lords to bring the issue of the poor laws before the King.[28] The 'noble Lord [most likely Brougham] has said that the principles of Malthus were sound and just, and he would defend them to the utmost extent'.[29] Malthus, Cobbett argued, would say to the indigent: 'There is no relief for you, no seat for you.'[30] Colonel Evans, MP, challenged the balance and representativeness of the appointees:

> We are told that the Commissioners have recommended the introduction of this extraordinary Bill; but who are the Commissioners? They consist of two Bishops, two political economists, and two gentlemen of the bar. Can these persons be quoted as authorities for such extraordinary propositions as these?[31]

Cobbett clearly took a critical stab at the selected men engaged in deciphering the problems and determining the outcome of the pending legislation. Their first attack aimed to expose the untrammeled growth of 'improvidence' in their parishes. Across London, indeed across the United Kingdom, the settlement of out-of-wedlock children and their mothers loomed largely. Who and which laws could curb this problem, the overseers asked. Although laws on the books, dating from the reigns of Elizabeth I and James II, called for the 'punishment of lewdness', the magistrates seldom invoked these laws. The law to punish an unmarried mother proved difficult to enforce. Moreover, the fathers of the 'bastards' were 'indeterminate', and therefore, not concerned about 'the welfare of their child'. In stark contrast, the more easily identifiable mother made prosecution much simpler. One Westminster administrator called Parliament to renew the old laws requiring punishment of 'lewd women'.[32] Indeed, he argued, a law must make it compulsory for every magistrate to commit unwed mothers to prison for three months of hard labour for every 'offence' after the first illegitimate infant. Paupers went from the gin shop to the workhouse and considered their admission a small victory. The poor had come to regard parish relief as their 'birth-right'.[33]

To address the complaints from local poor law parishes and the larger question of how to deal with the unfortunate, the Poor Law Commission set up a survey of 26 questions.[34] The men enquired as to whether parish administrators noted the character of the person and the causes for distress. They wanted to know whether they were on a first name basis with the recipients of assistance, especially single mothers.[35] Commissioners believed if they placed the burden of chastity and self-control on women, the law could diminish the problems of unprotected children and mothers fending for them.[36] Reformers claimed relief benefits demoralized the respectable poor, who married and lived together as man and wife. Certain changes were required; vestrymen and commissioners were concerned not only with who received the relief, but also with the amount of relief, and under what conditions they distributed relief.[37]

The published preliminary results of the Commission appeared in a collection of abstracts under the short title of *The Administration and Operation of the Poor Laws, 1831–1832*. Judging, sorting and highlighting the most egregious problems of the system, commissioners soon found the solution challenging. The reports recounted multiple incidents of social unrest during the winter of 1831–2, reflecting growing social divisions. Traditionally, scholars have emphasized the commissioners' aim to diminish the dependency of the able-bodied poor (generally thought of as men) by curbing reliance on outdoor relief. In fact, the commissioners' investigation and the poor law debates in the House of Commons and House of Lords placed equal emphasis on unwed mothers, their illegitimate children and the Irish. Many proposed reforms would be detrimental rather than a 'boon to the female population', as leader of the House of Commons Lord Althorp suggested.[38] Commissioners would commend their judgments to the public by citing 'case after case of injustice and cruelty to innocent young men at the hands of scheming prostitutes or husband-hunters'.[39] Clearly, the New Poor Laws addressed the condition of women differently than men. The law altered the burden for childcare, laying it squarely on the shoulders of the mother, rather than solely or jointly on the father. While some compensation would eventually become possible, it never proved easy, as will be explained.

According to London poor law overseers, hereditary poverty and moral profligacy posed the greatest problems, not changing technological realities facing the 'Luddites' in the countryside, or unemployed industrial workers in mill towns. A vestry officer testified for the London parish of Lambeth Walk, located south of the Tower of London near Lambeth Palace: 'We sometimes have pauper father, pauper wife, pauper son and pauper grand-children frequently applying on the same relief day.'[40] In Marylebone, the clerk reported 700 illegitimate children on the books. He had received payment for only 150 and found it next to impossible to garner support payments from fathers.[41] Parish overseers believed they had little 'moral restraint' upon 'lewd' women. Their solution proposed to make the poor law work as a 'preventive measure' or as a 'deterrent' rather than a set of criminal statutes sending unwed mothers to jail.[42]

St George Hanover Square overseers strictly applied all laws and statutes pertinent to relief. They had been more successful than other parishes in keeping unwed mothers out of their parish because they swiftly administered penalties, such as a jail sentence for mothers who delivered a second or third illegitimate infant. Their vestryman, Mr Chappell, even reported how St George Hanover Square magistrates sent unwed mothers to the 'House of Correction' in Cold Bath Fields. Chappell believed this practice served as a preventive measure. 'Children' proved to be the one drawback of concern.

He believed placing children in jail with their mothers marked a 'measure of bad economy'. If magistrates removed the progeny from the incarcerated mother, the parish had to provide alternative facilities. Otherwise, mothers who took their children to prison exposed them to 'unsavory influences'.[43] Mr Chesterton, 'Governor of the House of Correction' in Cold Bath Fields, affirmed these assertions, and concurred with Chappell's report. Commitment to the House of Correction removed the mother from the community and placed her in an environment where she could not get pregnant again. Unlike placing her in the workhouse, where she could intermingle with men.[44]

Punishment attained its end for lewd women. Prison administrators generally found, however, they could not 'put the mothers to other work, beyond the care of their infants'.[45] Confinement proved enough; the privation of everything other than food, shelter and housing served as a deterrent.[46] The lack of personal privacy and the co-mingling of all sorts of classes caused women who had gone to jail for bearing illegitimate children to be further stigmatized with 'the contamination inevitable from evil society'. Nonetheless, some women preferred jail to the workhouse because they received better food there.[47]

Other London parishes such as St Anne, Westminster, and St Martin-in-the-Fields reported they seldom sent women to the House of Correction for bearing illegitimate children although their districts had the fastest growing workhouse populations in London.[48] In a case where the mother could prove she was a victim of a 'breach of promise' and she could identify and locate the putative father of her child, restitution became possible. In St Clement Danes, the vestryman reported he paid 'seven shillings a week for one bastard child'.[49] He even gave as much as nine shillings a week to a mother who proved the father of her child had lived with her nine months before its birth. Women most frequently pressed charges against rich men.[50] Some parishes testified mothers received payments ranging from two to seven shillings from the putative father. The Lambeth 'Collector of the Poor Rates', Mr Sefton, reported he knew of one case where the father paid eight shillings a week, although the woman had since married. She had worked as a domestic, and the father of her child was her master's son. Sefton argued the penalty was too much for the father to pay and suggested authorizing the parish to retain some of the mother's restitution to pay for the child's apprenticeship.[51] Indeed, the engagement of local poor law officials in the private lives of families proved significant in the years before passage of the New Poor Laws.

The Poor Law Commission planned to change these long established practices, paying particular attention to the question of funding, who should pay for non-settled unwed mothers? Through their actions, they shaped gender roles and responsibilities according to the prescriptions of 'natural economics'.[52] The language used in the recommendations reflected assumptions surrounding 'natural motherhood'. The men believed the 'intractable nature of unmarried women's desire to consort with young men' posed a threat to the stability of society.[53] They deemed feminine, not masculine behaviour, a threat to morals, asserting women had full control over their fertility. The burden of avoiding the conception of an infant rested on her choices, not the father's ability to control his own sexual desires. Consider this case in point, according to recommendation 18: 'She has voluntarily become a mother without procuring for herself and her child the assistance of a father and a husband.'[54] The operative word 'voluntarily' should make this point clear.

In deference to Providence, the Commission argued God would put checks on such 'licentiousness'. Any policies providing help to unwed mothers weakened, or even perverted, the Divine Will, or God's authority.[55] The Commission proposed to restore things, in so far as possible, to the 'state in which they would have been if no such laws [18 Eliz. 1, c.3] had ever existed'.[56] Historically, the old Act of Settlement and Elizabethan poor laws held both father and mother responsible for the welfare of their children until they reached the age of majority, 16 years, or the child married. Traditional rights to relief stemmed from contributions made by working parents to the economy. Barring support from the mother, children followed the settlement of their father. The law made them eligible for food, coals and rent money, or outdoor relief, in the borough, parish, or county, wherein their father resided and paid taxes. If the father had abandoned the mother and child, authorities required the mother to report her circumstances, including a pending birth for purposes of public assistance. The Elizabethan programme held the father liable for support. Commissioners, however, believed this victimized men because women shamelessly petitioned courts for support using perjury and extortion.[57] On behalf of the fathers, commissioners wrote: 'It is the unfortunate young man who is brought before the justice; but when the mother is spoken of, it is her vice that forms the subject of complaint.'[58] Further, they believed 'punishment of the supposed father' was useless, if not 'worse than useless'. If justices of the peace or guardians of the poor pursued the father, punishment would fall upon a possibly 'innocent man'. Therefore, the arbiters of the new policies confined themselves to 'the effect produced on the woman's mind by her power of calling for that punishment'. In short, they thought it easier for the unwed mother to accuse the putative father than to face the problem on her own.[59] Concern about 'disgrace to the innocent [father]' pointed to the willingness of the men to forego placing the responsibility for paternity on him. Although he may have been more highly educated, or living under better circumstances than the mother and child, he would be under no obligation to help. The final article, number 21, summarized the intent of the new legislation, turning back the Elizabethan statutes:

> WE RECOMMEND THEREFORE THAT THE SECOND SECTION OF 18 ELIZABETH. CAP.3., AND ALL OTHER ACTS WHICH PUNISH OR CHARGE THE PUTATIVE FATHER OF A BASTARD, SHALL, AS TO ALL BASTARDS BORN AFTER THE PASSING OF THE INTENDED ACT, BE REPEALED.[60]

In short, commissioners, using capital letters for emphasis, ended all possible charges against putative fathers because as the Westminster overseers claimed above, they had to either track down the father, or put the mother in jail for lewdness, and the costs for such actions went to the ratepayers. Ideally, commissioners hoped to induce the unmarried mother to remain in the parish where she resided; and through self-sufficiency, help from friends, or local charities, however limited, she could survive. They believed this a better solution, permitting the mother to 'toil for her own and her child's subsistence, rather than to be dragged in shame to the scene of her youth'.[61] Failing outside charitable aid, they recommended magistrates offer the workhouse first, and make inquiries later, resolving the problem of parish settlements.[62] In theory, the commission assumed it possible to destroy 'improvidence at the root' by denying outdoor relief, such as rents, coal, bread and clothing, to unwed mothers at the start.[63] By halting material support for the destitute, the men believed they could help individuals plan for their future by encouraging a more cautious approach to their behaviour.

The proposed law held the mother-child duo inseparable and had decisive consequences for young women.[64] Unmarried mothers would find themselves facing the same lack of support as impoverished widows or abandoned wives with children.[65] And since, 'in the natural state of things', according to the Bishop of Exeter, 'a child, until emancipated, depends on its parents', the commissioners and nineteenth century courts argued unmarried mothers should bear the care and rights of custody until 16 years of age, or the child married, or died, whichever came sooner. Again, according to the seventeenth recommendation, the lone mother would bear the burden of child rearing because only one parent could be clearly identified, the mother.[66] In another step, the commission proposed the revocation of punishment of the mother and father for abandonment of their parental duties and taking it a step further, suggested repeal of the 'little used' statute requiring the incarceration of a lewd woman who bore more than one child.[67]

Lawyers, advocating for the poor mothers, argued the women had the right to the care and custody of their children because they were 'marked by nature' as the proper custodians. The Victorian courts ruled maternity provided enough proof, legislating an illegitimate child could not inherit titles, lands or personal property of the father until or unless the father admitted paternity. According to the language of the statutes, the illegitimate child should become a 'burthen [on its mother and where she cannot maintain it] on her parents.'[68] Afterwards, commissioners held maternal grandparents responsible, assuming they remained alive and had the interest or even wherewithal to rear another child.[69] Generally, women without strong family ties, or networks of friends, were defenseless and most likely to become victims of seduction. Although the act temporarily made outdoor relief available to women for a limited period, after passage of the new laws, commissioners hoped construction of workhouses and the introduction of paid administrators, or guardians of the poor, would make the asylum serve as the last choice. The men anticipated the amendments would see the bastardy clauses fall into 'desuetude', or disuse.[70]

These proposed legislative changes sparked heated debates differing in focus, form and content in the Houses of Parliament. Together with the commissioners, most MPs in the Commons aimed to keep the peace, preserve property and rationalize the welfare system by applying theories of political economy to a serious social problem: providing for the poor. Although a consensus existed on the urgency of the issue, arriving at the proper resolution created dissension. Ensuing debates reveal popular expectations regarding gender and class, providing a broader perspective on the passage of the New Poor Laws. Interest in separating the legitimate from the illegitimate and the labouring poor from the indigent who had fallen on the rates, received outdoor relief, or gone into the workhouse threaded together in a common refrain. Both houses heard loud protests. The Commons saw the poor rates as a threat to continuing economic growth. Debate in the House of Lords centred on preservation of rights and privileges for respectable and responsible members of society. Ultimately, the rights of property over the rights of the poor, the rights of men, who had no real stake in the rights of women, especially poor women, won out.[71]

The Commission Takes Recommendations to the Commons: Poor Law Debates

More than two years after the commission's appointment, the Poor Law Amendment Bill received a favourable reception in the House of Commons when first read on 17 April 1834.[72] Debates boiled down to who should pay for children born out-of-wedlock: able-bodied men, or improvident women. On the first day of debate, the second speaker on the amendments, Colonel Evans, read from the commissioners' report; but other MPs who followed him in the deliberations stated they had not been able to read the entire report, nor were they able to consider all the details.[73] Evans asserted the proposed measures would alter the 'Constitution', while at the same time identifying three evils in the existing system. The first flaw stemmed from distribution of outdoor relief. The next fault sprang from the Laws of Settlement and Bastardy. The final defect included the lack of interest shown by the upper classes in the moral education of the poor. Evans presented one of the most prescient critiques of the recommendations throughout the debate. He envisioned unwed mothers relying on the workhouse for confinement, generally the two weeks following labour and delivery. If she remained outside the house for delivery but stayed on outdoor relief for more than two years, then the guardian (former vestrymen) would have no choice but to offer her the 'house'. If the woman were offered the 'house', then who, meaning which guardians and which poor law union, should support her and her illegitimate offspring? As predicated by Evans, the reforms removed former legal rights to the *carte blanche* distribution of outdoor relief and forced unmarried mothers into the workhouses during the period of 'confinement', or childbirth.[74]

In the general discussion of the bill, Sir Samuel Whalley acknowledged the discomfort many felt in dealing with such sensitive issues. Upon standing to speak, the MP said he felt considerable pain regarding the problem, because he believed the government had a responsibility to relieve injustice, and the bill would bring nothing but evil to the country. Further, 'It would be prejudicial to property, and demoralizing to the laboring classes.'[75] Whalley gingerly broached the subject of the bastardy recommendations, acknowledging unwed motherhood had been a 'delicate subject' in polite society. The proposed laws, he continued, exonerated males, allowing 'the misery to be thrown on the mother of an illegitimate offspring; she had all the disgrace to encounter'. Empathetically, Whalley observed the mothers, not fathers, had to bear the 'pains of parturition'.[76] With this remark, the House of Commons broke into laughter; whereupon the speaker chastised his fellow MPs. 'Honorable Gentlemen might laugh, but he would not let false notions of delicacy prevent him from offering his opinion. This Bill went to offer a premium for immorality, and to encourage the crime of infanticide.'[77] Although he concurred with others that payment in cash to single mothers with several children should cease, unwed mothers should be eligible for at least 12 months of support.[78]

Whalley also articulated his views on men. All 'able-bodied' men, he said, had the right to the fruits of their labour, a view also espoused by Radical politicians, and elaborated upon by William Cobbett. If a man could not work, then the industry of others must support him.[79] George Grote, Radical MP, referred more frequently to 'poor and able-bodied workers – those labourers who work the hardest, and who defer the period of marriage from an anxious desire to maintain their independence'.[80] Grote acknowledged the thousands of artisans, craftsmen and skilled labourers who delayed marriage, either by engaging in a long courtship, avoiding pregnancy, or equally likely by not marrying any of the women whom they impregnated (although this point went unmentioned). The City of London MP argued the proposed measures, upon adoption, provided for the improvement of the moral condition, industrious habits and independent feelings of the labouring population.[81] Sir Francis Burdett replied, indiscriminate relief or almsgiving to the poor 'without any inquiry into their character or des[s]erts', or their worthiness to receive relief proved futile.[82]

William Cobbett, returning to the constitutional question, argued if the poor were willing to fight for the nobility, then they deserved support in time of need. The installation of poor law guardians, within an inherently cumbersome bureaucracy, broke the direct relationship between the nobility and the poor and it destroyed the power of the gentry, parish vestries and the local magistracy.[83] Some MPs such as Mr Walter conflated the destruction of the constitution with the demise of families on poor relief. Calling the proposed legislation a measure of 'fearful importance' with an 'anomalous and unprecedented character' impossible to hide. Walter suggested Parliament had written a 'new-made' constitution for the poor, which served to re-constitute laws of settlement and bastardy.[84] At the end of the first reading, the House divided: 319 'ayes', 20 'noes'.[85]

Commons debates addressed the first through thirteenth recommendations, with the latter transferring oversight powers from the parish vestries to a central authority comprised of three members known as the Poor Law Commission. The opposition feared commissioners, insulated from the day-to-day ills of the poor, would neither share their power with the local authorities nor understand local conditions. Lord Althorp allayed discontent regarding the transfer of power by referring MPs to the thirteenth amendment, which said the secretary of state and both houses of Parliament would review all rules, orders and regulations before issuance and publication of laws by the commissioners. Thus, reassured, opposition to clause 13 collapsed and the Commons accepted sections one through thirteen of the bill.[86] Members of Parliament then verbally approved clauses 14–20.[87]

The Commons debated the twenty-first clause, reserving the right of the commissioners to investigate the expenses of the poor in each parish, particularly as related to encumbrances generated by the malt tax, which raised funds through sale of beer and ale.[88] On 9 June, MPs debated clause 33, which regulated the election of the guardians and ostensibly widened the voting franchise, influenced several aspects of parish vestry administration, and established the conditions for election of the guardians. Additionally, it unified old poor law parishes, and consequently changed the boundaries established under the revised Law of Settlement. Moreover, the consolidation of multiple parishes into larger geo-political units established new spatial parameters for the location of workhouses. This clause allotted one vote for each ratepayer, and affected the town and rural districts differently, removing power from the hands of large landowners and concentrating it in the most populous towns. Several MPs challenged the value of such an arrangement, arguing it gave the 'lower classes of ratepayers' (who would significantly outnumber wealthier constituents) the same privileges as those held by proprietors and small business owners. Undoubtedly, changes proceeding from the Reform Bill heightened their concerns. Lord Althorp claimed it better to offer large landowners some extra weight in voting, because they were 'most interested in every parish.'[89] Rejected, Althorp's proposal illustrated the degree to which the wealthy men of banking, trade and industry, rather than the landed elite, now exerted considerable influence in local government affairs.[90]

Heated opposition soon appeared in the debate over workhouse provisions. In early May sessions, MP Edward Buller announced he understood the commissioners had been empowered to unite parishes for purposes of building workhouses. [91] He had also heard rumours of families risking separation, men from their wives and children, and children over the age of seven from their parents. Buller opposed this section but to no effect.[92] When the question of workhouses faced new discussions in June, Lord Althorp, leader of the House, claimed: 'The separation of man and wife must exist to ensure the proper regulation of the workhouses.'[93] MP Thomas Hodges broached the subject with Althorp, asking if workhouses might become 'houses of correction?' Althorp replied: 'The workhouses would be managed as they were at present, but more strictly: care would be taken to prevent disturbance which might annoy the sick and infirm. Measures would be taken to maintain regularity and good order.'[94]

In June, when the workhouse clause came up for discussion again, MPs Benett and Scrope tried to frame the debate to their advantage. Benett objected to the discretionary authority of the commissioners who could vest the guardians with the ability to send able-bodied workers, in need of temporary help, to the workhouse. The clause contained language requiring workers, single mothers and the elderly to sell all of their personal belongings, give up their cottage, and move into the workhouse. The commission designed the infamous 'workhouse test' to serve as a measure of a person's eligibility for relief. Ironically, the proposal would discourage inmates from leaving to take a job, which might pay only eight shillings a week, since they had given up their personal and household possessions before entering the asylum. Upon leaving, they would need to re-establish themselves with a food and shelter.[95] Considering the aforementioned circumstances, outdoor relief seemed the better option for the poor. Mr Scrope moved, no rule or order should prohibit guardians from distributing 'outdoor relief' to the needy.[96] He maintained:

> If the men so thrown out of work could obtain no relief unless they went into the workhouse, they must be either starved or degraded and ruined forever. In this commercial country, unfortunately, such cases were of frequent occurrence. A similar observation applied to widows, to orphans, illegitimate children, and others, who for a little temporary relief, which could be administered on the spot, might be confined to the workhouse for the rest of their days.[97]

Taking an oppositional stance, Lord Althorp, replied:

> Wherever the workhouse system had been introduced under good regulations, so far from their being objected to by the poor of the parish, the person who had introduced that good system, and who presided over the workhouses, had become extremely popular with the paupers.[98]

Althorp's comment did not lessen the concerns of William Cobbett, who vehemently opposed the workhouse clause, which proposed, 'No relief was to be given to able-bodied men out of the workhouse; and if placed in it husbands were to be separated from their wives'.[99] Additionally, the clause required the separation of children from their parents, with no communications from family or friends, head shaving and badge wearing. Cobbett wished to know 'what power the House had to pass such a law'.[100] Despite Cobbett's protests, the law passed with some of the provisions he most feared.

The poor law parishes held the primary responsibility of keeping costs down for the local ratepayer. In the House of Commons, very little debate centred on the distribution methods of the rates because the responsibility rested with local government representatives.[101] Clause 45 would have permitted the Poor Law Commission to distribute relief, but ultimately the provision suffered defeat by the majority of votes, thereby keeping the power to distribute relief the hands of local government administrators.[102] Clause 48 also focused on the distribution of relief, proposing magistrates and justices of the peace could no longer deliver poor relief; leaving the responsibility entirely in the hands of the guardians of the poor who faced triennial elections. In order to be eligible for candidacy, a man had to own or rent property with a ratable value of £40 or more per year and prove residency for a period of 12 months. Clause 48 passed with a majority of 102.[103] Debate on clause 60 in the House of Commons

(62 in the House of Lords) focused on the benefits of emigration as a solution to the surplus labouring population, a situation which purportedly further strained the current overburdened relief system.[104] It extended commissioner authority to raise money for emigration schemes. Labourers could be sent to North American colonies, Australia or the Cape where sufficient land existed for all.[105] Building on MP Wolryche Whitmore's suggestion, Colonel Torrens offered the emigration scheme should have a selection process, so commissioners could withdraw 'labourers with large families who were partly supported from the parish; this would reduce the supply of labour... and raise wages until they became sufficiently high to afford married labourers with families independent support'.[106] He thought it to be the ideal solution. 'In Ireland there was redundant labour; in England redundant capital, and in the colonies boundless tracts of rich and unoccupied land.'[107] Further debate continued on emigration and the condition of the poor in Ireland.

Then, on 18 June 1834, the Commons shifted their focus to unwed mothers, and when sections relating to the bastardy issue came to the table for debate, Althorp urged logic must replace 'feelings' in the discussion. The evils of the system required correction, and careful consideration must be taken. The Speaker said, addressing the situation of the community in general, the effects of the existing bastardy laws served to 'diminish all inducements to chastity to the greatest possible degree'. [108] Undoubtedly, Althorp claimed, the present state of the laws brought about 'general demoralization'.[109] In its present form, laws sheltered and even held out advantages to 'females of an abandoned character'. The system destroyed all 'moral feeling which otherwise might preserve their chastity'.[110] Frankly, Althorp observed, the law least affected men, who also had a limited notion of chastity. Furthermore, male self-control of sexual impulses proved unreliable. Therefore, women had to carry the burden of illegitimate children.[111] MP Charles Buller argued the bastardly laws 'perjury' and proposed taking measures to prevent this travesty of justice.[112] MP Wolryche Whitmore agreed, the 'practice of giving public support to illegitimate children was a cause of their increase'.[113]

By contrast, the opposition proposed punishment for the father rather than pardon from his responsibilities. MP George Robinson recommended clauses 69–73 inclusive, relating to bastardy and settlement be stricken from the bill. Instead, he favoured retaining the current laws. Robinson objected to the seventieth clause because it relieved fathers of child support. In the seventy-first clause, Robinson found 'to his astonishment as a man and a Christian, that the liability was removed from the father [and] was placed on the mother of an illegitimate child, and that she was bound to support it'.[114] Fraught with complicated suggestions, the seventy-second clause produced vehement objections. Robinson disliked it because it extended the responsibility of support for an illegitimate child, should something happen to the mother or father, on the maternal grandparents. In his view, this act contradicted 'every principle of justice and humanity'.[115] Robinson feared the clauses would lead to concealment of illegitimate births and infanticide, and strenuously objected because women had been excluded from participation in the legislature and had no voice in the proceedings on matters of most concern to them.[116]

MP Benett, a former magistrate who had served for 30 years in a rural county, vigorously supported Robinson, arguing: 'The clauses proceed on the principle, women would perjure themselves for the small premium of 1s. per week.'[117] Were they to assume, 'these poor, unfortunate souls, whom he perceived as honest women, intended to universally and publicly commit the crime of perjury for more than 2 s. 6 d. a week.'[118] Benett continued: 'The law merely intended that no child, however valueless it might be to some gentlemen in that House, and to some persons in the country, should perish.'[119] When brought to a vote, the bastardy clauses passed by a majority of 81. Thirty-three MPs favoured Mr Robinson's proposal to remove the bastardy clause from the Poor Law Amendment Acts, and 114 voted to retain the clauses as they stood.[120]

Perhaps the most controversial clause relating specifically to relief of unmarried mothers included a recommendation under section 55, which removed the power to grant relief to unwed mothers, from local magistrates to quarter sessions courts.[121] This move would make it extremely difficult for unwed mothers to receive a legal remedy against the father.[122] Sections 67–71 repealed acts relating to the liability and punishment of the putative father and the mother of an illegitimate child, while including language holding the mother liable for support. Sections 72–76 required overseers, soon to be poor law guardians, to apply, on behalf of the unmarried mother, for an order against the father for maintenance. The proceedings required testimony and corroborating evidence from the mother, with no part of the money serving to support the mother.[123] The commissioners acknowledged they intended the ruling to prohibit women from committing perjury and extortion, specifically by raising false charges against wealthy men. They recognized little chance of indemnification for a woman if she went to quarter sessions courts.[124]

The third reading of the Poor Law Bill took place on 1 July 1834. A closing shot fired across the bow included a point from MP Leech, who stated the nature of the bill 'must render the breech between the rich and the poor wider than it had ever been hitherto'.[125] Noting the House did not have a quorum with only 50 members attending on the day of the third reading, Mr Hodges rightly assumed members must have made up their minds on the bill. The Commons retorted, 'Hear! Hear!' Hodges submitted the bill intended to meet the needs of the agricultural interests, but failed on this count. Rather, it set out four main principles and measures: 'alterations in the law of settlement, alteration of the bastardy law, throwing into unions the various parishes throughout the country with the creation of workhouses, and after the 1st of June 1835 able-bodied persons would not be entitled to relief unless in the workhouse'.[126] Hodges believed the bill would change the poor of the country into thieves. He knew many gentlemen believed if the indigent could not receive outdoor relief, then they would emigrate.[127]

In closing, Lord Althorp remarked the problem of surplus labour could not be solved by the workhouse, but 'he was still of the opinion, as when he first brought the measure forward that they could no longer allow the present system to go on without attempting its amendment'.[128] Fears caused by surplus population, the threat of revolt nurtured by the impoverished condition of the English labourers, a noticeable rise in Irish immigration, and a desire to limit ratepayer spending by curbing outdoor relief contributed to the passage of the bill in the Commons on the third reading. 'Ayes for the third reading, 187, Noes 50; Ayes majority for the third reading, 137.'[129] The members of the Commons, who supported the final proposals, utterly abandoned discussions of the role of parish vestries, magistrates, the rates and the condition of England as a whole. Instead, it became a spending measure intended to curb improvidence and to prevent England from declining into to the conditions prevailing in Ireland, which they all knew too well.[130] The Commons sent the bill to the House of Lords where debate continued.

The Commons Sends Recommendations to the Lords: Poor Law Debates

On 21 July 1834, Lord Chancellor Henry Brougham rose in the House of Lords to introduce the Poor Law Commission's recommendations as amended by the House of Commons. According to *The Times*:

> He lent weight to their task, pronouncing it, of paramount importance, increased by its difficulties in principal and its complexity in detail.[131]

Brougham thanked the individuals who inspired the reforms, including Thomas Malthus in whom the 'Church of England possessed no brighter character'. Malthus' influence on the Poor Law Commission, including Nassau Senior and Edwin Chadwick, brought changes reversing 'the primal curse pronounced upon man', the Elizabethan Poor Laws.[132] The Lord Chancellor defended the magistrates, noting they were not to blame for the current condition of the poor laws. Rather, as the 'first judges in the courts of law', they had dispatched their duties in a liberal and generous a manner, straying from the original intent of the Speenhamland system. The law had not intended to:

> Proceed on the principle that every poor man had the right to be supported comfortably in his own dwelling, himself and his family, and to be furnished with a cow, a pig, or other animal yielding reasonable and sufficient food.[133]

Surely, the function of the legislature, Brougham argued, was not to make every man comfortable or to encourage idleness. Furthermore:

> A man [not necessarily women] should be paid according to the work he did, that he should be employed according to the demand of those who had work to give, that those employed should not live worse than those who were idle, and that the mere idler should not run away for himself with any portion of that which the industrious man had earned for his own support. (Hear! Hear!)... No man had a right to sit idle while the other man worked.[134]

When Brougham introduced debates on proposed changes to the Act of Settlement, the right to relief in the poor law parish of residence, he elicited a protracted discussion from the Lords. The settlement issue had come up at the time the Foundling Hospital opened its doors. Charitable institutions could not have existed in London parishes without a special dispensation relieving poor law overseers of responsibility for infants delivered at lying-in facilities or abandoned on the doorsteps of churches, private homes or other charities. Notably, he remarked, the Foundling Hospital charter freed the parish of St George Bloomsbury of all responsibilities for 'foundlings'. While charters at Queen Charlotte's Lying-in Hospital and elsewhere required administrators to keep records showing the birth of the child and the mother's name to ensure that if the mother gave birth in a 'non-birth parish', then the infant would follow her settlement. The 'Act for the Better Regulation of Lying-in Hospitals,'[135] deemed it 'prudent that no bastard child born in any such hospital or place be legally settled in or be entitled to relief from the parish wherein it is situated'.[136]

Therefore, the Lords focused on how to create a legal identity entitling an individual to relief. The Bishop of London, Charles James Blomfield, cited abuses among employers, particularly those who kept domestic servants. Blomfield observed domestic servants dominated the field of applicants at the Foundling Hospital, commenting they held positions for 'fifty-one weeks and one day'. If, after 51 weeks, the employer wished to retain them, they would need to be rehired. On the other hand, if the domestic lost her 'situation', she would be ineligible for help in the parish where she worked because she had not fully established residency by living in the parish for one year. Although not specifically designed to protect employees from exploitation by their employers, certain protections built into the Law of Settlement on this count would work in favour of the employee.[137]

Clear divisions existed on the issue of support for the abandoned mother, a would-be Foundling Hospital petitioner and her child. According to Lord Kenyon, the public considered the bill a 'measure of extreme harshness and cruelty'.[138] Bishop of Exeter Henry Philpotts, along with Lord Wynford, brought up provocative questions in debating the legislation with Lord Chancellor Brougham and the Bishop of London, both staunch supporters of Nassau Senior's views.[139] Exeter and Wynford believed the magistrates would feel uncomfortable and embarrassed if confronted with a pregnant woman seeking relief from the putative father. 'It would be disgraceful to any magistrate to suffer a woman to be so examined in a public room, and there is no law requiring such an indecent thing.'[140] Exeter charged the 'law of England – which ought to be a transcript of the law of God' – could not make the mother liable for maintenance of an illegitimate child simply because she was the only identifiable parent. In his opinion, the report placed the blame on her. Charging, 'illicit intercourse, in almost all cases, originates with the female'.[141] He regarded this harsh judgment with sorrow, noting how the report regarded fathers of out-of-wedlock infants and children as 'unfortunate'. On the other hand, magistrates charged the mother with 'vice'.[142] In Exeter's view, the child's legitimacy depended on both parents; it was the 'natural state' of affairs for a dependent child and 'a restraint of Providence'.[143] Lord Wynford agreed the crime of creating an illegitimate child 'common to man and to woman'. He questioned how the punishment of one party would solve the problem of illegitimacy when the other escaped culpability. He argued the amendments freed the man from the 'inconvenience of becoming a father to the child'.[144] He projected an increase in infanticide rates, if the charges of 'bastardy' fell to the mother, and quite possibly a rise in unwed mothers who entered the workhouses, where she would face further exposure to degradation. The Bishop of Exeter and Lord Wynford predicted the mother's alienation because society would cast blight on her character if she delivered her infant in a workhouse.[145] Brougham responded: the commissioners confronted the problem of how to preserve female chastity and how to prevent 'bastards' from becoming chargeable on the parish.[146] The Bishop of London countered that the bill did not prohibit the father from helping the mother. Further, Exeter and Wynford had overstated their case.[147] Exeter responded: 'Here cast upon the floor', (the bill) lay the fate of unwed mothers.'[148] He invoked his clerical authority to speak from the pulpit, as it were, asserting the law held both parents of an illegitimate child responsible, noting the law said 'parents' and not the singular 'parent'.[149] The burden and duty should not be removed from the father, though law bound the mother sustain her child. 'At that tremendous extremity of suffering in nature, woman must have assistance – she must have support – she must have it then, and from some time afterwards.' In Exeter's view, it was a mockery of the laws of nature and God to cast this 'undivided burthen' upon women, who were not designed or qualified to bear the full upkeep of children independently.[150] If the law forced the mother to pick up this burden, the bishop warned, women would try every expedient possible to place the burden for her baby into the hands of others.[151] Although he doubted more women would commit infanticide, he suggested the likely scenario to be abandonment. He forewarned of mothers nicely wrapping up their infants, nestling them in baskets, and placing them on the front doorsteps of vicars and overseers; or of many more mothers petitioning the Foundling Hospital. Who, he asked, was prepared to take up this responsibility.[152]

Exeter's plea failed. In a motion to exert their final imprimatur on the Poor Law Amendments, the House of Lords, led by the Bishop of London, rejected the Commons advice to remove the mother's appeal from quarter sessions courts to the lower courts. The Lords also required the mother pressing filiation charges to provide corroborating evidence, including two witnesses against the putative father.[153] In attempting to close the debates in August 1834, the Lord Chancellor stated the Lords were impatient 'to come to a division on the question'. It had already been debated six or seven times; besides, the Bishop of London's speech covered all the issues and it was a waste of time to continue.[154]

The Lords voted and the bill passed by a majority of 11: 93 in favour, 82 opposed.[155] The day after the Lords approved the Amendments and authorized their publication in the *Parliamentary Debates*, seven opposing members published a protest in *The Times* stating their opposition to the bastardy laws as central to their discontent.[156] The Duke of Wellington first stepped forward and protested the clauses directed against poor women. The Marquess of Westminster, Marquess of Lansdowne, Lord Wynford and the Bishop of Exeter supported Wellington. The Bishop of Exeter exclaimed he could not conceal his gratification for the support. The opposing voices included the Bishop of London and the Marquess of Salisbury. The Duke of Richmond took an indeterminate stance, arguing the language was too harsh. The point of the bill, however, was to stop the practice of 'giving women money to settle questions of bastardy by way of a bargain'.[157] Ultimately, the Lords most adverse to the amendments included the Bishop of Exeter and Lords Wynford, Penshurst, Falmouth and Mountcashel.[158] They launched final protests, joining company with the like-minded MPs in the Commons, who stood outside the chambers of Westminster Hall, but they remained in the minority. On 14 August 1834, 4 & 5 Will. 4 c. 76 s. 1–109 received royal assent.[159]

Commissioners who prepared the 1834 bill attacked the 'moral depravity of women', as evidenced in the reports from the survey and the bastardy recommendations themselves. Strongly influenced by Malthusian theories, the commissioners asserted, hitherto, the law had implicitly legalized pre-marital sexual relations and encouraged the celebration of improvident marriages, making socially undesirable births more likely.[160] The New Poor Law made it almost impossible for unwed mothers to obtain the necessary legal support or financial redress from the father. Lawsuits for child maintenance, tried in quarter sessions courts, required corroborating evidence as to the identity of the father.[161] The law limited maintenance costs for the father. It also required fathers to remit money to poor law guardians, not the mother. The commissioners expected the collected funds to apply to the welfare of the child and not to the mother, adding a layer of separation between the mother and financial support.[162] The laws placed the responsibility of childcare squarely on the mother's shoulders until the child turned 16 years of age, married, or died, whichever came sooner. If the woman married, the child would follow her husband's settlement. The commissioners intended these restrictions and limitations to serve as a preventive measure aimed at reducing illegitimacy and improving sexual morals. The new laws did nothing of the sort, but the amendments fundamentally rearranged the statutory codes.[163]

To Discourage the Poor from Improvident Habits: Further Legislation

Although subject to frequent criticism and occasional administrative-structural changes, the New Poor Laws remained relatively intact until the end of World War I.[164] Clearly, the 1834 Act held unintended consequences, demanding more institutionalized space for the poor than the legislators could have ever imagined. By 1850, the local workhouse provided a domicile for the destitute.[165] Three consecutive regulatory bodies headed the organizational hierarchy of the New Poor Laws after passage of the bill. For a period of 12 years, the Poor Law Commission, a centralized authority responsible to Parliament, oversaw activities at the local level of government, but commissioners petitioned to end their role, and to replace it with a Poor Law Board in 1847. Approximately 600 poor law unions operated as the basic unit of administration in England. In 1869, London poor law administrators divided the metropolis into 40 poor law unions and parishes. Ratepayers elected guardians, or overseers, who had considerable autonomy.[166] In 1871, the Local Government Board merged duties of the Board with public health services and a variety of other responsibilities.[167] Between 1834 and 1929, the central authority determined the amount of relief and audited the financial records.

The Board could disallow or refuse to pay for union expenditures, but it had limited ability to enforce policies on different unions.[168]

The authority invested in the guardians by their office to dispense aid also encouraged them to understand their role as arbiters of the common good. In the 1860s, vestiges of the outdoor relief remained, forcing guardians and MPs to revisit complaints, particularly the issue of 'improvident women'. According to Inspector Henry Longley, 'the mere existence of a poor law is unquestionably a discouragement, ipso facto, to the formation by the poor of provident habits'.[169] When put into practice, the new statutes often did not work or worked badly. The growing problem of abandoned mothers and infants without fathers caused many problems for guardians and magistrates. Calls for review of the bastardy clauses appeared within a few short years of the 1834 legislation. According to the historian Thomas Mackay, the public developed a strong distaste for the newly legislated 'inequities'. Soon after the passage of the bill, magistrates and others 'wished to strain the Act in order to provide a civil remedy for the woman and a penalty for the man'.[170]

The commission received countless letters from magistrates voicing complaints and raising questions. In 1835, Nottingham magistrates said the recommendations slowed a mother's appeal for affiliation, because the law made it too difficult for the mother to obtain corroborating evidence. Although the mother may have cooperated on her behalf, officers lacked the power to charge the father with failing to meet his duties. Because the time line for prosecution of putative fathers drove the process, the magistrates recommended that they should decide the remedy, if any, at the first hearing. Further, even if they charged the child's father for support, they lacked a standard method of computation in order to determine how much he needed to pay and for how long. If the child remained on the chargeable rates, commissioners suggested designating the father in default of support. Yet, by the time magistrates finally ruled on whether the case proved appropriate for quarter sessions, the father had departed.[171] Even with obvious flaws in the process of establishing paternity, commissioners held firm and in 1835 responded:

> The Poor Law Commission had no desire to force a 'father' into a marriage he was unwilling to uphold. Imprisonment, on the other hand, might also force the father to marry the mother, and this 'would always be an evil'.[172]

The commissioners queried: 'Is, or is it not, desirable to revert to the principle on which the bastardy laws stood prior to the Poor Law Amendment Act? Or is it better to follow out the recommendations contained in the Poor Law Report, and abandon orders of affiliation altogether?' The protesting guardians proposed alternatives, including support for the mother and pursuit of the father if he reneged on his duties. To which the commissioners scornfully commented:

> It should be borne in mind, that though more money may be expended in the applications to the magistrates at Quarter Sessions than can ever be recovered from the fathers of the children, it does not seem likely that the practice will discourage those it aims to oppose.[173]

Here, the Poor Law Commission inferred the poor law unions would spend more money seeking financial restitution than they could garner from an errant father. They also understood the guardians had no choice but to pursue the father if they wanted to keep the rates down. Therefore, in an indirect way, the Commission acknowledged the legislation placed burdens on the system for which they were ill prepared. Nonetheless, no other clauses demanded so much of the guardians' administrative attention.[174] In 1838, the House of Commons revisited the bastardy amendments under the leadership of Lord John Russell. The proposal sought to change the court of appeal from quarter sessions to petty sessions. Instead, two justices of the peace, at the local level of government would hear the case, removing another step towards appeal in order to expedite the cases more quickly. Russell's proposal failed, because the commissioners argued their point sufficiently enough against him to uphold the bastardy amendment.[175]

Bastardy continued to be a financial issue for ratepayers and an administrative problem for poor law guardians.[176] Consequently and despite earlier opposition, Parliament amended the bastardy or 'custody of infants' clauses three times before the end of the century, 1844–5, 1872, and 1873.[177] The Bastardy Amendment Act of 1844 removed proceedings from quarter sessions courts to the local magistrates and lifted the responsibility for affiliation proceedings from the guardians. The new Act provided for a 'summary' method of procedures in which the mother brought evidence and at least two witnesses against the putative father. The magistrate, unconstrained by the tenets of common law, adjudicated based on his knowledge of community norms and the presentation of facts.[178] The amendment still intended to hold the mother responsible. It stated:

> The mother of a bastard would be in the same condition as any other pauper, being bound to maintain her child to the best of her ability, and being entitled to relief if destitute; whilst she would have against the putative father a direct and summary remedy, independent of the [*sic*] chargeability of her bastard, and founded on a proceeding in which she found herself as the plaintiff.[179]

This legislation broadened the jurisdiction for pursuit of the putative father, and enabled the unwed mother, not the poor law guardians, to initiate the lawsuit. Magistrates in the lower courts would hear the cases, yet they had little legal jurisdiction over the father. They could not force runaway fathers to pay. As the venue of the court of appeals shifted, the guardians no longer held the responsibility for collecting money from the father and they would not pursue the father on the mother's behalf.[180] The statute, however, continued to require the destitute mother to recount her story to the guardians in order to receive relief. Therefore, guardians found it impossible to maintain emotional distance, because they found themselves drawn into personal crises when a woman appeared at the workhouse doors in straitened circumstances, pregnant, out of a job, abandoned by the father of her child, and without food, clothing and shelter. If the guardians believed they could follow the father, they occasionally petitioned the magistrates on the mother's behalf.[181] Later legislation confirmed this strategy when laws again permitted poor law guardians to ask the father for money through the magistrates.[182]

In an overstatement of the effects of the 1844 legislation, Thomas W. Fowle, a late nineteenth-century poor law historian, maintained, 'bastardy cease[d] to be a special part of poor law administration, and further mention of the subject may be spared'.[183] Poor law scholar Pat Thane argues the 1844 Poor Law Amendment Act marked a step forward because it 'allowed [unwed] mothers to sue for an affiliation order against the putative father in a magistrate's court'.[184] Only slightly positive, mothers still had to establish proof through witnesses, and she bore the full responsibility of the illegitimate child until it reached 16 years of age, she or the child died. The amendments did not guarantee full restitution because the mother gained only when and if the father agreed to cooperate. Throughout the 1860s, the problems posed by unwed mothers, illegitimate and abandoned children, and the impunity afforded 'unwed fathers' under the poor laws and statutory laws caused much debate. The Registrar General considered the problem of out-of-wedlock births and infanticide of such grave significance; it began tabulations of all reported cases in every poor law union. *The Saturday Review* pressed the issue by publishing essays linking seduction, illegitimacy and infanticide together.[185]

Public concern eventually resonated in Parliament when it again set up a committee to investigate infant mortality and baby farming. Both issues clearly related to the compromised situation of mothers and children who lacked financial support. Baby farming, or placing an infant with a wet-nurse while the mother worked, triggered an investigation of these practices, along with infanticide and concealment in 1872.[186] Findings from a select committee on provisions for unwed mothers influenced reforms of poor law statutes relating to 'bastardy' later in the year. At the hearings held by the Committee on Protection of Infant Life, Mr John Curgenven, a surgeon and secretary of the Harveian Medical Society, the group that had drawn up recommended changes for prosecution of errant fathers, explored the relationship between the laws and the condition of unmarried mothers.[187] When questions about affiliation proceedings for an illegitimate child arose, Curgenven responded: 'The mothers alone have to struggle with their children; the fathers do nothing for them.'[188] His questioner, Mr Jacob Bright, responded: 'Is that so? Very often they do not know who the fathers are.'[189] Bright argued it no use to try to make the father pay; worse, he believed, the mother simply wished to rid herself of her child.[190] Bright's claims went to the heart of the hearings. MPs experienced alarm after reading reports from the Obstetrical Society and Ernest Hart's collection of essays on 'infant life'. In some parts of the country, illegitimate infant death rates stood at 35 per cent and in London, the rates were as high as 75 per cent.[191] These questions and concerns eventually led to revision of the Bastardy Amendment Act of 1844.[192]

The 1872 Act provided aid to an unwed mother.[193] If she could prove the father had given her money for relief before the birth of the child, then she could start filiation proceedings at once, appear in petty sessions and attest to this. The justices of the peace could then summon the putative father to court. The law required the father to either pay the maintenance costs of the child, or to sit in jail for three months. The laws required paternal maintenance until the child reached 16 years of age. Section four stipulated that even if the unwed mother had not received any money, she was still required to provide evidence, testify and identify the putative father before a justice in petty sessions to be eligible for aid. Moreover, under section six, if the child had fallen on the parish and the mother appeared incapable of suing for support but willing to give a deposition, the guardians could charge the father for funding 'in certain cases' and place him in jail. Whether jail time deterred men from extra-marital affairs and abandonment is doubtful. The likely outcome of this legislation served to encourage the putative father to leave the county if not the country. Although the new law provided a modicum of legal support, difficulties remained in actually collecting money from the father.[194] In 1909, Parliament once again addressed responsibilities for children born out-of-wedlock. The 'Necessitous Mothers Assistance Act' empowered local authorities to assist women who applied before, during, and after their pregnancy.[195] The bill provided food, medical aid, midwifery and nursing care, and clothing for the mother and newborn for a period not to exceed one year. The law required local authorities to coordinate with all existing voluntary agencies. The right to apply for aid extended to married and single women, thus retaining the 'franchise, right, or privilege'. This act applied to England, Scotland, and Wales, but not to Ireland.[196]

Also at this time, Parliament amended the 'bastardy acts' to restore the father's responsibility for the creation of a child. In cases where a wealthy father had died before an unwed mother sued for support, the law permitted unwed mothers to bring a claim against his estate. In situations with a living father, the law required him to pay for maintenance of the child until the youngster reached 16 years of age. If the mother had received funds on behalf of her child and she died, then the child could inherit the money through his or her mother's estate. If the child became a ward of the state under the care of the Poor Law, then the guardians had the right to sue for maintenance against the father in sums not exceeding five shillings a week (the average sum paid to certified poor law facilities by administrators) until the child reached 16 years of age. The guardians or mothers retained the option to invest the maintenance money in government annuities at the post office. The mother could opt not to deal face-to-face with the father in the courts. The law permitted her to request the maintenance payments through the courts or any person nominated and approved by the court.[197] These revisions show that ultimately, the legislation dealt with the problem of who should pay for, protect and nurture an illegitimate child or 'nobody's child', the mother, while suspending the father's responsibility for his actions.

In the last quarter of the nineteenth century, Parliament passed more bills relating to the guardianship and custody of infants. By way of contrast, in civil suits pressed by married mothers for custody of their children, the father had control and responsibility for his children. A married mother had no legal authority over her offspring during their father's lifetime. Before 1839, upon the death of her husband, the children faced the possibility of transference to a guardian nominated in the will. Worse still, the mother risked not seeing her children through legal prohibition.[198] The two acts dealt differently with child custody cases depending on the marital status of the mother. The 'Custody of Infants Act' passed in 1873. Under this statute, a wife's adultery ceased to be a bar to entitlement, but the custody of legitimate children continued to be a matter decided by the courts as evidenced by the case brought by Mrs Annie Besant in 1878.[199] Married women seeking separation from their husbands and wishing to have custody of their children had little support from the courts at this time. The Act dealing with guardianship of children and paternal control of children dated back to the common law: guardianship in chivalry, abolished by law, in socage (infant under 14 inherits land by descent), by nature and by nurture.[200] Guardianship by nature was an incident of tenure in chivalry through which the privilege belonged primarily to the father. 'The right of the father except as limited by statute and the control of the courts [was] absolute even against the mother.' The Custody Act gave magistrates jurisdiction in child custody proceedings if separation occurred between married parents; if parents were not married and living separately, the authorities could take custody of an 'abandoned' child. The authorities could determine the religion of such a child. Amendments, to the legislation in 1884 and 1886, held both parents liable, despite other behaviours. On the death of either of the parents, the courts had the power to appoint the surviving parent as the guardian.[201] The 1886 change in the House of Lords ensured the courts were free to determine who should pay for the child, thus finally placing the burden of child support on the father.[202]

Gradual legal changes suggested a growing awareness and willingness to support young women who had been 'taken advantage of by men'. Acts to stiffen penalties for men took decisive steps on behalf of girls. A new law passed to address the 'forcible abduction of girls under the age of sixteen' by an older man, whereby the offender could be charged with a misdemeanour.[203] Under the Criminal Law Amendment Act of 1885, legislators increased the age of abduction to 18 years and strengthened the penalty for abduction. Yet, the case had to show clear evidence of abduction with the intent to rape or carnally know the victim. The jury, then, determined whether the girl was 'in possession of her person' at the time of the assault.[204] Cases such as these appear from time to time in Foundling Hospital petitions, but, are by no means common to accepted or rejected cases.

The New Poor Laws, as delineated in the recommendations by the Poor Law Commission, marked a sweeping and drastic piece of social legislation. According to the London Local Government Board Inspector Henry Longley, these aimed 'to combine the maximum of efficiency in the relief of destitute applicants, and the minimum of incentive to improvidence'.[205] This principle guided local authorities for the next 75 years.[206] If anything, since the law exonerated unwed fathers of responsibility for their offspring, society witnessed a rise in the abandonment of mothers and babies.[207] Instead of resolving the problem of 'unchaste women', as most legislators laid the blame on women for irresponsible behaviour, the law burdened mothers, and hardly improved circumstances for children. Because of these recommendations, relying on the workhouse for sustenance, the birth and care of children, would become ingrained in the minds of respectable and those respectability-seeking Victorians as a sign of failure. Before addressing the women and services made available at the London Foundling Hospital, it is important to understand the risks and circumstances of the wide majority of women who did not have the wherewithal to gain admission for their infant and instead, truly fell on the poor laws.

Oh the Dropped Child Is Dead!: Long-Term Outcomes of Poor Law Legislation

The new laws instructed guardians, clergymen and receiving officers to provide the poor, the able-bodied, women, children, the aged, infirm and vagrants (a largely male constituency) with tickets for admission to the workhouse.[208] Conditions were so repulsive in most places that some women would rather starve on the streets or turn to begging than enter the workhouse. If possible, anyone with a thread of pride avoided the 'house'.[209] Women with a special responsibility for children were most likely to require poor relief. To avoid the workhouse some engaged in part-time prostitution, begged for food, abandoned their infants, starved to death, committed infanticide, or ended a pregnancy rather than stigmatize their child with delivery in the 'house'. They often had few choices; they either could go to the 'house', or die, or watch their children die. Accounts of women, children, and families who tried to resist the constraints of the relief system appear in the press, parliamentary minutes of evidence, police reports, accounts of guardians, and the Foundling Hospital records. The impact of restrictions on outdoor relief and outright abhorrence of the workhouse highlighted here provide the backdrop to the admissions policy and services offered by the Bloomsbury institution.

The women who applied to the Foundling Hospital for admission of their infants had a will to survive; they struggled in the face of daunting challenges. A pending childbirth obviously removed a lone mother from the labour force, required her to find a shelter wherein she could deliver her baby, remain in bed until recovery, and receive food necessary for survival of her newborn. The birth of a child required extra money to pay for a midwife, doctor or surgeon to attend the birth. English poor law workhouses served as community-birthing centres and childcare sites where mothers received food, however poor the quality, a bed, however rough, and medical assistance. In most cases, the workhouse and attendant buildings remained the least desirable venue for childbirth for most of the century. Many women, especially those faced with an illicit pregnancy, often had no other recourse. Private charities, such as Queen Charlotte's Lying-In Hospital, required letters of recommendation attesting to respectability; while home deliveries were out of the question for most women faced with an out-of-wedlock pregnancy, primarily because of the risk of discovery. Indigent London women relied on poor law infirmaries for their confinement.[210] The limited maternity services offered there slowly improved, especially after the 1866 cholera epidemic and passage of the Metropolitan Asylums Board Act in 1867. Yet, 'any unchaste woman, whether a parishioner or not, when approaching her confinement has only to present herself at a workhouse door and she must be admitted', wrote a Lambeth Union guardian.[211] Indeed, according to this individual, the public viewed the workhouse infirmary as a free hospital where 'vice' always had the right of entry over which the workhouse overseers had no control, meaning the power to 'punish', or 'discipline'. The Lambeth guardian added his perspective by characterizing the place as 'Liberty Hall!' Single women sometimes reappeared there in a state of pregnancy as many as four times.[212] Admission to some workhouse infirmaries required an unwed mother to stand before the guardians, all of whom were men, and request relief during her confinement. In other unions, women were admitted without questioning.[213] Dora Downright, one of England's first married female guardians, recounted in her run for election as poor law guardian how several women approached her and complained: 'If you knew, ma'am, what we has to suffer, you wouldn't mind being a Poor Law Guardian for our sakes.'[214] Her prepared account offers a rare glimpse from a woman's point of view into workhouse admission practices in one rural community.[215] After her successful election as a guardian, she learned about poor women and their problems when she began to attend the board meetings. The first time she witnessed an unmarried mother appearing asking for relief, the humiliation and discomfort of the petitioner appalled her. According to Downright:

> As the poor young thing came into the board-room, accompanied by the beadle, and looking ready to sink to the ground with shame, I saw a glance of curiosity, quite as insulting as compassionate, go round the table.[216]

When the guardians questioned the workhouse petitioner as to why she requested admission, she almost buckled under their stares. Downright queried: 'How much less regard is paid to the class which is generally supposed, but I think erroneously, to have no feelings at all?'[217] After witnessing the insensitivity of the guardians, Downright offered to meet privately with the young woman and then to provide a report. She observed how some applying to the workhouse infirmary were poor married women who simply needed help. In *Why I Am a Guardian*, Downright empathized with women who went to poor law officials for help. She wrote that as the confinement approached, one could fancy 'what the feelings of a respectable married woman' must have been the first time she appeared before a 'Board of gentlemen'. The services for which the women petitioned were often rudimentary because the master and matron managed the workhouse, they were not professionals such as doctors and nurses. Downright described how the master and matron seemed to have settled everything themselves. She found the workhouse ill arranged and poorly ventilated. Downright claimed the cooking wasteful and careless, and the washing so badly done, the clothes looked nearly as black after as before laundering. Children frequently lacked sufficient clothing, something as simple as a flannel undershirt, for example. Disappointed, one of the first female guardians of the poor opined she would have expected the matron if not the master of the workhouse to meet the simple needs of the children.[218] Undoubtedly, her narrative explains why small-town unwed mothers fled to urban centres in search of aid during their confinement.

Many women who sought confinement at the workhouse left as soon as they were physically able because infant mortality rates were extremely high, and the stigma attached to remaining too long in the workhouse proved difficult to overcome. Some observers of the system considered the Marylebone Infirmary progressive because it separated patients based on their afflictions, rather than by character. In testimony taken by the 'Select Committee on Infant Life', guardians from the Marylebone Union testified almost unanimously that they never refused poor law infirmary services for a destitute woman in labour.[219] Of the total born at Marylebone workhouse between 1869 and 1871, 28 per cent of the infants were legitimate. Generally, the guardians conflated high infant mortality rates with illegitimacy; they reported that of the 72 per cent illegitimate infants born at Marylebone over 20 per cent died within one week after birth.[220] With this widely known reputation came the threat of public derision for the institution and the women served there. If her infant survived the first several weeks of life, the baby remained in jeopardy. Under these circumstances, some mothers abandoned their infants to the streets of London.[221]

The unwillingness of ratepayers and guardians to provide support to unwed mothers, and the stigma of illegitimacy encouraged self-induced abortions, infanticide, infant abandonment and child desertion, particularly in West London. For domestics who would lose their jobs on the spot should their mistress discover their pregnancy, abandonment posed an unattractive alternative. Most women understood, if they deposited their infants in an obvious setting where passersby would notice them quickly such as on the front doorstep of the vicar's house, they had a chance to survive. If passersby refused to pick up an abandoned child, the baby would most likely die. If rescued and turned over to a responsible individual, such as a police officer or vicar, the authorities transported the baby to the workhouse. The guardian then asked a pauper mother with an infant of her own to nurse the foundling. This child would then be considered a genuine 'foundling' or dropped child, the sort of baby Dickens's pauper nurse had seen too many times:

> 'Oh, the dropped child was dead!' The old pauper nurse turned around: With her shabby gown half on, half off, and fell a crying with all her might. In the deep grief and affliction of her heart; turning away her

dishevelled head: sobbing most bitterly, wringing her hands, and letting fall an abundance of great tears that choked her utterance. Oh, the child that was found in the street, and she had brought up ever since, had died an hour ago, and see where the little creature lay, beneath this cloth! The dear, the pretty dear![222]

Infant and child abandonment rates in London, during the last quarter of the nineteenth century, were as dismal as the infant mortality rates. Mr Daniel Cooper from the Rescue Society testified how Metropolitan and City Police reports listed 376 infant bodies found in the metropolis, and between 1 January and 19 May 1871 more than 105 dead bodies had been found. Some of the infants were less than seven days old; one infant was 21 days. Mr Cooper doubted the mothers could have abandoned the infants themselves. 'The 96 newly born could hardly have been left there by their mothers, but must have been left there by third persons.' Cooper most likely attributed this behaviour to the owners of the 'secret-lying in hospitals' and baby farmers.[223]

In Chelsea and neighbouring Kensington, both wealthy neighbourhoods, mothers knew the guardians would bring in their infants if they left them on the doorsteps of the workhouse. Alternative sites were the residence of the Sisters of Charity of St Vincent de Paul, or the house of a wealthy family, or a park. According to St Mary Abbot's (Kensington) baptismal register, parents had abandoned 61 infants and children between 1878 and 1901.[224] Between June 1875 and Christmas 1876, the Chelsea Workhouse received 71 infants and children whose ages ranged from three weeks to two years. Of these 71 infants, only two had died, because mothers in the workhouse infirmary took on the responsibility of feeding and caring for abandoned infants.[225] The emotional and physical conflicts single mothers faced are dramatized by the Mary Griffiths' 'child murder case' as publicized in the *Evening Standard* and the *Times* in 1889. Griffiths, 23 years of age, delivered her illegitimate baby in Marylebone Workhouse. The *Evening Standard* reported, 'Mary Griffiths, a domestic servant, was charged, on remand, with having feloniously caused the death of her illegitimate male child by drowning it in the Serpentine', a stream running through Hyde Park, on or about 14 September.[226] From Wales, she knew she was pregnant when she arrived in London in December 1888. She found a situation as a kitchen maid in elegant Sloane Square, Chelsea. Although the Marylebone workhouse provided shelter for her delivery, Griffiths feared the ruination of her 'character' if she remained in the infirmary past her confinement, a period of two weeks. Hence, she left, with the help of friends for the seaside town of Margate. While there, her weakly infant 'almost died from fits'. Griffiths revived the baby by placing it in a warm water bath. Upon her return to London, her former employer aided her in finding a place to stay at the Gladstone Home situated on Great Portland Street, a charity assisting out of service domestics.[227] Ordinarily the Gladstone Home would not have admitted Griffiths because she had a baby, but the Lady Superintendent at the home made an exception for the mother because she arrived with a good reference and her baby was so ill.

Residents at the Gladstone Home reported the baby cried many times and disturbed them while they were trying to sleep. The matron testified that she would have permitted Miss Griffiths to remain in the home until she found a *situation*, or employment, but she had a baby.[228] Griffiths constituted a burden to society.[229] She looked in vain for work as a kitchen maid, which would include food and a place to stay, and provide enough money to pay for a wet-nurse. In the meantime, Griffiths wrote to a friend that she was preparing to find a proper home for her infant. First, she went to the Foundling Hospital, trekking across London from Regent's Park to Bloomsbury, finding her way to Great Coram Street. At the Foundling Hospital, she learned about the petitioning process and her need for witnesses and a hearing. From Guilford Street, she made her way to Carlisle Place where the Sisters of Charity of St Vincent de Paul had opened an orphanage in 1859. The free orphanage for destitute children also provided a childcare facility for the children of the 'milk women' from High Barnet.[230] A few parents paid for their childcare, but most relied on the charity of the congregation. Carlisle Place would have been ideal for Mary because, if she could retain her job at Sloane Square, it would not have been too far to walk to see her child. When Griffiths appealed to the 'Sisters' Home', Sister Servant Chatelaine told Griffiths they could not accept any more babies because they were 'full up'. When Griffiths heard this, she fell into despair.[231]

The despondent mother returned to her friend, who reported Griffiths had stopped nursing her infant. They parted company about 9.30 p.m. and Griffiths began to walk aimlessly through Hyde Park where she purportedly dropped her infant into the Serpentine. Griffiths returned to the Gladstone Home where she reported to another 'inmate' that her baby was all right and a 'lady had got it'.[232] When questioned by Mr Angus Lewis, the prosecutor for the Treasury Department, she denied killing her baby. 'I did not do it. I left the child with a friend.' Then Griffiths changed her story and told Lewis that her son had another seizure and died in her arms. Griffiths remembered laying her baby in the stream.[233] The Hyde Park constable testified that he found the infant dressed in workhouse clothing and lying face-down in seven or eight inches of water. The police took the corpse to the workhouse mortuary where Dr Tweed pronounced death due to drowning. The coroner reported that he did not see marks of violence on the body.[234] Appearing before the magistrate, Griffiths pleaded innocent. She positively identified the clothing of John, her five-month-old infant.[235] When witnesses were asked whether Griffiths was fond of her child, they testified: 'Oh, yes sir; very fond of it.'[236] The magistrate ordered Griffiths held in custody. After her second hearing, the magistrate charged her with willfully murdering her child by drowning and set a date for trial.[237] At the second hearing, the mother again stated the infant had died in her arms. The counsel for her defense, Mr Matthew, asked the jury to consider the devotion and affection the prisoner had always evinced towards the child. He argued that the child had had another fit in Hyde Park on the night of 14 September, and believing the infant dead, Mary Griffiths placed her baby in the Serpentine. The jury found Griffiths guilty of manslaughter but strongly recommended her to the mercy of the court. Her defence attorney explained how arrangements had been made for her to return to the Gladstone Home. Justice Stephens, however, sentenced Mary Griffiths to three months' imprisonment with hard labour, not taking into any account her seriously afflicted baby and the high infant mortality rates for workhouse births.[238] Neither the magistrate nor the press mentioned the father during the trial. Mary Griffiths was an abandoned woman tramping the streets of West London with an infant in her arms.

The young woman left the scene of the death of her infant without reporting what had happened. Many other mothers left well babies in a public space with the intention of discovery, hoping them to become true foundlings. The degree of infant abandonment raised enough concern for *The Times* to publish a report on the treatment and naming of abandoned children by poor law guardians in 1867. One school of thought suggested foundlings could take the surnames of guardians or churchwardens under whose care they had been placed. Both the guardians and the churchwardens opposed this approach, arguing it 'uncharitable' in their opinion to name a pauper child after a respectable member of the community. While guardians and clergymen deliberated on what to name a 'foundling', the infants were temporarily registered with a forename and a pseudo-surname such as 'Mary Unknown'. Another strategy for naming the child provided the 'found' child with a common forename, and a surname reflecting the place where the passerby found the infant. For example, a name such as 'Polly Pancras' did the girl little good, since St Pancras remained a desolate slum community in West London. Obviously, 'Polly Pancras' had been found in the St Pancras Poor Law Union. On other occasions, at the baptism of foundlings the guardians christened the children 'Mary Smith' or 'Polly Jones'.[239]

After passage of a 'Bill to Amend the Law Relating to the Guardianship and Custody of Infants', poor law guardians kept detailed registers listing the date of the deserted child's admission, cause of desertion, name and last known address of parents, age at reception, date of resolution of the case, the ending date for Poor Law guardianship and religious creed for each case.[240] The passage of this law and further clarifications in 1889 marked early steps towards prosecuting the errant fathers.[241] In Kensington, St Mary Abbot's workhouse register reveals changing legal structures relating to women and children.[242] In 1881 workhouse clergymen baptized 82 babies listing no father, and the parents of only 12 baptized babies indicated they had married. The following year, a change in the law required the receiving officer to list the names of both parents, if they were cohabiting. Consequently, workhouse records saw a decline in illegitimacy and a rise in reported cohabitation. For example, the workhouse register for 1891 also listed four children as illegitimate, 32 couples as married, and 98 couples as cohabiting.[243]

The Chelsea Board of Guardians 'Register of Deserted Women and Children' for the year 1885 lists mothers and children, and children who were deserted and forced to enter the workhouse because their parent died, abandoned them, or one or both were in prison. Warrants for the arrest of the father or mother were filed in these registers. In one case, the guardians fined the father for desertion. Many children older than three years of age were listed as 'deserted'. Out of 27 families, seven were groups of two or more children admitted at the same time without their mothers. The youngest of these motherless children, a four-month-old female had a surname of 'Weston'. The guardians obviously knew the mother because the register noted a warrant for her arrest had been posted.[244] Whether the guardians wanted to assume the problems of single mothers or not, the burden fell on their shoulders. If older children appeared unattended on the streets, or someone reported his or her parents deserted him, the police took the children into custody and then turned them over to the poor law guardians. Sometimes relatives and neighbours brought 'abandoned' or 'jeopardized' children to the police station, just as they brought other problems and difficulties to the police. Desertion included leaving children at home unattended or in a 'disorderly' household. In the latter cases, the community, policemen, and magistrates aggressively removed children from 'disorderly houses' in the West End.[245] Police reports illustrate how increasing concerns for the welfare of children came to dominate social policy, and how poor law facilities became repositories for children endangered by the 'moral corruption' of their parents.

The New Poor Laws shaped strategies of the poor, particularly mothers. Their motivation in avoiding or having recourse to the workhouse, a place from which they could come and go, and their experiences in this institution highlights the constrained agency of the poor. Women tramped across London from place to place seeking assistance. While trying to care for a starving and crying infant, the mother's desperation sometimes led to infant abandonment or infanticide. Some mothers found a path leading them out of despair, others abdicated parental responsibilities, and still others struggled with little means until they met more favourable times. Many mothers sought some kind of institutional support for themselves and their children until they were capable of taking on childcare responsibilities. For the destitute, the Poor Law workhouse offered the only viable option. Only a small minority qualified for assistance from a private charity. Mary Griffiths' case is particularly telling. She could have chosen to go home, if she had a home, or a space for her, but then she would have had to face the humiliation heaped on her by her family, friends and neighbours. Alternatively, she could find a job, a 'situation', in order to afford a wet-nurse for her baby. Respectable orphanages such as the London Foundling Hospital were out of reach for an individual such as Mary Griffiths, as society deemed her character suspect; it would never pass approval. Moreover, association with the workhouse would have marked her character with disdain. In turn, for most of the nineteenth century members of the Poor Law Commission, poor law guardians and receiving officers had little respect for private charities, as these were said to promote improvidence. Even so, private charities offered an alternative to the workhouse. An analysis of the services, admissions procedures, institutional space, and population served by private charities, in contrast to those served by the workhouse is essential to gain a fuller understanding of the implications of space, values, gender and agency in the lives of London's poor.

2

Ornament of the Metropolis: Victorian Representation and Reality

> The Committee of Governors meet every Saturday Morning at Ten o'clock at the Foundling Hospital, to receive and deliberate on petitions praying for the admission of Children. Children can only be received into this Hospital upon personal application of the Mothers. Petitions must set forth the true State of the Mother's Case; for if any deception is used the Petition will be rejected, and the Child will not be received in to the Hospital. No application can be received previous to the birth of the Child, or should the child be above Twelve Months old. No person need apply, unless she shall have previously borne a good Character for Virtue, Sobriety, and Honesty.
> *Foundling Hospital Petition Form, 1813*[1]

Henry Brougham described the London Foundling Hospital as the 'ornament of the Metropolis', during the 1834 Poor Law debates in the House of Lords.[2] The Lord Chancellor praised the charity for its selective practices and efficient operations. Institutions such as the Foundling Hospital highlight political and social values associated with lived spaces of the charity and the people it served. The home for children had a long history dating from 1741, when Thomas Coram, a retired sea captain from Rotherhithe, opened its doors on Great Ormond Street. Charles Dickens described Coram in the following:

> Although the captain had made his fortune on the American plantation, and had seen sights in his day, he came out of it all with a tender heart; and this tender heart of Captain Coram was so affected by seeing blank children, dead and alive, habitually exposed by the wayside as he journeyed from Rotherhithe [where he had set up his retreat that he might keep a loving eye on the river] to the Docks and Royal Exchange, and from the Docks and Royal Exchange home to Rotherhithe again to receive the old shipmate, who was generally coming to dinner, that he could not bear it.[3]

Coram's sympathies for neglected children inspired him to provide a better chance at life by bringing them under one roof as infants. His aims included nurturing, training and preparing future British colonists.[4] Since the founder's attention pointed to the children, the 'foundlings', not the mothers, appeared in the forefront of public awareness because the eighteenth-century governors did not want to suggest their charity promoted vice, not to mention improvidence. A focus on the foundlings obscured the institution's more 'discrete mission' to unwed mothers. Several connecting and strong points need to be made about this history: the English Poor Laws formed the backdrop for assistance or lack thereof for all mothers, lone or married, leaving women, abandoned by the fathers of their children, in a highly vulnerable state of existence: the Foundling Hospital provided relief to a small percentage of those in need. The portion of the population who were eligible for the services diminished over time, as evidenced in the admission process, which selected only the most respectable applicants. This chapter pursues these themes by examining the history of the admissions process, the way in which the policy correlated to changes in the poor laws, and its impact on the beneficiaries of its charitable giving.

In 1741, the Foundling Hospital opened its doors in Hatton Garden, after receiving royal approbation from George II. At the time, the 'General Committee' decided not to give 'Preference to any Person'.[5] Mothers flocked to the doors on appointed days with their infants, indicating little advertising was necessary. Time barely passed before the demand for services rose dramatically.[6] When all the spaces for infants had been taken, the governors hung a notice on the door stating, 'The house is full'.[7] During the first year of operations, the governors received 113 children. The Foundling Hospital had to set intake limits because admitting an overwhelming number of infants strained financial resources it did not have and domiciliary care it could not provide. The governors appointed one day a month as 'taking-in day'. Crowds of anxious mothers appeared, and competition for available slots increased.[8] This approach lasted only until 1742.[9] Governors then chose to adopt a lottery, aiming at an equitable and even-handed admission process.

The method known as the ballot (as in vote by ballot) offered each applicant the same chance.[10] Table 2.1 indicates the number of infants accepted by the institution during the first 15 years of operations. Under the balloting system, the available openings determined numbers admitted. Governors called the mothers into a room, where they placed a proportionate number of white, red and black balls in a bag. The women then pulled a ball from the bag. A white ball signified an available slot; red meant being placed on the waiting list, and a black ball sent the mother from the hospital waiting room at once.[11] During the Seven Years War, the government called on the institution for assistance, which became known as the 'General Reception', lasting from 1756 to mid-1759. During this era, administrators received money from Parliament

Table 2.1: FH Admissions before the General Reception[12]

Admission Year	Number Admitted	Admission Year	Number Admitted
1741	113	1749	100
1742	47	1750	120
1743	23	1751	199
1744	0	1752	160
1745	45	1753	120
1746	52	1754	80
1747	101	1755	104
1748	80	1/1–6/1/1756	40
1741–8 Subtotal	461 Admitted	1749–6/1/1756 Subtotal	923 Admitted
1741–6/1/1756 Total			1384 Admitted

for veterans' children. In the first year in which this policy was in place, the hospital admitted 116 children, just over half as many as had been admitted in 1751.[13] Table 2.2 shows the arrival of an overwhelming mass of infants and children entering an ill-prepared asylum.

Table 2.2: FH General Reception Admissions[14]

Admission Year	Total
1756	1783
1757	3727
1758	4143
1759	3957
1760	1324
Total	14,934

Governors accommodated this many children by adding three country hospitals and homes at Shrewsbury, Ackworth in Yorkshire and Aylesbury near Oxford.[15] They also built houses at Westerham in Kent, and at Chester, Cheshire and Barnet, Hertfordshire in 1762.[16] The governors set only one restriction: children admitted could be no older than 12 years of age.[17] The liberal admissions policy proved counter-productive, because witnesses noted exorbitant mortality rates and the burden incurred enormous expenses.[18] On 3 May 1759, Parliament expressed reservations about the wisdom of providing funds for 'exposed and deserted' children stating simply: 'It would be pleasing to the public that they should be exonerated from the expense of maintenance as soon as possible.'[19] Sir Richard Lloyd's speech in Parliament recommended all persons in need would be best served by going to the workhouse, reflecting early ratepayer dissatisfaction with spending on the poor.[20] High infant mortality rates, labour costs, expenses for infant care, and perceptions that systematic state-sponsored help for illegitimate infants promoted licentiousness, made everyone skittish about funding this large social welfare project. The *Gentleman's Magazine* went so far as to claim the Foundling Hospital a 'Useless Burden'.[21] The annual cost to Parliament during the General Reception totalled £166,000. Worse, under the open admissions policy, the asylum 'put out' or graduated only 105 children from the apprenticeship programme. Moreover, the journalist also doubted such an institution capable of preparing loyal English subjects. How could children be loyal to their country if first they had not built up a loyalty to their parents? Further, many parents felt the overwhelming burden of out-of-wedlock children to the degree they were willing to give them up or abandon them to an institution. The article cast the infants as innocent victims and parents as the guilty parties. On 30 April 1760, a notice appearing under the letter 'D' in the *Gentleman's Magazine* served as an obituary for the period known as the 'General Reception'. The notice emphasized the disastrous loss of infant life between 25 March 1741 and 31 December 1759. Ultimately, this report undercut the public image of the Foundling Hospital as an effective institution dedicated to protecting children. The data, succinctly provided in a table, and reproduced in Table 2.3 doubtlessly shocked the public.[22] Although some discrepancies exist between Foundling Hospital registers and Table 2.4, the figures from the *Gentleman's Magazine* provide some valuable information. According to the *Magazine*, 14,994 infants and children entered during the General Reception. Actually, according to the Foundling Hospital register, the hospital admitted fewer children, 14,934, and the mortality rates were worse than reported.

A full accounting of the registers shows over 11,000 children or 68.3 per cent of the foundlings died. The deaths occurred for many reasons: a lack of

Table 2.3: The Disposition of FH Children, 1741–59[23]

Condition	Place	Number
Claimed and returned to parents	With parents	75
Boys apprenticed to sea service and husbandry	At service	87
Girls apprenticed out	At service	74
Alive in country		5,929
Alive in hospital in London		155
Alive in hospital in Ackworth		113
Alive in hospital in Aylesbury		40
Hospital at Shrewsbury		56
Total living children*		6,473
Died**	As of 31 December 1759	8,465
Children received	Before 21 June 1756	1,361
Total children received***		14,994

*Reported figures are not a summation of above numbers.
**Figures include infant deaths from opening date.
***Figure reflects infants received during General Reception per *Gentleman's Magazine.*

Table 2.4: Tally of FH Admissions Registers[24]

Condition	Children N
Total children received prior to 21 June 1756*	1,384
Total children received during General Reception	14,934
Total children received 3/1741–12/1759	16,318
Total infant deaths	≈11,000
Approximate number of survivors	6,318

money, improper care for infants and children, a dearth of wet-nurses, and the state of medical knowledge regarding infectious and epidemic diseases.[25] Presumably, the 6,473 living children who needed complete care for at least the next ten years of their lives including food, clothing, shelter and apprenticeship training most concerned the *Gentleman's Magazine*. Of course, Parliament covered the costs incurred for children received during the Seven Years War; these amounted to a staggering £33,000 per year, or £7 10 s per child.[26] George II provided an emergency grant of £5,000 in December 1759, but on 25 March 1760 (Lady Day) Parliament finally cut funding for new admissions. The last infant accepted under the 'general reception' policy was baptized as Kitty *Finis*, 'Kitty the last'. Payments continued for children until 1785 by which time the last wartime admittances had completed their apprenticeships.[27] In 1760, the Foundling Hospital register showed 6,857 surviving children. The termination of parliamentary funding meant the institution could not afford to take on more responsibilities.[28]

The 1759 financial crisis and public outcry over the dramatic decline in admission in the decade following the loss of state support appears on Table 2.5. Between 1761–2, the hospital admitted only 17 infants. Obviously, if the governors hoped for the charity to survive, they had to alter fund raising and admissions strategies. Ultimately, under a new and improved system, approximately 5,428 'foundlings' arrived between 1761 and 1907.[29] A slight rise in admissions, following the treaty ending the Seven Years War, would suggest these incoming foundlings were 'war orphans'.[30] The 1759 financial crisis and public outcry over infant mortality rates brought the Foundling Hospital governors a new understanding of their charity.

In 1762, governors began to develop a rationalized system of acceptance. They required the mother to complete a 'petition' for admission of her infant. By 1768, administrators demanded a completed letter of petition and a personal interview with Foundling Hospital 'committee men' for admission.[31] The petition and the development of a 'committee' to judge eligibility marked a radical departure from the ballot, the open admission during the General Reception, or for a short period through the poor law parishes. Between 1801 and 1813, governors ratcheted up the process and chose to become more selective by implementing a standardized form. In 1836, governors set further limitations. When Mr John Brownlow took office as secretary in 1849, the petition transcripts suggest a more vigorous attention to merits of petitioner in scope and detail.[32]

Jonas Hanway, an original thinker best known for promoting public policy changes in Parliament for women and children, became a governor in 1758 and forwarded a new approach for public-private relationships to benefit needy women and children. He proposed collecting parish funds, 'to make the Foundling Hospital more useful to the public'. Under his leadership,

Table 2.5: Decline in Admissions at the FH, 1761–71[33]

Admission Year	Admitted N
1761	11
1762	6
1763	41
1764	99
1765	4
1766	25
1767	33
1768	51
1769	36
1770	43
1771	18
Total	367

the governors met with parish officials and arrived at a plan whereby the hospital would serve as a go-between for poor law parish children and nurse mothers.[34] With the help of the governors, Hanway successfully shepherded an 'Act for the Better Regulation of the Parish Poor Children', better known as the Hanway Act through Parliament. The Act required poor law overseers to implement new wet-nursing practices at London's workhouses, a policy already institutionalized at the Foundling Hospital.[35] The Acts also addressed the problem of provisions for older children by limiting the years as an apprentice.[36] Hanway negotiated with the parish officials, offering Foundling Hospital wet-nursing and childcare services for a fee of 20 s. in advance, and 12 s. 6 p. a month per child. The monthly charge amounted to £7 10 s. per year, the sum Parliament agreed to pay for each child during the General Reception. In return, the Foundling Hospital covered arrangements between poor law overseers and wet-nurses, or nurse mothers. The twenty shillings provided enough money for clothing, transporting the child to the country, and burial services in case the child should die. Pricey and impractical for the time, nurse mothers received a weekly fee, a sum many parishes could not afford, while other asylums lacked the political will to take responsibility for an illegitimate child.[37] By 1770, parishes began to default on their payments, but the policy continued until 1796. The institution received about 50 parish children a year under this admissions scheme. Since the system proved eminently unprofitable, the governors negotiated with parish officials to end this programme.[38]

The poor law route to admission of an out-of-wedlock child at the asylum ended, prompting an alternative procedure. Significantly, the mother's personal history came to assess her worthiness in exchange for relief of her infant. Perhaps, Jonas Hanway had a hand in this adjustment, given the fact he was instrumental in setting up the Magdalen Hospital, a refuge for women who wished to turn away from prostitution in the 1760s, and had incorporated similar policies into the institution's by-laws.[39] In general, the governors grew to prefer the petitioning and interview process. Petitions took the form of a written statement requesting permission to do something, to acquire rights and privileges, or to confirm a binding relationship.[40] Petitioning Parliament for passage of private bills was becoming increasingly common at this time. For example, a married couple appealed to Parliament for legal separation of property and rights. Parliament's approval freed the couple of the legal obligations imposed by marriage.[41] Like Parliament, the Foundling Hospital governors selected a group of men, known as the 'committee', who performed comparable duties for the Foundling Hospital applicants. Mothers petitioned the Foundling Hospital for admission of their infant. The committee deliberated, and if they approved the petition, the men freed the mother of the legal obligations to her child.[42] Admission of one's infant evolved from an unrestricted acceptance policy into a negotiated practice between the mother seeking entrance of her infant, and the committee men. The criterion encased in the petition and interview process changed over time, reflecting both internal constraints at the Foundling Hospital and external social and legal changes. By extension, the contents of the petitions reflected the ways in which the hospital chose women as suitable candidates, worthy of Foundling Hospital beneficence. The governors instituted a set of standards measuring the 'goodness' of an abandoned mother's petition. In framing the issue of her character, the governors relied on and reflected contemporary standards for female behaviour; these extolled virtue, moral excellence, righteousness and chastity. Of course, an unwed mother was de facto at odds with the value of chastity. The form defined a good character as virtuous, industrious, sober and honest, with the exception of one 'fall' from purity.[43] Reform implied an ability to change; for the Foundling Hospital, it meant the following: 'The reception of the child will in all probability be the means of replacing the Mother in the course of virtue, and the way of an honest livelihood.'[44]

Wealthy West End men and women embedded their ideals regarding women and men (reflective of the Enlightenment view of the perfectibility of man) in the petition requirements. Like their peers who debated the poor laws in 1834, the governors tacitly assumed the wayward fathers were beyond the control of hospital committee men, and eventually agreed, as did the Poor Law Commission, the mother should bear the burden of responsibility for the illegitimate child. Again, the governors, members of London's elite, viewed their charge as a proper mission, serving at least two purposes: providing a refuge for an illegitimate infant and saving the mother's reputation from ruin by hiding her condition from public knowledge.[45] The hospital offered an alternative to infant abandonment in the streets of London or at the workhouse. Moreover, helping the mother to hide her unaffiliated infant would also minimize the influence such behaviour could have on other young women. Committee men worked on behalf of and with women to cloud, if not erase, a sordid past. If an unwed mother, a humble petitioner, could get a hearing, then her bid for admission of her infant progressed to the next stage. Governors required the mother to appear with a written testimony in hand explaining her reasons for seeking assistance. This alone could be prohibitive. Either the mother had to be able to read and write, or someone else could help to complete the form.

Rules required the mother to explain why she was petitioning for the admission of her infant, and to provide witnesses who could verify the truth of her story. The respectability test placed the burden of proof on the mother. If her story proved credible, then she was a candidate for the lottery, which the governors retained in conjunction with the petition until 1793. Under the lottery admission policy, the mother was both a gambler and a petitioner. Putting an end to the ballot in 1813 placed further weight on the mother's character, a 'Victorian' concept. The completed petition, references, and supporting evidence differentiated between the respectable and the non-respectable or undeserving poor.[46] Character, then, crystallized into measurable objectives. A committee could now interpret and analyze artifacts such as the petition form, a hearing transcript, recommendations from supporters *qua* witnesses, and eventually, the notes of a private investigator.

Deciphering the Form and the Oral Transcript

> Let him that is without sin, is the condition proposed by our Lord. Who has fulfilled this condition? Who is without sin? Who can say that he is free from the very sin which he is at the moment censuring?... Who can say that he has not been on the borders of it [sin] and arrested, if indeed he has been arrested, not by his own strength or resolution, but by God's great mercy which he has not deserved, which he has scarcely even desired.[47]

The petition and interview process mirrored changes in social rules and economic circumstances. In 1813, the governors reinforced the admission policy, refusing under any circumstances to accept an infant without the fully completed form. The Foundling Hospital printed the first forms on white folio paper. They printed later forms on folio-size, bi-folded light-blue paper. On the top recto side, the language explicitly spelled out admission requirements. The verso side of the first page remained blank. Here the secretary occasionally made comments on some pertinent aspects relating to the case. For example, John Brownlow frequently recorded the name of the 'workhouse' in which the mother delivered the infant. The recto side of the form registered the mother's name, age, address, the child's name, sex, date, and place of birth. The form did not allocate a specific space for the mother's 'occupation'. Between 1842 and 1892, the secretary informally recorded this category under her surname or within the petition transcript. The form required the father's name, occupation, address, when the mother, or anyone had last seen the father, and his whereabouts, or purported destination.

The secretary transcribed the woman's oral testimony, as she stood in front of the committee at a Saturday morning interview, on a single sheet of folio-size paper and inserted it between the pages of the form. Additional items relating to the case, such as newspaper clippings, letters from recommenders, doctors, midwives, workhouse officials, clergymen and love letters were enfolded within the petition. Altogether, the petition looked like a packet of deed papers or a personal will and testimony. Foundling Hospital petitions and the application process mirrored the evolution of the law of evidence. During the nineteenth century, defendants gave evidence, proof of the circumstances and facts surrounding their case, and supplied witnesses who corroborated or denied the defendant's deposition. The petitioner presented their case before a jury who based their decision on whether the accounts given by the defendant confirmed their knowledge and understanding of life in a certain situation. Similarly, the Foundling Hospital committee heard the petitioning mother's testimony, weighed it in light of corroborating evidence including character witnesses, and rendered a settlement or verdict, which, at bottom, reflected the governors' own moral perspective and experiences.[48]

In tightening the rules regarding the petitioning process, the Foundling Hospital governors wished to ensure selected infants were the offspring of virtuous, hard working, sober, and honest women. Significantly, Foundling Hospital policies supported or confirmed the perspective of the Poor Law commissioners who framed or constructed issues involving illicit pregnancy, childbearing, and childcare as private matters, best handled within the family.[49] Changes in the construction of public policy necessarily influenced Foundling Hospital policy. With the passage of the landmark legislation, the law placed the burden of proof on the mother, not the father, requiring the unmarried mother to go through affiliation proceedings in quarter sessions court. The committee expected the woman to provide the evidence about the man who had fathered her child, proof that he promised her marriage in the customary fashion, and further proof he had abandoned her and the baby. Appealing to the magistrate for child support was intimidating and almost impossible for labouring poor women to accomplish without support from others. As Lord Wynford and the Bishop of Exeter argued in the House of Lords during the Poor Law debates, if a woman appeared before a magistrate, then her character was damaged forever. Lord Wynford stated: 'It would be disgraceful to any magistrate to suffer a woman to be so examined in a public room.'[50] Until 1834, no law required such an 'indecent thing'.[51] The 1844 amendment did little to help women, leaving the problem of unmarried mothers in the spotlight of social politics. It is notable, with the removal of affiliation proceedings from quarter to petty sessions, Foundling Hospital committee men increasingly asked petitioners whether they had first been to the magistrate.

In the magistrate's court, the mother needed to provide the father's identity, witnesses against him, and evidence of a breach of promise to marry. The law compelled her to verify that the man accused of fathering her child had deserted her. A heavy burden fell on her because magistrates demanded more proof than circumstantial evidence. Collecting evidence against the putative father proved challenging, because unencumbered, they could easily catch a ferry to the Continent, or sail to North America. If the court ruled in favour of the mother, the allowance was a pittance: 2 s. 6 d. a week. The offered compensation was barely enough even to pay 5 s. per week in 1871 for a wet nurse. Even if, the mother received an 'affiliation order' from the magistrate, she could not be guaranteed financial support; because the law did not yet require justices of the peace to pursue the father. Fathers could simply depart, leaving women and children in destitute circumstances. The Foundling Hospital, for some, represented a double-edged sword: it offered attractive terms at a grievous cost. Nonetheless, in Parliamentary testimony, the hospital treasurer made it clear, the governors had no intention of picking up where the poor laws left off. They thus adhered to a stringent admission procedure.[52] Even though, as Brownlow wrote, Thomas Coram knew impending what every man who studies the human heart must know, indigence was more than dereliction of duty. The father of her child had first abandoned her.[53]

In the wake of the New Poor Laws, the institution combined sympathetic understanding with a stringent no-nonsense approach to the petitioners. This strategy emerged during John Brownlow's tenure as secretary. The hospital admitted the man, himself, as a foundling with private number 18,607 in

August 1814. Upon reaching the age of majority, the hospital hired him as an employee. He joined the officers' table for dining in 1818. In June 1828, governors appointed Brownlow as treasurer's clerk.[54] He then served as under-secretary, until his appointment as secretary, a position he held between 1849 and 1872. By the time of his retirement, Brownlow had matured into the grand patriarch of the institution. His experiences as 'under-secretary', when responsbilities required him to make inquiries into each petitioner's case and to transcribe the oral testimonies, probably had a strong influence on his sensibilities and resulted in further amendments to the petition form in 1856. Guided by experience, the governors transformed the simple paragraph requiring 'virtue, sobriety, and honesty' into something more explicit:

> No Child can be admitted unless the Committee is satisfied, after due enquiry, of the previous good character, and present necessity of the Mother, and the Father of the child has deserted it and the Mother, and that the reception of the Child will in all probability, be the means of replacing the Mother in the course of virtue, and the way of an honest livelihood.[55]

Brownlow's experiences taught him about the different strategies women used to gain admission for their children. Of course, he needed the full support of the committee to eliminate loopholes in the rules and regulations. For example, for the first time, under Brownlow's tenure, married women and widows were strictly forbidden to apply. Only first-time mothers had this privilege for their infants, who had to be older than two months, but not one year of age.[56] Moreover, more intense scrutiny of each case emerged. Significantly, when Brownlow took office as secretary, petition transcripts also lost their formulaic qualities, as details of the courtship became more explicit. If witnesses contradicted the oral testimony, the committee rejected the application. One thing was certain: the mother could never have lived with the father.[57] If the committee accepted the petition, the mother agreed not to attempt to retrieve her child, unless she could prove able to provide for it.[58]

Even in the midst of hardening legal constraints relating to women with out-of-wedlock children, the Christian perspective could be at odds with the law. Although the institution did not have a resident cleric, they invited leading London clerics to preach on particular occasions. In 1862, James Augustus Hessey delivered a sermon to governors and committee men. The language in the homily represented a Christian interpretation of the petitioner's condition. As is clear from the details found in transcript testimonies, his text also paraphrased the questions posed by the committee during the interview. In fact, this text helped to crack the code and unlocked understanding of the petitioner's transcript responses.

Most Victorian sermons began with a verse from the Bible, 'Let him that is without sin' throw the first stone. 'Who,' Hessey asked, 'is without sin?' He exhorted people to examine their consciences, were they free from sin at the moment they passed judgment on the young woman? Have they, themselves, ever been tempted and stopped in their tracks, if not by temperance, but 'by God's great mercy?'[59] More than offering an injunction, calling on governors and committee men to reflect and be even-handed, he represented the ideals at the heart of Victorian values. Indeed, the sermon identified attitudes towards sexuality, childbearing and unmarried motherhood. Although Hessey advocated compassion, he did not slip into moral relativism. He preached: 'She has become a mother; she is a scandal and disgrace to a decent household; she belongs at once to a class which is a shame even to mention.'[60] She strayed from the 'paths of purity'. He articulated the questions aiming to reveal the woman's character and the implicit circumstances of her 'fall' or 'seduction'. Hessey asked, 'What is her history?' Had she been overcome by a sudden temptation? Had she been deceived? Had she been the victim of unscrupulous associates who corrupted her heart and soul long before she yielded her body to an act of sin?[61] Had she 'a home full of holy influences?'[62] Here, he made reference to whether or not the woman's family attended church. Testimonials from her clergyman and or her 'respectable' employers would be used to gauge her 'character'. If such witnesses confirmed the petitioner's sterling reputation, was it possible her pregnancy was caused by one fall, similar to Eve's in the Garden of Eden? Hessey asked: 'Was she overcome by a sudden temptation?'[63] If the unwed mother had a 'deserving' character, then she was worthy of another chance. The above language speaks to the sermon heard in the church; it demonstrates how religion influenced and shaped the committee decision-making process. Moreover, the homily illuminates the petitioner's experience during the interview by inference. These standards played into the calculus of respectability, measuring whether the candidate deserved the benefits of the institution. Ultimately, however, for the mother, admission of her infant required a confession, not before a cleric, but to the men on the committee in the courtroom on the Foundling Hospital estate. In offering a service for women who met the criteria, the committee could not grant spiritual absolution, only freedom to go and start afresh.

The hospital appropriated both legal and Christian terms in the oral testimony; this language found in every transcript also aided in describing the petitioners' experience. The Christian position pervading the petition transcripts casts the 'act' of sexual intercourse in Biblical terms. Consistent characterization of the woman's seduction as the 'petitioner's fall' reminisces on a fall from grace or purity. Theologians blamed both Adam and Eve for the fall from the Garden of Eden at various times throughout history.[64] Biblical scholars, churchmen and philosophers have explained the fall from grace in different ways. For example, while the stain of original sin came from Adam, the pain suffered by women during childbirth signified complicity in the fall from grace. The transcriber of the oral testimony termed the relationship between the petitioner and the father of her child as the 'seduction'. Although the Foundling Hospital petition narrative associated the fall from grace with seduction by the father, the transcriber never referred to the impregnator as anything other than the 'father.' In stark contrast, the oral testimony never attributed the term 'mother' to the petitioner. Instead, the transcriber always cited the biological mother as the 'petitioner', a categorical reference common to courtroom proceedings.[65]

Legal overtones combined with biblical language complicated the tenor of the documents. The committee referred to the act of sexual intercourse outside of wedlock as 'criminal conversation', 'crim. con.', or simply 'c.c.' Legally, criminal conversation referred to an adulterous relationship between a man and woman, with either one or both in the state of marriage. By law, a man engaging in sexual intercourse with a married woman trespassed on another man's property. Under the Married Women's Property Act, Parliament repealed laws pertaining to criminal conversation in 1857.[66] Why the transcriber used this term is not explained in the available Foundling Hospital archives, but in all probability, the language represents the legal training of the Foundling Hospital committee.

In Parliamentary testimony before the Infant Life Protection Committee in 1870–1, the Foundling Hospital representative believed magistrates' decisions regarding illegitimacy cases too harsh, because the law required more evidence than required against the father. They also believed the magistrates unresponsive to the needs of unwed mothers. They concurred that the petitioning process at the Foundling Hospital was indeed similar to what went on in the magistrate's court, only the remedy different. If the Foundling Hospital men accepted the petition, a sure and final remedy existed: the committee relieved the mother of her infant. The admitted infant received the best care the administrators could afford and maintain, and the mother could proceed with her life, unencumbered, and preserve her character and reputation.[67]

Foundling Hospital authorities, however, did not wish to pick up where the Poor Law left off. 'We do not like relieving the parish', testified Foundling Hospital Treasurer George Burrows Gregory.[68] The administration clearly framed their charity as something more high-minded and efficient than the poor law workhouses. In fact, the Foundling Hospital served only a 'selected' group of women.[69] Mr Gregory's testimony before the Select Committee indicated that he and his colleagues relied on the practices established by the

English legal system to determine the validity of the mother's testimony. The committee judged applications on a case-by-case basis, in a reasoned and orderly decision-making process, based on a formal written petition and a cross-examination, in a courtroom-like fashion. The governors applied their vision of case law in the English common law to the petitioning process, as they evaluated each petition. Essentially, they judged the woman's 'character' in a courtroom-like setting to determine if she deserved the benefits of the Foundling Hospital. The committee relied on their legal expertise in their deliberations, and they incorporated the law's power and form of inquiry to investigate the case. In effect, these men acted as arbiters of morality, at least in the cases before them.

Charles Dickens provides glimpses into the realities of the hearing day. The committee ushered the mother into the courtroom. The interior was 'wainscoated with the names of benefactors, set forth in goodly order like the tables of law'.[70] Oblong in shape, dark wood paneling, elaborate plasterwork on the ceiling, and a huge crystal chandelier hanging in the centre adorned the room. A large fireplace, with a carved wood mantel, provided heat. Paintings from the famous art collection hung on the walls. Housekeeping arranged extra chairs against the wall.[71] Not exactly a private affair, they examined her 'minutely as to the facts of the case'[72] The hearing required the woman to answer questions regarding the most intimate details of her personal life and to maintain her composure during the grueling experience. As they deposed the petitioner, the secretary transcribed her responses to the questions in the first person.[73] Others could not represent the applicant's case, nor could she have legal counsel with her.[74] The Foundling Hospital enquirer referred to the process as an 'examination', similar to 'cross-examination', as in a trial.[75] If they found the petitioner lied, the men dismissed the petitioner immediately. The confidentiality of the woman's case depended on the jurists. A smaller group would have been less 'satisfying', according to Treasurer Gregory, because case dispositions were left to the discretion of 'every gentleman on the committee'.[76]

In referring to the petitioner, the transcriber used the abbreviation 'pet', as a form of shorthand. This is not amusing in light of the British penchant for pet dogs and horses. Interestingly, Dickens, sustained a close relationship with Foundling Hospital governors and was even aware of the petitioning process. Because a character named 'Pet' in *Little Dorrit*, who he writes, had an 'air of timidity and dependence, which was the best weakness', giving her 'a crowning charm'.[77] Use of the term 'pet' also suggests the gender assumptions embedded in the discourse between the committee men and the petitioner. In sum, the deposition process operated in casework-like fashion, exploring the factors contributing to the mother's seduction. It ascertained whether it had been her first fall; if the father had deserted her, and whether she had maintained an 'otherwise good character'.[78] Gregory listed the questions in precise order as they appear on the transcripts.

> We take the mother's statement as to the father, where she met him, how long she knew him, where they had been together, under what circumstances the seduction occurred, who had seen them together, where the father resided, and what business he carried on. Then that is followed up by our inquiry; and we also ask her, 'What inquiries have you made of the father, when did you see him last, where was it, and what have you done since', and so on.[79]

The committee left no stone unturned in the investigation of the mother's reputation. Contrary to Gregory's testimony, provided for public consumption, the committee asked many more questions, with even more answers provided. In an era predating digital recorders, the transcript revealed only information the transcriber was able and willing to record. The petitioner's testimony, insofar as she was able to provide details about the most intimate facets of her life, was second-hand. The transcriber limited elaboration on the part of the petitioner to 'just the facts, please'. The 'legalistic approach' most likely removed the emotional aspects of the case. Most petitions began, 'When first acquainted with father… '. One question led to several others. How had she met the father: at work, as a lodger in the house where she lived or worked, as a neighbour in the village? Where had she met him: on the street, at church, in a museum, at Hyde Park, or Crystal Palace? These represented popular meeting places for young people growing up in London. The most fundamental questions included: How long had she known the father? Had she received a promise of marriage? Had she given her consent? The committee wanted to know the details about the venue where 'criminal conversation' occurred, and how many times they repeated sexual intercourse. Had the father used drugs or alcohol to induce the seduction or did the young woman consent freely? They wanted to know whether the father used force to 'achieve his purpose'. Had the father given her money?[80] The committee queried the petitioner regarding the age of the father, his occupation and address. When had she last seen the father? Where was she confined? Who assisted her in her delivery? How had she paid for her confinement? How long had she been confined? How much money did she have in savings? Had she told anyone about what had happened? If so, whom did she tell? Had she gone to the magistrate? Did she know whether her parents were aware of her situation? If relieved of her infant, could she promise that she would be able to find steady employment in the future?[81] At the end of their examination, they had to be assured of the quality of the petitioner's character and whether, if 'relieved of the child', she would be set 'in the course of virtue'.[82] The men asked the woman to provide names of recommenders and or witnesses who would and could vouch for her story, and to provide any tangible evidence such as love letters, tokens of affection, or newspaper clippings.[83] According to Gregory:

> Having taken down her statement, we then refer it, if we consider it a case proper for reference, to an officer of the institution who conducts those inquiries, and during the week he follows up this case by all the references that we can obtain from the girl.[84]

The committee required official testimony from doctors, midwives, employers and landlords regarding the respectability of the candidate. By the mid-nineteenth century, the Foundling Hospital investigator visited some of London's most fashionable West End homes in St George Hanover Square and Bloomsbury, met with highly regarded employers, and asked questions about the petitioner after her appearance. Landladies and landlords, employers, and family members testified to whether the petitioner's fall was a case of seduction or a broken promise to marry. Employers told how the father of the infant deserted the mother. The enquirer collected written affidavits regarding the mother and the delivery of the infant by going from doctor to doctor, midwife to midwife, and workhouse to workhouse for testimony as to whether this was the woman's first pregnancy. Occasionally the investigation took the investigator out of town in his quest for the truth; this could prolong the process. The enquirer reported to the committee on the details of the case as he had discovered them. After this, the committee deliberated, deciding on 'the reception of the child', which of course depended on whether the information provided in the oral testimony could be substantiated by an investigator's findings and recommendations from individuals who knew the case. The secretary sent a message to the mother by post as to whether or not the committee would accept her baby. If eligible, the secretary set a date for admission of the infant.[85]

During the Foundling Hospital's long history, a direct relationship existed between the sources of funding, admissions policies, and the commonly held values of the society. The committee used a red tape investigation to filter out women with fewer qualifications. The form essentially discriminated against those mothers who did not have the wherewithal to complete it. Another salient aspect of this part of the Foundling Hospital study is the way in which it demonstrates changes in public opinion regarding assistance to unwed mothers, and how these changes shaped policies. Initially, few qualifications for admission existed, but changing social conditions and values reflected within the larger society as exemplified by the New Poor Laws, yielded little appreciable benefit to unwed mothers. The ways in which the administration interfaced with the lives of the women who applied emerge in the next chapter, which begins with the petitioner's account of how she met the father. Evidence shows that women who appealed for help did so because they saw no alternative; the stigma of illegitimacy and burden of care for the child was too overwhelming. Society deemed an illegitimate child a burden to society, one more inmate in the local workhouse. The next chapter analyzes the demographic aspects of petition forms and transcripts and thus begins an exploration of the mother's account. Her story provides us with the other side of this 'negotiated' relationship and illustrates the tension between 'constraints' and 'agency' in the lives of Victorian women.

3

Circumventing Social Geography: The Unwed Mother's Search for Respectability

> It has been appositely remarked that whereas the City is the heart, Westminster is the head of our great metropolis; while the suburbs in general constitute its limbs and extremities... The City is the centre of all commercial transactions, Westminster is the residence of the Court and the seat of the Legislature which directs and controls the affairs of the nation.[1]

On average, 200 women per year found their way to the porter's gate on Guilford Street, located just off Russell Square. The ability to cross social and spatial boundaries on behalf of their illegitimate infant demonstrates her power to choose one path over another. The unexamined social geography and its ability to intimidate those who would feel out of place in the rarefied atmosphere of the Foundling Hospital estate forms the core of the following discussion. The power of 'space' as a product of a lived environment raises several valuable points of understanding for the London Foundling Hospital. In the Victorian metropolis, the widest extremes existed between the living conditions of the wealthy and the poor. Journalists consistently emphasized the west to east divisions. This began in the 1830s when wealthy merchants who succeeded in the imperial trade, moved north and west of the City, away from the commercial centre located near St Paul's and to the west of the Tower of London.[2] The social geography of London, a geo-political configuration of two spaces, both with different purposes, the City, organized for trade, and Westminster, established for politics and state ceremonies, adds to an understanding of the world in which Foundling Hospital mothers lived because most worked in the service industry as domestics. Even a modest household required a retinue of servants in order to display the wealth produced at the Royal Exchange, the East India Company, the West India Dock Company, or Lloyd's of London. Into this landscape, we insert ourselves as time travellers to uncover the everyday lives of the women forming the focus of this study.

At the end of the eighteenth century, commercial traders, bankers and entrepreneurs lived in the immediate vicinity of the City, maintaining businesses and residences in the same building. Offices occupied the first floor, entrepreneurs and their families lived on the second floor, and domestic servants and apprentices had a space in which to sleep in the loft, garret or kitchen.[3] The City soon hosted expanding offices at the Royal Exchange, the Bank of England and Lloyd's of London. Dwelling spaces turned into commoditized, saleable or capital space, prompting commercial classes to shift westward to Bedford Square, and many other squares including Tavistock, Russell, Gordon and Fitzroy squares, best characterized as garden parks surrounded by homes of the wealthy, in what became known as the West End. By 1837, fashionable Victorians preferred the growing suburbs to the narrow streets of the City, home to the financial district; as they moved to the West End, domestic servants and liverymen accompanied them.

In its material form, respectability existed most perfectly in neighbourhoods that wrapped around St James Park, Hyde Park, including Knightsbridge, Kensington, Mayfair and Belgravia, and then it extended northward to Regent's Park.[4] Owners capitalized on George IV's (1820–30) 1825 reconstruction of Buckingham House, making adjacent West End real estate extremely attractive to buyers.[5] Indeed, the location of the palace increased the prestige of the powerful lived spaces, radiating outward to the south, west and north. By contrast, in the East End, or 'darkest London', most casual labourers occupied two-storey brick houses amid warehouses, canals and large dock complexes. Although many proprietors owned country estates, and frequently engaged more in the social and political affairs in their home districts than in the metropolis, this locale provided a centre from which the London season – lasting from Eastertide until August – played itself out.[6] Furthermore, accompanying business establishments, providing exclusive goods, constituted another part of the social milieu. A service class – doctors, lawyers, government administrators and educators – and a working class, comprised of skilled domestics, store minders and caretakers, provided necessary accoutrements for gated-urban estates.[7] For example, the *Building News* elaborated on the latest amenities for the home in 1857:

> The first class residences [under construction] will comprise family mansions of the best description, great care being taken to have them built in the most sound and substantial manner, and appropriately decorated… In these houses more than usual ingenuity seems to have been brought to bear in the planning of the basements for domestic comfort and convenience; for, in addition to commodious kitchens and sculleries, with a profusion of fittings to them, there is a housekeeper's room and butler's pantry to each, two wine cellars, beer cellar, larders, and servants' water-closets, together with a cistern capable of holding 300 gallons of water.[8]

In turn, the property description clearly shows the need for significant support staff to maintain such an operation. The magnificence of palaces, parks and statues in the West End bespoke a Victorian London at the pinnacle of imperial greatness. Walter Thornbury's entertaining articles in the journal *Belgravia* further explored the luxuries of life for exclusive residential areas, with their attendant squares filled with statues and benches, rolling parks and streams. Sketches of young couples, young men and women walking through parks and the countryside, carrying picnic lunches in large wicker baskets filled to the brim, suggested a life of affluence and leisure. Images also framed the ideals of domestic and romantic bliss in a bucolic setting, where subjects posed casually in fashionable attire. Missing were representations of the domestics who made this lifestyle possible, illicit amorous liaisons among members of the household, or any mention of the rag-tag affairs of political life. Instead of strolling through Hyde Park on a Sunday afternoon, some women made their way across London to the porter's gate in Bloomsbury to retrieve a petition for their infant in the hope of its admittance to the Foundling Hospital and thereby, a respectable upbringing.[9]

As an institution, the Foundling Hospital provides an example of representational space, embodying complex symbols communicated through the cultural mediums of art, music, literature and architecture. Each medium carries with it certain messages about social values and develops meaning in a unique way.[10] The asylum clearly imprinted itself as part of London's cultural landscape during the early nineteenth century. It had a massive physical footprint on the West End in a way similar to a church or government building. Knowledge about Foundling Hospital services spread to distant counties by word of mouth through the *Penny Magazine*, Charles Dickens's novels, his news magazine *Household Words*, or the chroniclers of London's historical places such as John Timbs and Edward Walford.[11] Like Dickens, many domestics and others learned about its services simply by walking along the pathways enwrapping the perimeter of the estate because they lived in the neighbourhood. An exploration of the relationship, between Greater London and the Foundling Hospital women and children served there, provides a new and better understanding of the ways in which this particular estate served as a crucible for English charity and respectability.

Throughout most of the nineteenth century, Londoners read about, created and abided by social and spatial identities. Take, for example, the Foundling Hospital estate, long regarded as a beacon of efficient charity for infants and children. Its closest neighbours included the governors of this charity, other wealthy families, along with their respectable domestic servants, and homes for hapless women; but the foundations of the Foundling Hospital estate predated the rise of the West End. A wise decision to purchase 56 acres from the Earl of Salisbury by administrators in 1745 paid off handsomely in the future by helping to fund hospital activities well into the twentieth century.[12] Early lithographs show the Foundling Hospital as an open estate. The porter monitored two gates situated on Guilford Street. Not to confuse issues, delivery men used a service entrance on the northeast corner of the estate; while visitors and petitioners entered the estate through the main gate off Guilford Street. Two squares, named for aristocratic families – Tavistock, and Mecklenburgh – flanked the estate.[13] On the north side of the property, the parish maintained St Georges' Gardens as a large public meeting space.[14]

Deep in debt by late 1759, because of a dramatic increase in admissions, the governors chose to use their attractive property as collateral in order to develop the area surrounding the Foundling Hospital by signing 90-year leases with property owners. Officers built four new streets: Tavistock, Great Coram, Bernard and Guilford streets. These linked up on the south side with Southampton Row.[15] Lofty brick walls, creating a secure dimension of 'privatized space' in the public realm similar to those on the neighbouring Bedford Estates, obscured the grounds from public view.[16] London chronicler Edward Walford described the site as one of the most open and healthful spots in the metropolis, standing alone in the centre of Lamb's Conduit Fields: 'The squares that flank the institution on either hand have no house on the sides next to the hospital, and that consequently these large enclosures act as supplementary lungs to the ample gardens and grounds of the institution itself.'[17] A large expanse of manicured lawns with wide gravel footpaths and driveways stood before Georgian-style-brick buildings trimmed with wooden colonnades. The complex included a central house situated between two wings, each large enough to maintain between 300 and 400 children and servants. Girls and boys domiciled in separate wings. The facility required two large kitchens, a laundry facility, living quarters for instructors, and workshops that served as classrooms for spinning, weaving and other handicrafts. The governors situated the chapel between the two wings, housing the children on the south side of the property with an entrance onto Upper Guilford Street.[18]

Governors reduced debts incurred from the construction projects through extensive leases, and savvy real estate investments that supported the charitable mission in a business-like fashion. In years following, unlike other Victorians who did not understand real property to be a lucrative means of capital formation, the institution survived nicely on an annual income ranging between £3,000 and £5,000 per year in rents.[19] The substantial profits enabled the charity to maintain its place in a neighbourhood with well-heeled neighbours. Weekly offerings collected from chapel-goers contributed around £687 per year. Concerts by foundlings and a few 'blind children' accompanied by a professional choir raised as much as £1,000 a year.[20] By 1901, the income amounted to over £25,000 per year.[21] Part of the attraction to this estate included the music accompanying the Sunday liturgy at the chapel, observed a Frenchman in 1851.[22] Indeed, the Foundling Hospital had a reputation for music since the eighteenth century, when George Frideric Handel directed the first performance of the Messiah in London. Musical training comprised a part of the curriculum at the school, and the children frequently performed for the public. The foundlings and the choir sat together in the loft on the east end of the chapel next to Handel's organ. Visiting preachers offered the Sunday morning and evening sermons.[23]

The architect designed the interior of the chapel in 'low' not high Anglican church style. Pew boxes faced each other across a wide central aisle.[24] Corinthian columns supported the second storey loft extending the full perimeter of the sanctuary. Sunlight could flow in from the round or rose window situated above the organ. The remaining windows, on the second floor of the chapel, extended the full length of the building, and atop the long windows sat half-moon shaped windows characteristic of Georgian architecture. Administrators hung a large painting below three arched-stained-glass windows illuminating the west end of the chapel.[25] Attendance at the Foundling Hospital chapel increased over the nineteenth century, because Secretary Brownlow added extra pews between 1845 and 1870.[26] The layout of the church situated the pulpit immediately below the children, so all eyes could gaze on the officiating clergyman, as well as the children. The governors and their wives sat opposite each other, separated by the 'Communion Table'. Candles, a crucifix and altar linens, characteristic of the High Anglican tradition, did not appear in the lithographs.[27] Instead, large oil paintings on permanent display showed Christ in infancy and manhood. Benjamin West's donated eighteenth-century portrayal of *Christ Presenting a Little Child* hung above the altar. The painting evokes the Christian view of Christ as a father figure who came to the assistance of all little children.

Foundling Hospital chapel-goers were expected to do the same, to come to the aid of the indigent. By contributing to the charity, patrons provided financial resources and became more Christ-like. Eighteenth-century governors commissioned Andrea Casali to paint another large piece of work for the chapel depicting the adoration of the Christ child. *The Adoration of the Magi* hung above the chapel altar for the remainder of the century.[28] *The Adoration* portrays the Virgin with the infant Jesus and the worshipping kings. This painting carried another message; since Jesus was born of the Virgin, he did not have a known biological father, but one who stood in as proxy, Joseph. Moreover, the mystery of the Virgin birth seemed to coincide with the mystery of the parentage of every foundling. Although they had biological parents, they, like Jesus, had surrogate parents. Hospital staff taught the children that the governors, committee men and nursemaids were their parents. They knew their country mothers, or wet-nurses, as their nurse mothers, and the male figures on staff at the Foundling Hospital took on a fatherly role in their upbringing.[29]

It is not likely that families moved to the Foundling Hospital neighbourhood to be close to the charity, but it did uphold an air of respectability and offered concerts and Sunday services. Yet, the Foundling estate itself, compared favourably with its neighbours in architectural appearance, layout of the estate, and access. In reality, people moved to this part of town because of proximity to power, the historical significance of the place (frequently the consequence of its proximity to power), parks, clean air and water, social appearances and the pleasure of having like-minded neighbours.[30] These included the duke of Bedford, whose family was responsible for aiding Coram with the establishment of the asylum. Both his son and Lord Mansfield, a brilliant and popular lawyer, established the Bloomsbury sector of London as a respectable place for wealthy West Indies traders.[31] Other neighbours included the Marquis of Tavistock, baronet and chairman of the East India Company. City merchants and rich retired West India planters resided on Bedford Square, which derived its name from the duke whose London home he situated there. Sitting adjacent to the Foundling property, the Bedford estate carved out an area next to the Southampton estate and restricted street traffic from nearby large arteries such as Euston Road and Oxford Street.[32] Like the Foundling estate, large iron gates protected the properties; brick walls surrounded it, marking a pointed example of the growing spatial separation of the classes.[33] Like the porters at the entrance to the Foundling estate, managers blockaded streets to keep undesirables, those looking for a hand out or part-time employment, away from residences. According to P. J. Atkins, one observer opined that the Bedford Estate houses were 'externally as alike as peas'. Long rows of brick-fronted structures stood side-by-side along the streets. The homes had four floors, the length of the window sashes shortening with each floor. The uniformity of the houses created a sense of social orderliness frequently associated with respectability. The regulation of architectural style design and the controlled access enabled estate managers to retain fastidious control over their estate.[34] In addition to the fashionable residences, we learn from the Foundling Hospital papers that charities for indigent women established homes along Marchmont Street. Other neighbours included the British Lying-in Hospital on Brownlow Street, the Great Ormond Street Hospital, and Mrs Gurney's home, a refuge for 'Deserted Mothers and Their Infants'.[35] This neighbourhood also had a long association with the world of culture, where the British Museum, a magnet for tourists, stood only blocks from the institution.[36] The legal world, beginning with Russell Square, named for Lord John Russell, dominated the neighbourhood to the west. The Royal Courts of Justice, Grays Inns, and Lincoln's Inn Fields populated Holborn, situated to the south.[37] The proximate location of the state law offices enabled several committee members to attend the Saturday hearings in the courtroom of the Foundling Hospital. Like the Bedford Estate, porters guarded the gates to the estate on Guilford Street, ensuring only people with permission to pass could cross the threshold. This included the governors and committee men who attended the weekly hearings for petitioning mothers, their infants, nurse mothers and deliverymen.

Location: A Measurement of Respectability

Visitors entered the Foundling Hospital estate during the nineteenth century either through gates on Guilford Street or Gray's Inn Road.[38] When the unwed mother learned about the Foundling Hospital and decided to start the admission process, she was required to go to the hospital gates. Rules approved by the governors prohibited others from requesting a petition on behalf of a mother. Rules forbade guards from issuing a petition to anyone but the mother; rules prohibited hospital officers from discussing the case with the mother, a proscription that some women, unfamiliar with the admission process, unwittingly violated.[39] Upon request, the porter handed the form with instructions regarding the application process to the would-be applicant. It is unknown as to how many petitions porters distributed each year. One thing is certain, rules advised applicants not to seek alternative routes to admission for their infant through letters to the secretary, hospital governors, committee men or employees. Instructions admonished mothers against attempting to bribe officers.[40] Likewise, regulations forewarned all employees and those associated with the hospital against assisting prospective petitioners. Governors promised, if discovered, the offending party would be immediately dismissed.[41] Again, the hospital emphasized that everyone associated with the admission process swore a promise to maintain absolute secrecy in all cases.[42]

What sort of women were most interested in petitioning the Foundling Hospital; and who were the committee men likely to accept? According to John Brownlow, in 1801, the Court of Governors resolved they would no longer take payment for admission and the character of the mother would determine admission of an infant. This step reinforced the rationalization of services based on respectability. As time passed, a calculus of respectability developed to aid in the decision-making process. Throughout the era under consideration, 1842 to 1892, governors attempted to 'decide each application for admission of children on its own merits'.[43] Therefore, the question becomes, what does the term 'merit' mean under these circumstances? To answer this and come to a better understanding of the mothers whose children played out their lives behind Foundling Hospital walls, the following analysis relies on information provided by a 50-year statistical survey of petitions submitted between 1842 and 1892.

The petition form contained pertinent data including: the mother's address, occupation, age, baby's birth date and sex, and the father's name, occupation, age, and his last known whereabouts. Profiles, created by collating these details, help describe a 'calculus of respectability', or acceptable and unacceptable circumstances, situations and standards of behaviour for these women.[44] The entire packet provides valuable information on Victorian efforts to categorize and measure all elements of social life and the circumstances of an intimate relationship. These discrete pieces of information helped to determine whether a mother's request would be fulfilled. The significance of 'lived space' in London underscores the fact that the Foundling Hospital petition began with questions relating to the mother's address. Appropriately, profiling Foundling Hospital mothers begins with questions about their residences. How many petitions were submitted from the metropolis, from regions outside of the immediate metropolitan area (Kent and Essex), and from Greater England, Scotland and Wales? To what degree did acceptance rates reflect pockets of deep poverty and in what ways? To what extent did her address result in the success or failure rate of the petition? That is, were women from the region lying east of the Tower of London disqualified? How did the petition-address mix change over time? In cases where the mother was a recent arrival to London, the transcripts usually provided enough information to determine how long the petitioner had been in London. If the petitioner had lived in London longer than three years, her London address counted as her domicile; if not, her town of origin counted as the correct address. This study categorizes Foundling Hospital petitions by street, according to London parliamentary registration districts, which, divided London into five divisions as listed in Table 3.1. Petitions from outside the metropolis have been separated into two groups: those from Kent and Essex are in one group; in the second category are petitions from Greater England, Scotland and Wales.

According to this analytical geo-spatial configuration, the North London division included the Foundling Hospital.[45] Table 3.2 reflects the concentration of the mothers' addresses between 1842 and 1892. Districts comprising a sizable portion of the petition pool included North and West London, Kent and Essex, Greater England, Scotland and Wales. The findings show that of any single district, North London produced the greatest number, or 25.56 per cent of accepted and rejected petitions. It is likely the high percentage

Table 3.1: Parliamentary Registration District Regional Divisions[46]

Divisions	Registration District
North London	Hackney, Hampstead, Islington, St Marylebone, St Pancras
East London	City of London, East London, West London, Bethnal Green, Poplar, Shoreditch, Stepney, St George in the East, Whitechapel
South London	Bermondsey, Camberwell, Greenwich, Lambeth, Lewisham, Newington, Rotherhithe, St George Southwark, St Olave Southwark, St Saviour Southwark, Wandsworth
West London	Chelsea, St George Hanover Square, St James Westminster, St John and St Margaret, Kensington
Central London	Clerkenwell, Holborn, St Giles, St Luke, St Martin in the Fields, Strand

Source: David R. Green, *From Artisans to Paupers: Economic Change and Poverty in London, 1790–1870* (Aldershot, Hants: Scolar Press, 1995), appendix 1.1.

Table 3.2: FH Survey of Mothers' Addresses, 1842–92[47]

Divisions	Accepted and Rejected Petitions N	Accepted and Rejected %
North London	91	25.56
East London	29	8.15
South London	20	5.62
West London	64	17.98
Central London	36	10.11
Kent and Essex	57	16.01
Greater England, Scotland and Wales	59	16.57
Total	356	100.00

from North London could be influenced by the hospital's proximity to wealthy households. Obviously the asylum was widely known among North Londoners, who found it convenient to make application there. Its closest competitor, West London, lagged behind by 7.58 percentage points. The data also shows petitions from outside the metropolis, Kent and Essex, and Greater England, Scotland and Wales combined to yield 32.58 per cent of all petitions. Extra-metropolitan requests included county and town names such as Devon, Sussex and Lewes, situated south of London, Yorkshire, and Buckinghamshire to the north. The poorer sections of London – South, East and Central London – ranged between 5.62 and 10.11 percentage points respectively and accounted for less than 25 per cent of all petitions.[48]

Table 3.3 represents the 17 years for which both accepted and rejected petitions were available; it shows the distribution by per cent of accepted and rejected petitions between 1842 and 1859. The accepted and rejected rate demonstrates the strength of the mother's address and illustrates how changing locations in the petition mix reflected shifting centres of wealth and poverty in London. The greatest number of petitions arrived from North London in the 1840s and 1850s. Common addresses included Islington, Finsbury, Marylebone and Hampstead. At the time, North London represented a growing centre of wealth, particularly around Hampstead; about 3 per cent of accepted petitions listed a home street address from there. North London also accounted for a high percentage of rejections because its district included poverty-stricken areas in St Pancras and St Marylebone parliamentary registration districts. In 1851, 6.3 per cent of the St Pancras population and 9.5 per cent of the St Marylebone population were Irish born. These districts also included the Strand Union and Marylebone Union workhouses, large institutions tending to attract destitute mothers to their facilities during their confinement.[49] North London's closest competitor for accepted petitions came from West London. Central London constituted its nearest competition for rejections for these decades.

In *Notes on England,* Hippolyte Taine described St Giles and the Strand as socially, politically and culturally pockets of poverty separated from the great buildings of state that had been standing in Westminster for centuries. Table 3.4 specifically examines petition breakdown in the 1840s and warrants special attention because of the figures for Central London. The Central London registration districts, including Clerkenwell, Holborn, St Lukes, St Giles and St Martin in the Fields, prove helpful for comparison with West London and its representative social spaces.[50] The principal pocket of poverty in West London coalesced around St Martin's Workhouse and Soho. The 1840s, the era of the Irish potato famine, marked the only decade in which Central London accounted for a sizable percentage of the petition pool (21.65

Table 3.3: FH Mothers' Addresses, Accepted vs Rejected, 1842–59[51]

Divisions 1842–59	Accepted N	Accepted Petitions %	Rejected Petitions N	Rejected Petitions %
North London	21	27.27	35	27.13
East London	7	9.09	12	9.30
South London	7	9.09	7	5.43
West London	14	18.18	18	13.95
Central London	5	6.50	27	20.93
Kent and Essex	10	12.99	15	11.63
Greater England, Scotland and Wales	13	16.88	15	11.63
Total	77	100.00	129	100.00

per cent). Percentages fell from their high in the 1840s to less than 1 per cent in the 1850s. Overall, Central London accounted for 10.1 per cent of all accepted and rejected petitions, at least 20.93 per cent of all rejected petitions, but only 6.50 per cent of the accepted petitions between 1842 and 1859. The region trailed North London most notably in terms of rejected applications in the 1840s, but these also sharply declined in the 1850s.

West London included the parliamentary registration districts of Chelsea, St George Hanover Square, St James Westminster, St John and St Margaret, Westminster and Kensington; these districts accounted for 18.18 of all accepted and 13.95 of all rejected petitions between 1842 and 1859. West London, especially the area around St George Hanover Square, differed from the gated community of Bedford Square in Bloomsbury. There, homeowners had other ways of maintaining the security of their streets. They kept their residences some distance from the parish workhouses and all other charities in their neighbourhood and made sure to supervise them staunchly. Moreover, according to the 1851 census records, the districts supported a considerably higher percentage of women than men. For example, in St George Hanover Square, women outnumbered men by 7.7 percent.[52] By contrast, the high application rate in the 1840s suggests Central London women were aware of the Foundling Hospital services; yet, their knowledge of the institution was to no avail, as evidenced in Table 3.4. Here, North London petitions had more favourable acceptance rates, surpassing those for Central London, and Greater England, Scotland, and Wales.

Table 3.4: FH Mothers' Addresses, Accepted vs Rejected, 1842–9[53]

Divisions – 1842–9	Total Applied		Accepted Petitions		Rejected Petitions	
Districts	N	%	N	%	N	%
North London	28	28.87	11	31.43	17	27.42
East London	10	10.31	4	11.43	6	9.68
South London	7	7.22	4	11.43	3	4.84
West London	15	15.46	4	11.43	11	17.74
Central London	21	21.65	5	14.28	16	25.81
Kent and Essex	5	5.15	2	5.71	3	4.83
Greater England, Scotland and Wales	11	11.34	5	14.29	6	9.68
Totals	97	100.00	35	100.00	62	100.00

Table 3.5 represents the breakdown of 1850s petitions, whereby survey figures show less representation from Central London in the 1850s. The Foundling Hospital received 10.09 per cent of all applications from there, but accepted none. Further, it accounted for at least 16.42 per cent of all rejected petitions. Not coincidentally, the Central London figures for the Irish-born population in the 1851 census listed Holborn at 16.9 per cent, Strand at 9.5 per cent, St Martin's 8.7 per cent, and St Giles at 20 per cent.[54] Table 3.5 represents the breakdown of 1850s petitions, showing a stark decline in Central figures.[54]

What contributing factors may explain this stark reality? The needy women probably lived in the growing Irish communities. If not Irish, their addresses were associated with the Irish. The stigma of originating from Ireland and professing Roman Catholicism factored into the petitioning process; although religion was never included as part of the questioning by the committee men. In some cases, a reference to race or ethnicity carried enough weight to stop a petition in its tracks. Occasionally, during the process, if the mother or the father were Irish or African, the secretary recorded this in his comments. In 1874, one testimonial noted, 'Pet.'s father and mother, who appeared to possess every characteristic of the Irish race, stated that Pet. is the eldest of their family of six, all living. She has been an excellent daughter up to the time of her fall and had rendered them every assistance in her power in supporting their family.'[55]

Table 3.5: FH Mothers' Addresses, Accepted vs Rejected, 1850–9[56]

Divisions – 1850–9	**Total Applied**		**Accepted by District**		**Rejected by District**	
Districts	N	%	N	%	N	%
North London	28	25.69	10	23.81	18	26.87
East London	9	8.26	3	7.14	6	8.96
South London	7	6.41	3	7.14	4	5.96
West London	17	15.60	10	23.81	7	10.45
Central London	11	10.09	0	0.00	11	16.42
Kent and Essex	20	18.35	8	19.05	12	17.91
Greater England, Scotland and Wales	17	15.60	8	19.05	9	13.43
Totals	109	100	42	100	67	100

Although the committee accepted this petition, the late date shows the residual prejudice. Irish women faced unique employment difficulties because the signs reading, 'no Irish need apply' were common. If they could not be hired as maids, then the mothers were unlikely to have a respectable employer willing to write a favourable letter of recommendation for their cause.[57] Gainful employment and the potential for return to a respectable situation figured into the committee's formula for admissibility. In the 1860s, admission rates for Central London rose slightly to 4.0 per cent, and in the 1870s to 4.35 per cent, but this part of the Metropolis never recovered a greater share of admissions. In the 1880s, Central London acceptance rates again fell to less than 1 per cent. In addition to extreme poverty, other factors contributing to the reductions in admissions from Central London may include declining population in the area due to redevelopment projects and the sealing off of communities with gates and walls, as in the cases of Bedford Square and Woburn Place.

On the other hand, North London was a growing centre of wealth, particularly around Hampstead, wherein about 3 per cent of accepted petitions listed a home address in the leafy green district. North London also accounted for a high percentage of the rejections because its district included poverty-stricken areas supported by the Strand Union and St Marylebone workhouses. The large asylums associated with the area, especially St Marylebone known for its lying-in services, attracted destitute mothers to their facilities during their confinement as explained in the case of Mary Griffiths.[58] In neighboring West London in general, housekeeping staff constituted between 23 and 24 per cent of the adult female population in Chelsea, St George Hanover Square, St James Westminster, St John and St Margaret.[59] Moreover, proper ladies' apparel entailed fancy hats and milliners to make those hats; fitted and fancy dresses called for skilled dressmakers. Suits for professional men required tailors, and fresh white shirts employed thousands of seamstresses and laundresses to provide the requisite accoutrements for the respectable family. Drapers and upholsterers were also in demand in London. In short, the majority of applicants provided rather fashionable postal codes. According to Booth's *Life and Labour in London,* by the 1890s, domestic service opportunities in the registration district of St George Hanover Square represented the highest concentration in the country, standing at 8.7 per cent; this data directly correlates to the higher percentages of Foundling Hospital petitioners from West London (Table 3.6).[60]

After 1880, committee men selected a larger percentage of cases from outside London. Could they have regarded London women as too worldly or cynical, inclined to play manipulative games? Alternatively, could it have been that small-town women encountered other difficulties when coping with an out-of-wedlock infant? Was it possible that the extra-metropolitan petitions arrived with stronger recommendations, or the committee men thought women living outside the corrupting influences of the metropolis were more malleable and thus more likely candidates for reformation, and better able to take advantage of a second chance? Whatever the precise answer, clearly, the arbiters for admission became increasingly more selective about their choices.

Table 3.7 shows the figures for total petitions received, wherein North London stood at 25.56 per cent; West London accounted for 17.98 per cent, while the heavily populated regions of London stricken with poverty stood at only 23.88 per cent. Kent and Essex and Greater England, Scotland and Wales accounted for 32.58 per cent of the survey. North and West London shared similar characteristics in terms of acceptance rates, but West London experienced considerably fewer rejections; indicating the noted respectability of the petitioner's employers. Rejected petition rates from East, South and Central London stood at 9.30, 5.43 and 20.93 per cent respectively, reflecting similar geo-social characteristics. While the practical guidelines had not changed in the 50 years, the selection process based on the mother's address changed. Committee men deselected petitions from the inner parts of the metropolis, and selected those from elite addresses, the periphery and beyond.[61] Upon reception of the official petition form, officials reviewed the

Table 3.6: FH Survey of Accepted Petitions by Divisions, 1860–92[62]

Divisions – 1860–92	1860–9 Petitions %	1870–9 Petitions %	1880–92 Petitions %	1860–92 Average %	Total N
North London	28.00	23.90	18.50	23.47	35
East London	10.00	4.35	5.56	6.64	10
South London	2.00	4.35	5.56	3.97	6
West London	24.00	32.62	9.26	21.96	32
Central London	4.00	4.34	0.00	2.77	4
Kent and Essex	18.00	13.04	31.48	20.84	32
Greater England, Scotland and Wales	14.00	17.40	29.64	20.35	31
	100.00	100.00	100.00	100.00	150
Total London	68.00	69.56	38.88	58.82	83
Total outside London	32.00	30.44	68.52	41.19	67

general information; culled out all incomplete forms, and sent a note advising the mother as to whether or not she was eligible for a hearing.[63]

The power of place and space and the associated authority that comes with a respectable address could not be more evident than in the findings of the survey. The Foundling Hospital intently framed itself as a respectable institution, the ornament of the Metropolis as Lord Chancellor Brougham remarked.[64] It operated as the pre-eminent charity of London, ordained to serve the needy and unfortunate domestic servants of the wealthy. Clearly, the question of London's social geography plays into the profile of the petitioner. For example, the committee men knew exactly the street from which the

Table 3.7: Comparison for All FH Addresses, 1842–92[65]

Divisions	Accepted Addresses 1842–92 N	Accepted 1842–92 %	Rejected Addresses 1842–59 N	Rejected Addresses 1842–59 %	Accepted and Rejected Addresses 1842–92 %
North London	56	24.67	35	27.13	25.56
East London	17	7.50	12	9.30	8.15
South London	13	5.73	7	5.43	5.62
West London	46	20.26	18	13.95	17.98
Central London	9	3.96	27	20.93	10.11
Kent and Essex	42	18.50	15	11.63	16.01
Greater England, Scotland, Wales	44	19.38	15	11.63	16.57
Total	227	100.00	129	100.00	100.00

following 1841 petition had arrived, Great James Street, situated north of Gray's Inn Field and south of Great Ormond Street, more or less in their own neighbourhood.

Mary T. (aged 21) worked as a 'servant of all works' on Great James Street.[66] When she met the father, he was a coach maker. 'He paid her attention proposed to keep company with her', and accompanied her home. A week later, he visited her at Hoxton upon which occasion she 'consented to keep company with him'.[67] They walked out to public gardens. 'Acquaintance' continued until January. Mary T.'s 'mistress had knowledge' of this affair and it was understood the father intended to marry her. [68] In January, 'c.c.' took place in 'her master's house in the absence of her master and mistress but not the children'.[69] This scenario would have, most likely, raised eyebrows.

The transcriber reported that 'Connection was repeated', and the father continued to visit until June. When he learned of her pregnancy, the father departed for France.[70] The questions then become, how did Mary's case, her choice to seek admission to the hospital for her infant, her age, occupation, the father's occupation, and the place to which he absconded, compare with other accepted petitions? These questions frame the context of the following chapter.

4

'When First Acquainted with Father I Was. . . ': Foundling Hospital Mothers and Fathers

> Persons who present Petitions to the Committee, must not previously apply to any Governor, or to any Officer or Servant belonging to the Hospital on the subject, on any pretense whatever; but they themselves must attend on Saturday Morning at the Hospital at Ten o' Clock, with their Petitions; all of which will be considered in rotation, whilst the Petitioners are expected to remain in attendance.[1]

> No Child can be admitted unless the Committee is satisfied, after due enquiry, of the previous good character, and present necessity of the Mother, and that the Father of the child has deserted it and the Mother, and that the reception of the Child will in all probability, be the means of replacing the Mother in the course of virtue, and the way of an honest livelihood.[2]

For a young mother, the admission of an infant born out-of-wedlock at the Foundling Hospital was highly sought after; it offered a stepping-stone to social rehabilitation in a world where respectability equalled employment. No matter how unattractive, unwed mothers had choices besides petitioning the Hospital. A mother could have gone to the workhouse and then abandoned her infant, where, chances were high the infant would die within a few weeks. She could have left her baby on the doorstep of a wealthy West End family. The mother could have concealed the birth of the child and placed it in a dustbin. She could have withheld her breast milk, simply stopped nursing the baby, or she could have deposited the infant with a 'baby farmer' or wet nurse while she worked. 'Overlaying' or suffocating the infant while the mother slept with her infant could also have occurred. As a quiet reminder, a desperate struggle to control one's body through safe abortion proved beyond the realm of possibility in the nineteenth century. Many women felt desperation when confronted with a conception that would create burdens unique to themselves alone.

In a study of the Royal London Hospital maternity ward, where the first clinical records observing women's efforts to abort a fetus are held, suggestive details emerge. The hospital recorded 'abortion' cases separately; in 1901, 23 of 82, or 28 per cent pointed to reasons other than clinical causes for death of the foetus. In the same sample, 42 of 82 cases, or just over 50 per cent of the women reported one or more 'abortions'. These records permit us to back date this information into the past, making it concurrent with the dates for this study. Recorded non-clinical causes included 'scrubbing, lifting a heavy weight, quarreling, fell upstairs, laundry work, fall, induced, strain, fright, worry'.[3] In one case, a matron expressed her shock with an '!' and explained the woman's desperate 'attempt to remove the fetus from outside'.[4] Thus, we might conclude the woman had attempted a self-induced abortion. If details presented clear or unknown issues, the matron recorded these details.[5] One account reported the mother had a 'hairpin' inserted in her uterus. The doctors removed it using with the help of an anaesthetic. Listed among the clinical reasons for abortion were syphilis, albuminia, fibroids, anemia, influenza and vesicular mole.[6] At Mile End Poor Law Infirmary, the first in the East End to offer obstetrical and gynaecological services, matrons reported six cases of 'macerated foetuses' between 1899 and 1909.[7]

If the working mother carried the infant to term, her options ran along a spectrum that ranged from bad to worse. Obviously, the woman under consideration here chose a different route. She made a calculated choice that diminished the agony of discovery; she wanted to retain her own self-respect and the good opinion of family and friends. How did mothers learn about the requirements for admission of their infant? Women discovered the promises of this institution through respectable women's networks such as Queen Charlotte's Lying-in Hospital, Mrs Marchmont at Urania Cottage, Mrs Ranyard's Bible women, clergymen, employers and friends.[8] She may also have read about the services through novels and journal articles written by Charles Dickens. Other than those who had been through the petitioning process, few knew the details of the admissions policy. Nonetheless, word had spread as far as Brighton, via small town vicars, who were among the recommenders providing needed support for women in trouble. Some learned by word of mouth, for example, a petitioner who had already had her infant admitted wrote a note on behalf of her friend:

> Dear Sir, I beg of you to know if you could inform me respecting a young woman a friend of mine who has been taken in the same way as I was now living in Brighton and her young man has moved away and left her and she has lately been confined with a male child and she does not know what to do as she is I believe a good woman.[9]

The sisterly feeling of this woman for her friend is apparent: 'I should like very much to do something for the poor young woman... as her friends have turned their back upon her'.[10] Thus, demonstrating the degree to which Victorians ostracized young women for their 'bad' behaviour and misfortune.

Another London curate, Claxton by name, enquired about services for a child in his parish, writing: 'There is in my parish a poor little illegitimate child. The mother is an infamous character and the father disowned him. He is a very nice little fellow.'[11] He further explained that another woman had taken care of the boy for some time, but she could barely maintain herself, let alone someone else's toddler. Therefore, the parish women asked Claxton to write on behalf of themselves and the child.[12] He suggested that women could make a small donation on behalf of the unfortunate in order to gain admission.[13] Although, receiving money for care of a 'foundling' may have been the practice in the eighteenth century, by the mid-nineteenth century, the institution refused to accept cash for care of any child, relying instead on its real estate investments and pew rents from the chapel.

Then there were the medical doctors who tried to open the door for mothers. For example, a young woman's physician advised her to seek help:

> I have a littel [*sic*] boy 5 months old which I am unable to support, I have therefore applied to a medical gentleman who is well acquainted with my circumstances and who has advised me to apply to you [about] the necessary particulars required to get an infant into the Foundling Hospital[.] [I]f you would kindly forward them to me as I am unable from circumstances to apply personally.[14]

Lady Superintendent Ellen Davenport, who operated the Female Refuge for unwed mothers, also sent a letter requesting information. She wrote:

> Dear Sir, Will you oblige me with one of your printed forms, as I am anxious to get a child into the Foundling Hospital if the case proves eligible which I think it will. I quite forget the way in which an application ought to be made, though you were kind enough some time ago to send me a paper.[15]

Given the rising numbers of 'asylums', or homes, run by women for women, a query incorrectly assumed that women served on the admissions committee at the Foundling Hospital. Addressing the secretary as madam, for example, bespeaks this assumption.

> Madam, Will you be so kind as to inform me as soon as convenient what influence is required to get a child admitted into the Foundling Hospital also at what age a child is taken and what is required of those to whom the child belongs.

> I hope Madam you will pardon the liberty I have taken but I am quite ignorant of any rules or what is required of any person addressing any of the officers of that institution. Waiting a reply, Ann E.[16]

If the mother chose to apply on her own accord, then we can turn to Charles Dickens, who offers a simplified view of the process in 1853. The 'deserted mother' obtained a form from the hospital porter at the Guilford Street gate. She took the petition home, completed it, and returned the document to the secretary. If successful, she brought her child to the hospital and received a piece of parchment inscribed with a figure between 20,000 and 22,149. The number provided identification, or a 'personal number', for infants admitted between 1854 and 1907.[17] Retrieval of the form, however, was only the first step. Rules approved by the governors prohibited others from requesting a petition on behalf of a mother. No mother's petition, Dickens reported, was allowed to be issued other than from the 'porter's lodge; no previous communication with any officer of the Hospital must have been held by the mother'.[18] Ironically, both parties strove to maintain confidentiality for different reasons.[19]

What sort of women would be most interested in petitioning the Foundling Hospital, and who were the committee likely to accept? To answer these questions, the following analysis relies on information provided by a 50-year survey of petitions submitted to the Foundling Hospital. Analysis of data from the form provides a separate profile of the case. Further, information relating to whether the woman received an invitation to a hearing or not, also yields fascinating insights to a function of Victorian society, the 'calculus of respectability', or acceptable and unacceptable standards of behaviour for women.[20] The mother's address provided important clues as to whether her petition would be accepted by the committee. Women from North and West London districts, as well as those from Greater England, Scotland and Wales had better chances for admission of their infant, than those who lived in Central, South or East London. Another measure of normative behaviour includes the age at which women marry and or become pregnant for the first time. This survey examines the mother's age and the age at which the 'risk of pregnancy' became a reality in the young woman's life. How do the ages of Foundling Hospital mothers compare with other studies examining similar issues such as occupation and address?

In an 1851 to 1881 study measuring illegitimacy in the rural Devonshire village of Colyton, Jean Robin found the mean age at which women gave birth to an out-of-wedlock infant was 21.89 years.[21] When comparing the Colyton data with the Foundling Hospital data for the same years, it shows petitioners' mean ages were similar between 1860 and 1879 (Table 4.1).[22]

Table 4.1: FH Mothers' Mean Age on Application, 1850–79[23]

Decades	1850–9 N = 109*	1860–9 N = 50	1870–9 N = 46
Mean age at application	23.10	22.22	21.89

*The 1850 decade included accepted and rejected petitions and shows a higher mean age on application. The explanation for this may rest with the fact that rejected petitions counted for about 75 percent of the total received; and more mature women received higher rejection rates. The 1850 data could be higher since older women might have been rejected more, as in they are old enough to know better.

A plausible explanation for similarities between the data sets is that over time petitions arrived from counties surrounding London, including Kent and Essex, and accounted for 31.84 per cent or close to one-third of the total. Perhaps, committee thought, the younger the mother the more necessitous she was because of the social pressure she faced living in a town or village outside of London, or, the younger the mother, the easier to reform her behaviour as her whole life was ahead of her.

This study also analyzed Foundling Hospital mothers' ages by cohorts, or five-year increments, 15–19, 20–24, 25–29, and over 30 years of age for survey years between 1842 and 1892. Girls aged fourteen or younger are grouped in the 15–19 cohort. Table 4.2 shows that the majority of the youngest group, those aged between 15 and 19, lived in North London. Similarly, the most common address for those aged 20 to 24 years, or 27.84 per cent, lived in North London. Over 43 per cent of mothers, aged 25 to 29 years listed North London and Greater England, Scotland, and Wales on the form.

In Table 4.3, 19.66 per cent of all mothers fall under the 15–19 years of age cohort. Over the 50-year period, there was a dramatic rise in this group from a low of 16 per cent in the 1860s to a high of 33.03 per cent in the 1880s. In every decade, however, committee men received and selected the greatest number of petitions from the 20–24 cohort, which stands at an average of 54.49 per cent. As a reminder, the figures represent a self-selected and selected group; first, the mother chose to apply and second, the committee either accepted or rejected the request for admission of her infant.

Unlike an earlier generation, during the mid- and late-Victorian era, young women opted for a lifestyle different from their mothers including employment outside of the family, and living apart from their families before marriage.[24] Pre-marital sex resulting in pregnancy undercut rising ambitions to become part of the respectable middle class; thus, the pressure to give up an illegitimate child. Further, the New Poor Law legislation of 1834 clearly ratcheted up pressure on the mother to prove paternity for support of an out-of-wedlock

Table 4.2: FH Age Cohort vs Location, 1842–92[25]

	15–19 Years		**20–24 Years**		**25–29 Years**		**+ 30 Years**	
Location	N	%	N	%	N	%	N	%
West London	16	22.86	36	18.56	12	16.22	–	
East London	6	8.57	15	7.73	6	8.11	2	11.11
South London	4	5.71	9	4.64	4	5.41	3	16.67
North London	16	22.86	54	27.84	16	21.62	5	27.78
Central London	5	7.14	20	10.31	10	13.51	1	5.56
Kent/ Essex	16	22.86	29	14.95	10	13.51	2	11.11
Greater England, Scotland, Wales	7	10.00	31	15.98	16	21.62	5	27.77
% of Total	70	19.7	194	54.5	74	20.8	18	5.0

child, placing more social and economic pressure on young women and their families. This may also indicate that teen mothers were unwilling to accept their condition, or to jeopardize future prospects of a respectable marriage and family. Certainly, the younger the petitioner, the more likely committee men were to believe that some man had taken advantage of her innocence.

Clearly, age and address were not the only operative factors in the calculus of respectability; the form also requested information on the mother's occupation. This question weighed heavily the minds of committee because they wanted assurances that if relieved of her infant, she could return to full employment in a 'respectable fashion'. To place the statistics of the Foundling women in context, it proves helpful to review 1891 census data when compilers divided all labourers by gender. In that count, only 35 per cent of all women over ten years of age versus 83.9 per cent of men over ten years of age worked outside the home. Census keepers assumed the other 65

Table 4.3: FH Petitioners' Age Cohort by Decade, 1842–92[26]

	15–19 Years		**20–24 Years**		**25–29 Years**		**+ 30 Years**	
Decades	N	%	N	%	N	%	N	%
1842–9*	18	18.6	47	48.5	23	23.7	9	9.3
1850–9*	18	16.5	61	56.0	24	22.0	6	5.5
1860–9	8	16.0	30	60.0	11	22.0	1	2.0
1870–9	8	17.4	30	65.2	7	15.2	1	2.2
1880–92	18	33.3	26	48.1	9	16.7	1	1.9
	70	19.66	194	54.49	74	20.79	18	5.06

*Reflects accepted and rejected petitions.

per cent were married women who worked as mothers and housekeepers, rearing children and managing domestic life.[27] Wealthy households employed 44.5 per cent, or 1,386,167 women as domestic servants. Only 6 per cent of men worked as domestics because the occupation belonged 'exclusively or preferentially to women'. Livery and coachmen, usually employed by large households, were included with cabmen.[28] The cotton industry in Lancashire and the worsted wool industry in Bradford employed the second largest group of single, married and widowed women.[29] The service industries, charring, laundering, hat and dress making businesses occupied another 20.4 per cent of employed women.[30] By this time, the industrial and commercial revolutions had reshaped the labour force to the point that only 6.1 per cent of the population, ten years of age and older, earned a living in agriculture.[31]

Clara Collet, a colleague and female counterpart of Charles Booth, the great surveyor of London poverty, published *On the Money Wages of Indoor Domestic Servants* for the Board of Trade. She surveyed 5,338 women, 1,867 of whom lived in London, comprising just about 35 per cent from 1894 to 1898. The remaining workers lived in England, Scotland, Wales and Ireland.[32] Collet, like Booth, highlighted geographical and gender differences between the lives of East and West End workers. Of note, Collet asserted that chances for marriage were better in the East than in the West End.[33] Tying this information to the Foundling Hospital data, statistics show that East London women comprised 8 per cent of those who applied; and they tended to be older, rather than younger mothers. Furthermore, East London 'factory girls' earned their living at the match factory, in confectionery, making jams, candy, cigars, and as needle workers, laundresses and beer bottlers. Few if any women claimed their occupation as matchbox makers, charwomen or beer bottlers in the Foundling Hospital survey.[34] Collet regarded women working in factories as lacking in respectable social skills, possessing nomadic tastes, and having low expectations for comforts of a good home. They were improvident, failing to save their hard-earned money, plentiful in good times, for the inevitable rainy day. 'The [factory] girls never do save.'[35] Nevertheless, she noted, factories employed only the best workers on a regular basis. She argued that when times got tough, the women's reliance on parish relief and private charities lowered wages and raised poor rates.[36]

Significantly, Collet placed specific emphasis on domestic service, noting that 'any statistic of average wages in various trades in which so important an occupation as "Domestic Service" is entirely neglected must therefore be seriously defective'.[37] Nonetheless, she admitted, arriving at an accurate assessment was difficult because of the uneven distribution of domestic employment at various households. Depending on the wealth of a household, a wide range of perquisites, in addition to wages, may have been available. Benefits included food, lodging, occasionally uniforms and gifts at Christmas.[38] While many households could afford a domestic, and she makes this point in her survey, not every household could afford a cook. Therefore, the women working as cooks were likely to be fairly well skilled if in a wealthy home, particularly if part of the London social set, entertaining guests during the London season.[39] Cooks' wages had not risen appreciably from mid-century. In 1848, cooks earned £15–£16 per year. Harriet Martineau projected that cooks earned between £12 and £18 per year in 1859. On the other hand, housemaids earned between £11 and £14 per year in the 1840s and 1850s; while nursemaids earned as little as £5 and as much as £30 per year, although the high figure was most likely the exception.[40] Most cooks could not qualify as a domestic. Collet reported that London 'indoor domestic servants' earned £17 16 s. per year. Thus, a woman aged 17 could garner a starting wage of £13 per year, if she wished to pursue this path. If the woman continued in her profession, she earned only £1 less than a nurse, and the same amount as a 'ladies' maid' after 20 years of service. Collet's tables indicate that more money and benefits came with age. Employers paid general servants the least. At 16 years of age, they annually earned £6 8 s. After 40 years of age, a general servant could hope to earn at most £14 8 s. per year.[41]

Foundling Hospital petitioners reported more than 42 occupations.[42] The jobs have been divided according to Collet's six categories and wage scales.[43] Class 1 shows that 9.55 per cent of the women were working in a family business, or living with their parents.[44] Class 2 stood at only 1.4 per cent and consisted of teachers, day care teachers, governesses and foreign language tutors. Class 3 included cooks, upper housemaids, nurses, milliners, embroiders, tailoresses and seamstresses and yielded 31.46 per cent of the

Table 4.4: FH Mothers' Occupation by Class, 1842–92[45]

Class	Occupation	N	Occupation %
Class 1	Family business, living with parents	34	9.55
Class 2	Teacher, foreign language instructor, creche teacher	5	1.40
Class 3	Cook, embroiderer, maid, nurse	112	31.46
Class 4	General Servant	123	34.55
Class 5	Kitchen and laundry maid, bar maid, flower seller	21	5.90
Class 6	Deserted wife, widow, and unknown	61	17.14
	Total	356	100.00

total, and comprised a valuable and visible part of the service class in West and North London, that of general servant. Collet categorized the remaining groups according to a general understanding of the degree of competency entailed in each listed occupation. Class 4, the largest group, representing 34.55 per cent of the petitions, constituted general servants, lodging housemaids and needlewomen. Kitchen helpers or scullery maids, who did the dirty work such as scrubbing pots and pans and peeling vegetables, flower sellers, and bar maids were included in Class 5, and comprised only 5.9 per cent of all petitions surveyed. While Class 6 was probably not what we might think of as an occupational group, it reflected women's responses in the petitions to the question of occupation. These women provided answers such as 'deserted wife' or 'widow'. Class 6, by default included the 'unknowns'. Earlier in the century, governors elected to disallow petitions from deserted wives and widows. Indicating their priority was to help young women get back to work, not to help a married housewife. In this group, 17.1 per cent either made the fatal mistake of listing their occupation as housewife, widow or deserted wife; it also includes those who became disillusioned with the process and withdrew their application, or submitted an incomplete petition.

Conceivably, Collet and the Foundling Hospital committee men shared the same values that surrounded the Victorian visions of respectability. Both understood how essential it was for an aspiring young woman living in West London to protect and maintain her respectable 'character' at any cost. If a woman became pregnant as a domestic, she lost her 'situation', or job. Out-of-wedlock pregnancies were highly unacceptable in a respectable household and inappropriate for public discussion. Moreover, to retain a 'situation' or employment in a respectable household, West End and North London domestics had to avoid marriage and children. In this way, domestic servants and middle-class women shared something, Collet argued – diminished marriage prospects.[46] Noticeably absent from East London petitions were any references to housemaids or upper housemaids, not to mention cooks. South London figures ranked second from the bottom in terms of housemaids. North London and Kent and Essex produced the highest percentages of housemaids, a far more respectable situation than that of a general servant, but not as respectable as that of a cook.

While 44.5 per cent of all British women were employed in domestic service in 1891, at least 72 per cent of the Foundling Hospital petitioners surveyed between 1842 and 1892 worked as domestics (Classes 3, 4 and 5) as shown in Table 4.5. Surprising were the numbers of petitioners from Kent, Essex and outlying regions in Class 1 who reported residing with their parents. North and West London shared similar results. Families employed 9.55 per cent of all petitioners. The percentage for Kent and Essex and Greater England, Scotland and Wales stood at 15.25 and 12.28 per cent, respectively. It appears, the committee accepted the baby to assist the mother by saving her 'character' or reputation and to meet the wishes of a wealthy employer, or to preserve the parents' social standing within their community (Table 4.5).

North London and Greater England, Scotland and Wales shared four of the five Class 2 cases, where women reported employment as teachers or instructors of some sort. For example, a wealthy family employed one woman as a foreign language instructor. Teachers accounted for only 1.4 per cent of all occupations. Class 3 comprised of general servants, cooks, upper house maids and nurses, represented over 66 per cent of all reported occupations. Homes in North or West London and Greater England employed the majority of these women. In North London, 34.1 per cent of all petitioners were respectably employed as cooks, upper house maids, or nurses. An even greater percentage, 34.55 per cent, of North London petitioners described their occupation as general servants. Petitioners used the term 'general servant' repeatedly. These women were most at risk. Although they had the skills to work as maids in a small household and could perhaps manage several domestic tasks at one time, they were not in a position to garner much authority over other household employees, or a kitchen for that matter. This made their skills, although in demand, very generic. Greater England, Scotland, Wales and North London returned the highest percentages of general servants, 27.12, and 29.7 per cent respectively. The data makes a compelling point. It is not to say that women in these districts were not equally in need, only those more respectable women, such as upper house maids and cooks, were given preference over general servants. Indeed, these findings reinforce the conclusion that employment

Table 4.5: FH Mothers' Occupations by Address, 1842–92[47]

Classes	**Class 1 Family Employee**		**Class 2 Teacher**		**Class 3 Cook, Upper House Maid, Nurse**		**Class 4 General Servant**		**Class 5 Laundry and Scullery Maids, Flower Sellers, etc.**		**Class 6 Deserted Wives, Widows, Unknowns**	
	N	%	N	%	N	%	N	%	N	%	N	%
North	8	8.8	2	2.2	31	34.1	27	29.7	3	3.3	20	22
East	3	10.3	0	0	9	31.03	9	31.03	1	3.45	7	24.14
South	3	15	0	0	8	40.00	6	30.00	0	0	3	15
West	3	4.7	0	0	22	34.4	30	46.9	6	9.4	3	4.7
Central	1	2.78	1	2.78	6	16.67	13	36.11	3	8.33	12	33.33
Kent and Essex	7	12.28	0	0	15	26.32	22	38.6	3	5.26	10	17.54
Greater England, Scotland and Wales	9	15.25	2	3.4	21	35.59	16	27.12	5	8.47	6	10.17
Totals	34	9.55	5	1.40	112	31.46	123	34.55	21	5.90	61	17.13

coupled with chastity had become more important than family building among many of these Foundling Hospital applicants.[48]

Class 5 (including flower sellers, street vendors and scullery and laundry maids) comprised only 5.9 per cent of all petitioners. These women worked on the streets of London where shoppers could afford luxuries such as fresh-cut flowers, but at the same time, exposed, shall we say, to passing of folks from all walks of life and not protected behind the doors and walls of a respectable household. While working, they most likely did not have a steady stream of income or an employer who could write a respectable letter of support. As mentioned before, scullery and laundry women worked in the lower reaches of a household removed from view of the family, not to mention guests.[49] Under Class 6, the highest percentages of deserted wives, widows or unknowns, standing at 33.33 and 24.14 respectively appeared under Central and East London categories. Clearly, the mother's age and occupation, in addition to her address, set successful Foundling Hospital petitions apart from unsuccessful petitions (Table 4.5).

Although the committee placed a spotlight on the mother, they also took interest in the relationship between the petitioner and the father.[50] All petition transcripts started the narrative with the following statement: 'When first acquainted with father I was… ' While the men focused on the mother's account, the hospital investigation gathered information on the fathers, but not in as detailed a fashion as they had on the mother; after all, they were concerned with her not his character. The form required the mother to identify the father's occupation, age and address; the committee aimed to reassure themselves that the father abandoned the petitioner; and that her partner was not waiting in the wings after their child had been admitted. This information appeared at the end of the oral testimony, preserved as part of the transcript, with the leading sentence: 'The last time the pet. saw father… '.[51]

Analysis of the demographic data for fathers provides fascinating details. The Foundling Hospital fathers' mean age was 25.9 years. Over time, the committee became increasingly unwilling to admit babies sired by men over 40 years of age. They assumed that senior men had been married by that stage of their lives, and therefore, unwilling to accept offspring from an adulterous affair. Only four cases involving married men entered the surveyed petition pool; this is not to say married men did not serve as impregnators, rather, they were not a significant part of the statistical pool. In two of the four cases, the petitioners claimed not to have known that the father was married. The committee accepted these cases between 1858 and 1860.[52] Importantly, survey ages of the partners grew closer together as the mother's age dropped. Five teen-aged fathers appeared in the second half of the 50-year survey. A few cases appeared in which the petitioner was older than the father, a point that usually elicited a comment from the transcriber.[53]

Table 4.6: FH Fathers' Occupations by Class, 1842–92[54]

Classes	Class %	Father's Occupations
Class 1 – Elite	4.8	Gentleman, 'no occupation listed', i.e. wealthy
Class 2 – Professionals	10.4	Commercial traveller, medical doctor, dentist, surgeon, surveyor, architect, Italian opera singer, artists, civil engineer, lawyer, tea/wool broker, shipwright
Class 3 – Highly Skilled	43.3	Upper house servant, teacher, printer, municipal servant, detective, draper, jeweler, taxman, medical student, lawyer's clerk, tailor, gas fitter, construction site foreman
Class 4 – Skilled	23.3	Skilled craftsmen, railway man, tobacconist, cigar maker, toll-keeper, farrier, food service worker, building trades, i.e. carpenter, plumber, stone mason
Class 5 – Labourer	16.6	Fish seller, fisherman, farmer, labourer, dock labourer, shopman, courier, bus conductor, enlisted man in army or navy, sailor
Class 6 – Unemployed	1.7	Unemployed, dead, in workhouse, unknown

The occupations of the fathers, as with the mothers, serve as an indicator of social class. His socio-economic class, however, made little difference in determining whether the committee accepted a petition. Table 4.6 lists the occupational classes for Foundling Hospital fathers divided according to the socio-economic divisions devised by Gareth Stedman Jones in *Outcast London*. The greatest percentage, 43.4 per cent of male occupations, fell under Class 3, which included the following occupations: upper house servant, teacher, printer, municipal servant, detective, draper, jeweler, taxman, medical student, lawyer's clerk, tailor, gas fitter and construction site foreman.[55]

Within Class 3, domestic servants comprised the greatest percentage or 17.7 per cent of the employed fathers. Food service employees, butchers, cooks and restaurant workers made up 9.6 per cent of the survey. The butcher frequently appeared in this sub-group; because, they were likely to show up at the back door of a wealthy household selling their meats and chickens. This daily interaction between cooks, domestics and butchers provided a natural venue in which to start up an affair. When the young woman had a day off, the couple set a date for 'walking out' together. One thing led to another. When the woman found herself pregnant, she also usually found herself out of a 'situation'. Then a woman chose to either search for a solution to the illegitimate infant or managed to deal with the problem later. According to the Poor Law Commission, unwillingness to plan was a sure sign of improvidence, and those who failed to prepare for the future, embarked on a path filled with risk.[56]

London's building boom and railway construction in the 1860s and 1870s, particularly in West London, attracted carpenters, plumbers and stone and brick masons. London employed 24 per cent of all builders and 38 per cent of architects in England and Wales during this era.[57] In the survey of accepted petitions, men working in the building trades and as skilled artisans comprised 11.5 per cent of the Foundling Hospital fathers. Common labourers comprised 6.5 per cent, a much smaller group. Missing from the list, almost entirely, were dock labourers, which further emphasizes the paucity of petitions accepted from Tower Hamlets, or East London. According to the 50-year survey, 5.3 per cent of the men were already serving in, or may have later joined the army or navy. The likelihood that they would leave within days or weeks of starting a relationship was high. All fathers had the freedom to leave the mothers of their children, so military men proved no different. All mothers, on the other hand, faced the cleanup of their shared activities, whether consensual or not.

The length of acquaintance and date when the mother last saw the father of her child after conception reveals important information on Victorian working-class relationships. Table 4.7 indicates the length of time between conception and the father's abandonment of accepted and rejected petitioners between 1842 and 1892. The majority of fathers, or 68.17 per cent, abandoned the mother within six months of conception.[58] Breaking this statistic down a bit more, petitioners reported that 44.1 per cent of the fathers left within 0–3 months of conception, while 65.9 per cent left after four months, some remained until after delivery of the infant. The more complicated and involved the relationship, the longer the fathers remained in the picture. Mothers who

Table 4.7: FH Fathers' Time to Abandonment, 1842–92[59]

Date of Abandonment after Reported Conception	Date of Abandonment after Reported Conception %
0–3 months	44.0
4–7 months	24.2
8–9 months	21.1
+10 months	10.7

reported meeting the fathers of their babies after their confinements were suspect. The most questionable fathers appear in the last category, or the +10 months; because, committee men worried that their presence indicated a 'family strategy'. Perhaps, they thought, couples may have intended to continue their relationship without the burden of a child. This explains exactly why the committee wanted to know when and where the petitioner last saw the father.

Options at home and abroad, not afforded the mother, readily presented themselves to resourceful fathers. As Table 4.8 illustrates, the 'reported destinations' of fathers fell into several categories. The 'unknown' category comprised 36.2 per cent of the responsible parties. Initially, this group was most highly represented in rejected petitions; but lack of knowledge relating to the whereabouts of the father increased over time. Approximately 24.2 per cent reported the father was in England, Scotland, Ireland or Wales. The Continent, being proximate and offering a choice place to which an errant father could have absconded, absorbed 11.8 per cent of the fathers.

The United States and Canada, lands of opportunity, proved attractive to 9.3 per cent of the men and increased in popularity over time. The colonies, Australia, India, New Zealand, South Africa and other far-flung reaches of the British empire – absorbed 8.4 per cent of the fathers. While 4.8 per cent lived in the workhouse or a prison, or they were reported as deceased. The survey did not find significant differences in the fathers' destinations over time. Thus for the 50 years surveyed, men resorted to very similar strategies insofar as 'escape' was concerned. Obviously, their choices were far more wide-ranging than the petitioners'. Apparently, these fathers felt little personal obligation, even in those cases, representing 21.07 per cent of petitions, in which the relationship lasted more than a year.

Table 4.8: FH Fathers' Destinations, 1842–92[60]

Reported Destinations	Destination %
Unknown	36.2
England, Scotland, Wales	24.2
Continent	11.8
United States and Canada	9.3
South America, New Zealand, Australia, India	8.4
Workhouse, Prison, Infirmary	4.8
Military or Sea	5.3
Total	100.0

The nature of the father's relationship with a Foundling Hospital petitioner sheds additional light on another contested issue: prostitution. When the father remains in the text, as is the case with many accepted Foundling Hospital petitions, it seems unlikely that the pregnancy was the result of prostitution. Foundling Hospital Treasurer Gregory testified before a Parliamentary Select Committee in 1871 that the Foundling Hospital accepted only respectable young women who had been taken advantage of in 'the most cruel fashion, and who were most concerned about hiding… [their] shame'.[61] His assessment of the admission process supports the information above. The truly poorest women were not accepted because, as Gregory testified, the committee guarded against those women, the so-called workhouse cases. 'Women who have been four or five months in the workhouse, and utterly of the lowest class, in whom the moral sense is very much deadened' would not have been permitted to set foot on the Foundling Hospital grounds.[62] Gregory also averred that the Foundling Hospital would not approve a petition from a woman who had a history of prostitution.[63] If this sort of woman ably duped the porter into giving her a petition, the secretary rejected the petition at the review stage. If not then, certainly it was rejected after the oral interview.

Successful Foundling Hospital petitioners represented a sector of the respectable working class, seeking a viable alternative to the burden of raising an out-of-wedlock child. Table 4.9 provides a comparative profile of the petitions as discussed above. The mother's ability to sign her name and work at a minimum level of a general servant contributed to the acceptance or rejection of the petition. Both indicators suggest that the petitioners had a higher than average skill level when compared with East End women. Successful applicants had maintained a high level of respectability, with the exception of this one 'fall'. The institution held to the notion that if a woman could be relieved of her illegitimate infant, she could move back to a respectable situation. The applicants represented a broad spectrum of well-paid occupations, 42 in all.[64] As institutional practices evolved, Foundling Hospital committee men selected women aged 15 to 24 who were either employed by, or living with their families, especially during the last 20 years of the survey. This indicates a willingness, on the part of the committee, to aid those who were sincerely fearful and frightened of the stain an illegitimate child could have on their family reputation, as well as their own. The Victorian working-class woman regarded her occupation as part of her claim for respectability. When an infant compromised this option, choices had to be made. By successfully petitioning the Foundling Hospital for relief of her child, the young woman received a reprieve, redemption, so that she could reclaim her job, her reputation, and possibly marry one day.

This research seeks to show a clear example of Scott's argument that 'gender

Table 4.9: Comparison of Variables for All FH Petitions[65]

Categories	**Accepted Petitions 1842–92 %**	**Rejected Petitions 1842–55 %**
Mothers' Address – North London	24.67	27.80
Mother Could Sign Name	93.40	80.60
Mothers' Occupation – General Servant	38.80	27.100
Father's Occupation – Skilled, Class 3	46.30	38.0

is a constitutive element of social relationships based on perceived differences between the sexes, and gender is a primary way of signifying relationships of power'.[66] Patriarchy, class and the legal system placed strictures on the sexual behaviour of women not men. Biological realities also shaped the woman's reality; a father could leave, however a woman, short of an abortion or abandonment, could not leave her child. These choices, such as the refusal to end the pregnancy through an attempted abortion, or to commit infanticide, sent mothers in search of help to the Guilford Street gate. The committee had the power to decide the worthiness of each case and to provide a solution to a vexing problem for young women. To protect against the possibility of admitting the infant of a 'lewd' woman, the men assessed respectability of a petition by address, the mother's age and occupation. The place of the father in the petition proved essential to support true abandonment. The selection process ensured the mother would be capable of returning to work after the officers accepted her baby.

Regarding the public face, Foundling Hospital committee men, wished to portray petitioners as redeemed women, unlike others facing similar circumstances. They were different. Their choices and those of administrators spared them the humiliation of rearing an illegitimate child because they met the criteria of respectability. The Foundling Hospital mother preferred marriage before child bearing, or an independent life. Work, gainful employment, was often part of the formula for a successful petition. The next chapter analyzes the many questions asked of petitioners during the oral interview. It will further clarify the 'construction' of respectability for Victorian London's working poor, relieving the mid-Victorian petitioners of charges that they freely engaged in lewd behavior.

5

'Is My Own Name Really Required, for on that Everything Depends'

> Does not the character test fail in 'its most essential condition – that of enabling us to distinguish the genuine and the spurious in our domestic economy'.[1]

In mid-century, one of the few petitioners who could read and write, because she worked as a governess, asked Mr Brownlow: 'Is my own name really required for on that everything depends?'[2] Her character, which according to social reformer Helen Bosanquet, determined life's future circumstances, making some families rich and others poor.[3] An out-of-wedlock child marred a woman's reputation. Yet, belief in their own good characters steered like-minded women to the children's asylum for more assistance than the poor law and civil courts could provide. They made very difficult choices, some even risked travel to London with a newborn to be on hand in case the secretary called them for a hearing. If their courtroom testimonials – regarding the circumstances surrounding courtship, pregnancy and birth of the infant – met standards of respectability, then the institution agreed to accept the baby. The petitions reveal personal qualities that set these women apart from others in similar circumstances. One thing is certain, if they had not felt the extreme social pressure of shame and humiliation, the mothers would not have made application.

Social conventions prohibited women working as domestic servants from being married. If they wed, they had to leave service. Likewise, if they reported a pregnancy, the head of the household discharged them. The mistress clearly regarded the woman as a threat to the reputation of her family.[4] The parturient woman breached the bond of trust, the silent or unspoken contract between the employer and employee had been tested beyond reason, calling the respectability of both the maid and the household in jeopardy. As discussed above, the widest majority of applicants worked in private households, cleaning, cooking, laundering, nursing and tending children. Yet, their reputation, as measured by Foundling Hospital governors and committee, represented the definition of 'character' for over a century. This chapter analyzes petitioners' answers to questions raised at hearings in the Foundling Hospital courtroom as to how they found themselves pregnant and abandoned.

Respectable society, represented in this case by the men at the Foundling, created a moral calculus, which gauged future outcomes or consequences. According to the elite, this was the problem of the labouring poor; they were improvident and did not look forward to a time when they needed to provide for children, before they engaged in sexual activities.[5] Such preparations added considerable pressure to Victorians' lives, especially if society deemed their behaviour aberrant and the only recourse for help turned out to be the public workhouse. Such bleak prospects fostered a sense of despair in some.[6] John Brownlow expressed the challenges quite well:

> When a woman, with a sense of honour, finds herself the unsuspecting victim of treachery, with the witness of her disgrace hanging about her neck, in the person of her child, left to the reproach of the world and her own conscience, and seeing no other means of saving her character, she becomes delirious in her despair, and vents her fury on the consequences of her seduction, the child of her seducer! Hence the murder and desertion of children become alarming evils – evils which were produced and perpetuated 'for want' [to use the words of Captain Coram] of proper means for preventing the disgrace and succouring the necessities of their parents.[7]

Yet, her shame and efforts to hide the humiliation does not suggest that she led the life of a woman of the night, who suddenly found herself pregnant and full of remorse; or that she was always the saucy young woman who just happened to become pregnant. In *Love in the Time of Victoria*, Françoise Barret-Ducrocq portrays Foundling Hospital women in such a manner, either as manipulative prostitutes or youthful and unsuspecting victims. She suggests the women presented themselves 'in a pathetic light in order to secure material help'. She also argues that the hospital's main concern was 'to redeem prostitutes', based on their conviction that the mothers' lives were ruined.[8] Perhaps, the women could be charged with indecent flirtations and extra-marital sexual relations, but selling their bodies for money, or participating in a bigamous relationship was uncommon practice for women who had infants admitted to this institution, unless they were skilled mistresses of deception.[9] This study investigates the lives of these women, by challenging Barret-Ducrocq's description of the candidates as immoral, profligate, impure, animal-like and far from virtuous.[10] A short review of the literature on unwed or prenuptial pregnancies and a deeper analysis of the documents creates a more nuanced understanding of Victorian petitioners and their lives.

The questions of courting practices ending in out-of-wedlock births have been the subject of social historians for well over 40 years. Peter Laslett and Anna Clark significantly contribute to an understanding of this issue in Victorian society. In *Struggle for the Breeches*, Anna Clark observes that a promise of marriage meant a commitment; it meant that intimate relationships were possible between courting couples; society understood that should a woman become pregnant, her partner would marry her.[11] Peter Laslett examines four types of 'extra-marital' conceptions. The first arose because the courting and marriage process took a long time, and perhaps there was some interruption in the process, for example, the death of a partner, which stopped the couple from taking public vows. In *Bastardly and Its Comparative History*, Laslett does not suggest how long the courtship might have lasted. The 'shotgun wedding' describes a scenario where the couple made some move towards marriage; a pregnancy occurred, and the couple married. In the 'spouse entrapment type', the woman deliberately became pregnant and then induced the partner to marry. Finally, in the early modern period, the 'fertility testing type', or the process of getting pregnant first, to ensure reproductive capabilities, according to Laslett, was widespread. Demographers theorize that children, resulting from the latter three relationships, reflected the English social and legal construction of the term 'bastardy'. This label describes a concept unlike a prenuptial pregnancy that resulted from a prolonged courtship period. Laslett argues that the difference between a pre-nuptial pregnancy and the latter three pregnancies rests in the intentions of the partners. 'Such intentions,' Laslett asserts, 'are almost inaccessible to the historian,' because as mentioned above, most working-class people did not write about their views of the world and their particular situations, they worked for a living.[12]

To shed light on the 'inaccessible', we can turn to the Foundling Hospital petitions, which reveal intrusive questioning about the most intimate details of relationships. From their testimony, we learn about the private decisions and intentions obscured within less revealing sources. By using a process known as concatenation, or analysis of a series of interconnected events and consequences drawn from answers to questions provided by the petitioner, we can extrapolate the limits and extent to which mothers could exercise personal freedom (or agency shaped by constraints). To paraphrase E. P. Thompson's thesis, individuals make history in a world that is not of their own choosing, petitions provide glimpses of inaccessible details, but more importantly, illustrate choices and constraints in the socio-cultural milieu of Victorian London.[13]

Analysis of oral transcripts illustrates how closely the committee scrutinized petitioners' desperate circumstances with the following questions: How had she become pregnant? How had the couple met? Did a promise to marry accompany the affair? How long was the courtship? Had the petitioner received a promise to marry before giving consent to sexual relations? To gain relief, the women had to answer these questions as honestly as possible. She also knew that if she attempted to deceive the committee, they would find the truth through other means, including letters from recommenders and their private investigator. Hence, if sexual intercourse relied on a promise to marry and consent to an intimate relationship, the seriousness of the couple to marry in the future can be gauged, to some extent, by the length of acquaintance; or how long they had known each other before the woman received a promise to marry and gave her consent. Returning to Laslett, in *The Bastardy Prone Sub-Society*, sometimes courting relationships lasted a long time and based on answers to these questions found in oral testimonies, we can discover a quotient of 'respectability' to guage this claim.

This study divides the length of acquaintance by months into four periods: less than one month, or 0 months means 'no established relationship'; 1–3 months indicates the couple was 'acquainted'; 4–6 months suggests a 'possible relationship'; 7–12 months points to a 'steady relationship'; and 13 months or more implies a 'courting relationship'. In some cases, length of acquaintance does not actually reflect a relationship, only the petitioner and father knew each other. For example, the couple may have known each other from childhood, worked together, lived as neighbours, or passed each other on the street. Frequently, the woman said, 'I knew the father since I was a young girl', making it difficult to ascertain the nature of this particular relationship. Although arbitrary, these time-bound categories provide a useful measure of the strength or commitment between the mother and father of her child. One thing is certain, length of acquaintance clearly mattered to the committee. They frowned on very short-term acquaintances, favouring petitioners involved in long-term relationships as indicated by answering the question, when were you first acquainted with the father?

Table 5.1 illustrates changes in reported 'length of acquaintance' between 1860 and 1892 for all petitions. During Brownlow's tenure in the 1860s, few petitioners who reported knowing the father of her child less than a month succeeded. In the 1860s, the >12 month category stood at 28 percent. In the 1870s, under the >12 month category, the percentage rose by .26 percent. Between 1880 and 1892, however, the >12 month category rose to 31.48 percent. Looking at 1860 onwards, the trend shows a steady decline in the 7–12 month category, over 50 per cent between 1860 and 1892. This may be attributed to the extra caution the committee began to take with the help of the private investigator, who went to find the fathers. It may also be attributed to the fact that if the mother reported the presence of the father during the last months of pregnancy, the suspicions of the men would be raised. Again, they thought the father was actually waiting in the wings, until the couple found a more auspicious time to marry. The 1–3 month category rises sharply, over 40 per cent between 1860 and 1870 and the >12 category rises by 10 per cent, while the 4–6 months remains relatively stable.

Table 5.2 illustrates the length of acquaintance for accepted petitions between 1842 and 1892. A relationship of less than one month negatively influenced a woman's chances of having her petition accepted. Relationships of one to three months still commanded the highest percentage, standing at 27.88, but acquaintances longer than 12 months trailed by 0.58 per cent. More than 71 per cent of the accepted petitions indicated the woman had known the father for more than four months. Although the length of acquaintance for accepted petitions increased slightly between 1842 and 1892, significant differences existed between the accepted and rejected petitions.[14]

Of course, a smart girl might take a chance and lie about the length of the relationship, but it was risky because the Foundling Hospital investigator

Table 5.1: FH Acquaintance by Month, by Decade for Accepted Petitions, 1860–92

Length of Acquaintance	**1860–9 %**	**1870–9 %**	**1880–92 %**
0 months	0.00	2.17	1.85
1–3 months	22.00	30.44	29.64
4–6 months	24.00	23.91	24.07
7–12 months	26.00	15.22	12.96
>12 months	28.00	28.26	31.48

Table 5.2: FH Length of Acquaintance for Accepted Petitions, 1842–92

Time	**N**	**Acquaintance %**
0 months	3	1.32
1–3 months	63	27.75
4–6 months	53	23.35
7–12 months	46	20.26
> 12 months	62	27.32
Total	227	100.00

interviewed family members, employers and professionals who knew the case. If the investigator's report contradicted some part of the petitioner's account, it placed the petition in jeopardy. Table 5.3 shows petitioners reporting short-term relations constituted a significantly higher percentage of rejected petitions.

An acquaintance of 1–3 months has the highest percentage of accepted petitions, 27.75 percent, but is next to last in percentage terms when comparing accepted petitions with total petitions. The 4–6 months' length of acquaintance ranks as the most accepted relationship. The conclusion is that 4–6 months marked the ideal time in a relationship for a successful petition. Among the rejected petitions, 17.83 per cent reported acquaintance with the father less than one month. Among accepted petitions, only 1.32 per cent reported an acquaintance of less than one month. The greatest percentage of rejected petitions, 56.59 percent, was in the one to three months category. This compares with 27.75 per cent of accepted petitions. Less than 25.58 per cent of all rejected petitioners knew the father for four months or more (Table 5.3).

It also proves helpful to examine how women who delivered their infants in the workhouse fared in terms of length of acquaintance. Among the 356 petitions, 72 workhouse cases constituted 20.23 per cent of the pool. Among all petitions, the majority of workhouse women knew the father of their child for 1–3 months before becoming pregnant (Table 5.4). These data illustrate the extremely compromised position of women in society. Should they become pregnant out-of-wedlock, they relied on the poor law workhouse for delivery of their infant. The primary benefit of delivering in the workhouse was the assurance, provided by the attending midwife that this was the mother's first baby, always a concern for the committee. Further, at least authorities could not charge the unwed mother with infanticide if her

Table 5.3: FH Length of Acquaintance for Rejected Petitions, 1842–59[15]

Time	N	Petitions %	Accepted to Rejected Ratio
0 months	23	17.83	11.54
1–3 months	73	56.59	46.32
4–6 months	8	6.20	86.89
7–12 months	12	9.30	79.31
> 12 months	13	10.08	82.67
Total	129	100.00	63.76

Table 5.4: All FH Workhouse Cases by Length of Acquaintance, 1842–92[16]

Length of Acquaintance	N	Petitions %
0 months	8	11.1
1–3 months	32	44.4
4–6 months	11	15.3
7–12 months	8	11.1
> 12 months	13	18.1
Total	72	100.0

infant died during delivery or if she suffered from post-partum depression, as illustrated by the case of Mary Griffiths.[17] The other 79.77 per cent of the Foundling Hospital women, who had not relied on public assistance, were either more independently resourceful, or they had saved a sufficient amount of money to cover the costs of confinement, or they had a better family support system.

The Foundling Hospital transcriber recorded the hearings, within which he embedded important kernels of information. Questions about this material include: Is there a new set of values represented in the petitioner profiles? Were prescriptions for proper behaviour in transition from a pre-industrial pattern to a code adapted to urban living? To what extent can we see a shift in Foundling Hospital policies regarding admission of problematic cases, such as incest? To address these questions, the following analysis moves between the narratives, roughly arranged in chronological order, and the data. By extrapolation, several general conclusions about the lives of Victorian working-class women are possible. For example, in some cases, petitioners reported a tentative promise to marry if they became pregnant. In other cases, marriage was clearly out of the question, because in others, the father used force to achieve his 'purpose'. Subtle nuances in the text and tone make each petition distinctive. A universal theme, however, appears in most petitions: the woman's effort to preserve her character. She chose the Foundling Hospital option, and most fiercely desired to hide the new born and to move on without the father of her child.

The extended account of Sarah F. exemplifies a woman who clearly deliberated on her actions, selected a plan of attack, and then pursued it. According to her testimony, Sarah F. became pregnant after a short and illicit affair; the humiliation was overwhelming. She went to the Foundling Hospital gatehouse to pick up a petition. Upon arrival, she did not first ask for a petition; she asked the porter for a list of governors, apparently hoping to gain influence with them. Sarah wrote, 'On inquiring at the porter's lodge where I could obtain a book containing a list of the governors to the Foundling Hospital, I was informed that eleven applications should first be made known to you.'[18] This meant, 11 cases preceded hers.[19] Sarah F. completed the form by herself; a very rare occurrence. She listed her occupation as governess. According to M. Jeanne Peterson, in *Suffer and Be Still,* a governess 'had no social position worth attention. She was at best unenvied and at worst the object of mild scorn, and all she sought was survival in genteel obscurity.'[20] A woman with this profession, however, ranked within an entirely different class and stood apart from the poor and obscure Irish women living in the East End or around St Giles in central London. Further, this individual believed her life worth something more than a polite dismissal into 'genteel obscurity'. Apparently, Sarah F. hoped her ability to read and write would so impress the committee men that she could avoid full disclosure of embarrassing personal information. She was mistaken. In a letter to the committee, the candidate claimed she was unable to 'fill up', parts in the petition, specifically the father's name, age and occupation. While other petitioners understood the rules, in order for the committee to consider their case, the form had to be completed in its entirety, which meant the father's name had to be supplied. Sarah F., planned to get the petition passed the review process without naming the father or supplying names of recommenders. Therefore, she took the 'liberty of addressing the committee by letter'. She provided a detailed story, writing that on the way home from London on a Saturday afternoon:

> I was arrested by a gentleman quite a stranger to me with whom I entered into conversation. I was asked to take some refreshment which I did and for some time after I was unconscious. I feel sure something very strong must have been mixed with the wine I drank. The next day we parted[.] I never saw him again I was miserable![21]

Sarah F. volunteered information about her family; in particular, her father was a medical man who had had a reputable medical practice in London before he died. Immediately, this implied she came from a respectable family, which set her apart, at least in her opinion. She reported she could not attend her interview because 'feelings would prevent' her from answering the questions properly. Moreover, Sarah wrote:

> If I expose the matter to my friends I am disgraced forever, never can I enter home again and all friends will shun me. It is in this extremity that

> I thought of your institution… My only hope is in concealment[.] [O]nce discovered I must wander alone with my child. I know not whither.[22]

Living in fear and hiding, she worried what might happen if friends discovered her condition. She disclosed she could be contacted through an alias, 'Miss White', at Kennington Cross Post Office. Continuing, she explained how she shrank from 'appearing before a committee as the scalpel'.[23] To undergo the 'scalpel' of a surgeon in 1853 held many dangers, not the least of which was the pain caused by cutting into flesh that had not been anesthetized, and should the patient survive the incision the threat of infection after surgery posed a real possibility.[24] Sending mixed messages, Sarah controlled the information by mentioning a surgeon and scalpel as though she had considered an abortion. In a subsequent letter of appeal, Sarah revealed a disability. She was deaf. Hence, she asked the committee to consider her disability because it created 'timidity amongst strangers'.[25] Still bargaining, Sarah wrote: 'If my child can be admitted into the Hospital I have resolved to give a full account of myself.'[26] Her bid for special treatment failed to this point.

The Foundling Hospital secretary responded to her letter in a matter of fact way; her case would be heard at 9.30 a.m. on Saturday morning, at which time she would be expected to appear in person before the Foundling Hospital committee men to answer their questions. Sarah F. replied to the Secretary: 'After thinking over all the information you have so kindly given me concerning the hospital I feel that I cannot do better than inform you of my determination which I can express to you better by letter than by word of mouth.'[27] Still fighting the interview, Sarah agreed to give a full accounting through correspondence. She challenged the very mission of the Foundling Hospital, asking whether the institution was for deserted children, and was not her child deserted? Then she confessed. After meeting the father, she chose not to see him again because he was a married man.[28]

> I thought not of the result or I should have acted differently and it was not for some months that I fully realised all. I implored him to desist and leave me by myself but he remained with me the next day. The account he gave of himself is this. He is married not living with his wife they had been separated some years. Unable to marry again not being divorced his propositions were these to leave my family and commit myself to living with him. He intended to go abroad.[29]

Sarah could not accept this proposal. Given her situation, Sarah F. wrote about how she had entertained thoughts of suicide, but concern for the infant saved her:

> When I fully realised the whole my first thought was self destruction, this I attempted twice but was miraculously prevented and afterwards when better thoughts prevailed love for my child prompted me to make some effort to leave home and thus conceal the whole.[30]

Therefore, she left her position as governess before her confinement and went into the country, where she posed as a married-homeless woman. A poor old couple took in the mother and baby. She gave this account:

> Having very little money I never can forget what I endured there. [N]o one can tell what a person may be led to do when suffering from hunger and now when I hear of some poor creature stealing for absolute necessities I cannot wonder for had my temptation been put in my way I cannot really say how I should have acted. That is the horror of starvation.[31]

Starvation was another possibility for Sarah as it had for so many other women. If she wanted to survive, then she needed to save her 'character'. The charitable couple gave her food, shelter and maintained her infant while she returned to London to find a new situation as a governess. During this time, after several missives between Sarah and the secretary, Sarah conceded: 'I will be at the Hospital on Saturday next at half past nine. Will you show my letters to the Committee as it will inform them of my case and save me much explanation.'[32] She signed the letter using an alias, Miss White. In order to provide for her infant, Sarah submitted to a 'hearing'. Obviously, this lone mother viewed the Foundling Hospital as the most viable alternative for survival of her baby and herself. She could not leave the infant with the poor elderly couple, and she refused to go into the workhouse. Only with great reluctance, however, was she willing to submit to an interview. The committee accepted Sarah F.'s baby.[33]

The above case is exceptional. Sarah F. could read and write; she assumed a more direct role in the petitioning process than others. She understood, if she wanted to succeed, she needed to prove her respectability to the committee. For this, she needed willing recommenders to testify on her behalf. While the widest majority could read to a certain level, they could not express themselves in writing to the extent as could Sarah. If nothing else, the ability to write, to communicate your innermost thoughts on paper can be liberating and release a person from dependency. In most instances, however, mothers relied on a literate person for information on admission criteria and help with completion of the application form.

Inability to control a situation leads to hopelessness. We saw it before in the case of Mary Griffiths. If there was a sense of sheer desperation in Sarah

F.'s case, then, hers was but one example. Despondency overtook some single mothers because confinement and bearing an illegitimate child placed heavy psychological and emotional burdens not only on her, but also on families as illustrated by the following cases. Petitioner Elizabeth S. (aged 20) met her suitor on Oxford Street. They began to 'walk out' together; this marked the beginning of their courtship. They drank tea together, and he proposed marriage. She consented to his overtures, and when she discovered she was pregnant, with her partner nowhere to be found, she went to live with her parents in her fifth month. She told her mother what had happened, who persuaded her father to permit Elizabeth to remain with them through her confinement. In the petition application, the strain on the petitioner's mother had been extreme; the family took her mother to Bedlam Hospital, the insane asylum, the day Elizabeth delivered her baby. Elizabeth's former school teacher recommended her to the Foundling Hospital. He reported, 'the melancholy loss of the protection of her mother' in her youth, because of mental illness (suggesting Elizabeth was somewhat of an emotional orphan), was partly to blame for her circumstances. The Foundling Hospital committee admitted Elizabeth's baby.[34]

Perina P. testified the father refused to believe she was pregnant when she last saw him. This reluctance on the part of the father to accept what his girlfriend had told him appeared frequently in petitions. The petitioner recounted how she told the baby's father that if he would not marry her, she would commit suicide. He did not marry her. Crushed by this humiliation, she apparently had an emotional or mental breakdown. Someone who could help the hapless woman sent her to Gloucester House in Lockes Fields, an institution for 'depraved females'.[35] She remained there until her confinement. Thereafter, the Gloucester House committee helped her find lodgings at 25 Trafalgar Place in Kensington. The transcript also reported, 'as soon as she is able she will return to the institution where she will be provided with a "character" [letter of reference], and return to work'.[36] The committee men accepted her petition.

Her father employed Ann P. (aged 29) as bookkeeper and paymaster. She and her family lived in South Devon. One day in February 1846, when she returned from 'tea' in a carriage driven by one of her father's farm labourers, they had sexual intercourse. The petitioner did not exactly spell out the circumstances. Ann explained how she resisted and fainted, but told no one except her sister a few months later. Then the mother reported she was unwell. Mr Gardiner of Marlbro', a homeopathic doctor, not suspecting Ann P. was pregnant, gave her medicine. The medicine did not help her; so the family sent her to their doctor. When he discovered she was pregnant, the medical man told Ann P.'s mother. Fearing loss of respectability, the petitioner's mother then sent her away to the matron, Lady Elice, at the Hanwell Lunatic Asylum. There, she was confined; and the doctor removed the infant from her side immediately. Throughout this nine-month episode, Ann's father had not been informed of all that had transpired. Her mother fired 'Huntley', the farm labourer, for intoxication. After delivering her baby, Ann P. returned to work.[37] A short note from her family doctor testified:

> Nothing could have excited more surprise or regret in my mind, than to discover the degraded situation of that young woman, whom I had been attending from time to time during the spring and summer, there were symptoms in her case which might from the first, to have made me suspect of her situation, but I must acknowledge, that such was my opinion of the correctness of her conduct that I had not an idea of it.[38]

The asylum doctor claimed Ann P. had threatened to commit suicide. The family physician, however, had not seen any such behaviour. She had 'shewn great sorrow and repentance for her crime'.[39] Her doctor confided to the enquirer: 'Her position had preyed upon her mind possibly never of the strongest'.[40] Why Ann P. assumed responsibility for her 'crime' is a question deserving further consideration; perhaps she felt guilty because the farm labourer was fired. Nonetheless, she was intelligent, adequately educated, and from a respectable family who protected the mother's character, without her father learning of her circumstances. Her petition was accepted.[41]

In an 1865 petition, the transcriber explained that Annie C.'s employer, a solicitor, completed the form for her. Annie C. (aged 22) worked as a general servant and had known the father nine months before she discovered her pregnancy.[42] Annie recounted: 'When pregnant I told him and he slighted me and told me to drown myself and that he would help me to do so. He did not deny the paternity.'[43] This sort of response from a partner surely struck a chord of despondency in an unmarried mother, both because of the rejection and her loss of character. A sensational newspaper story from 1889 indicates continuity in the agony experienced by unwed mothers between the 1840s and 1890s. *The Evening Standard* reported how a young cook had disappeared from her position at a wealthy home in Hampstead. Witnesses told the reporter: 'On Friday night a splash was heard in one of the Hampstead Heath Ponds, which are large and deep, and on the bank a woman's hat was found. On the same night the dead body of a newly born child [was found] in some bushes on the Highgate side of Parliament-hill fields.' Attached to the newborn baby's garment was a note attributing the mother's tragic behaviour to the father's abandonment. Several days later, her employer identified the cook's body. The coroner's report indicated the infant suffered 'from [a] hemorrhage, through neglect at birth'. The victim, Eliza Butler aged 28, unable to swim in a weakened state after the delivery of her child, drowned in the pond.[44]

The shame and humiliation experienced by women such as Annie C. often stemmed from the duplicity of the father. Typically, in return for a promise of marriage, the woman gave her consent to a sexual relationship. The interviewer asked the petitioner whether she had received a promise of marriage and given her consent to sexual intercourse with her 'seducer'. For the sake of analysis, responses to this query were divided into 'yes' or 'no'. Nonetheless, some women gave ambiguous answers, or none at all. Table 5.5 indicates 47.20 per cent of all petitioners had received a promise to marry; if not a ring, at least some form of verbal agreement had been reached. Those reporting they had not received a promise to marry constituted 36 per cent of the petitioner pool, while 16.80 per cent remained indeterminate.

Table 5.6 shows at least 60.80 per cent of the accepted petitioners had received a promise to marry. If we take accepted petitions that had a promise (N = 138) and divide it by accepted and rejected petitions with a yes – promise to marry (N = 168), the data yield a ratio of 82.14 per cent. Meaning, if the woman said 'yes' on the question of promise to marry, she had an 82 per cent chance of having her infant accepted. If the woman said no, her chances diminished. Saying yes increased chances for admission by 13 percentage points. The committee men admitted the most candidates from those who provided evidence of a 4–6-month relationship and with an affirmative promise to marriage.

Table 5.5: All FH Petitions, Promise to Marry, 1842–92[45]

Promise	**N**	**Promise %**
Yes	168	47.20
No	128	36.00
Unknown	60	16.80
Total	356	100.00

Table 5.6: FH Accepted Petitions, Promise to Marry, 1842–92[46]

Promise	**N**	**Promise %**	**Accepted to Promise Ratio**
Yes	138	60.80	82.14
No	89	39.20	69.53
Total	227	100.00	

Table 5.7 illustrates committee choices that rationed slots based on respectable notions of marriage. Only 23.26 per cent of rejected petitions stated that they had received a promise to marry. Thirty per cent of the women reported they had not received a promise, but in 46.51 per cent of the rejected petitions, the answer remains indeterminate, because these petitioners were never interviewed.

Determining whether the mother had given consent to sexual relations is not a simple task. Clear and unambiguous testimony affirming consent appeared in 55.9 per cent of the cases as shown in Table 5.8. Extenuating circumstances, if given at all, clouded the degree of consent. If the woman had not given consent, committee men elicited other responses relating to whether or not the father had used force to 'effect his purpose', or whether the woman placed had herself in a compromising situation.

In 21.3 per cent of cases, the 'father' clearly forced the woman into a sexual relationship. In 2.5 per cent of surveyed cases, the petitioner reported a married man impregnated her. In several accounts, the petitioner never clearly stated, or it was not reported, whether she had given her consent. Another way of examining the question of consent is to divide the petitions

Table 5.7: FH Rejected Petitions, Promise to Marry, 1842–59[47]

Promise	**N**	**Promise %**
Yes	30	23.26
No	39	30.23
Unknown	60	46.51
Total	129	100.00

Table 5.8: All FH Petitions, Degrees of Consent to Sexual Relations, 1842–59[48]

Degrees of Consent	**N**	**Consent or No Consent %**
Consent	199	55.9
Force used	76	21.3
Compromising situation	9	2.5
Unclear	72	20.3
Total	356	100.0

between accepted and rejected; then, taking a conservative approach, divide all responses into 'yes' and 'no', putting all cases that did not clearly fall under the 'yes' category into the 'no' category.

Of interest in Table 5.9 is the comparison between accepted and rejected reports for consent. The percentages are almost evenly reversed. Petitioners who told the committee they had not given consent were rejected; while those who said yes, they had given their consent, were more likely to have their petition accepted. Clearly suggesting that other factors such as virtuosity, the mother's age, occupation, and even her recommendations, played into the decision-making process.

The following examples illustrate the ways in which the transcriber described mothers' consent to sexual intercourse. In the case of Margaret M. (aged 23), a general servant, working and living in Camden Town, the transcriber reported the father seduced the petitioner in a public house with her consent. The mother replied: 'I did not see him for 8 months, when I was 8 months gone with child, c.c. was repeated. I was living with Captain Rankes of Gloster St, Camden Town, but I left immediately after and went to lodge at 26 Pratt St, Camden Town.'[49] In the case of needlewoman Sophia W. (aged 23), the transcriber reported the petitioner had been acquainted with the father for three months. Criminal conversation 'took place in the pantry with my consent' and was repeated four or five times. During this time, the father 'promised to fix a day for our marriage but failed to do so'.[50]

An 1891 petition details the narrative for a 'promise of marriage' in a typical petition.[51] Its completeness illustrates gendered differences in respect to marriage. The case may also be considered as transitional, moving from the mid to late Victorian era, in part, because the petitioner's occupation has a modern ring to it. The vignette might be titled 'just a waitress in a vegetarian restaurant!' According to Elizabeth M. (aged 22): 'When first acquainted with the father, I was a waitress at the Vegetarian Cornucopia Restaurant, Newgate Street, E. C.'.[52] She had been working at the restaurant for exactly

Table 5.9: All FH Petitions, Consent to Sexual Relations, 1842–59 and 1842–92[53]

Consent	Accepted Petitions (1842–92)		Rejected Petitions (1842–59)	
	N	Accepted %	N	Rejected %
Yes	157	69.16	51	39.53
No	70	30.84	78	60.47
Total	227	100.00	129	100.00

two years and ten months, a respectable amount of time for any employee, when she met Daniel B. on the street in the City. The father, a foreman at the Farringdon office of the Firen Mann dairy, held a respectable position. Soon they shared a pledge to marry and engaged in sexual intercourse. The couple went out to Luton on the Easter Bank Holiday, when he had 'c.c'. with her. (The petitions continue to refer to out-of-wedlock sexual intercourse as c.c. more than 30 years after the Married Women's Property Act had removed criminal penalties.) The couple continued their intimate relationship; until Elizabeth found herself pregnant and reported this to the father, Daniel B.

Interestingly, this late nineteenth-century petition provides the first mention of the physical discomforts associated with pregnancy. Elizabeth said she suffered morning sickness and found it difficult to work. Therefore, she went to live at sister's house for several weeks. When she returned, Daniel B.'s feelings had cooled, especially after she had delivered the baby. He was no longer her lover, but the father of her child, and this entailed responsibilities. Although he said they should get married and had promised to meet at a church on a Sunday in November, he never appeared. When Elizabeth M. went in search of him, he could not be found. Since passage of new laws had improved a mother's chances to press charges for child support, she went to see a solicitor on Chancery Lane; she learned the father had gone to America and was completely out of reach. Following this, the abandoned woman applied to Miss Pye's Home for Unwed Mothers. From there, she decided to make an application to the Foundling Hospital. The unwed mothers' home saved Elizabeth from the humiliation of the workhouse, and the Foundling Hospital preserved her character for the rest of her life, as her case was accepted. Elizabeth's work record, her respectable recommenders, and her proven promise to marry, as vouched for by witnesses at the chapel, worked in her favour.[54]

The question of the promise of marriage and consent were central to every fully investigated petition, and represented the standards set by society; the committee men applied these norms to the young women whose testimony they heard. In many cases above, little mention of force, or sexual intercourse under duress appeared. In some petitions, however, clear and outright abuse of physical power appeared.[55] Under the veil of secrecy, committee men and the investigator uncovered details of each case to determine whether the woman had been raped or had been a victim of incest. They wanted to know whether the father had given the mother drugs or alcohol. They also examined the question of money, whether or not the father had given the petitioner any kind of compensation for services, shall we say. These circumstances emerged even in the petitions involving formal and informal promises to marry. Nonetheless, many ambiguities surrounding the relationships existed; in some cases, even where mutual attraction clearly existed, the father reportedly used force to 'have his way', which calls for a gingerly interpretation of the transcripts as interrogations. Further, transcriber asides complicate interpretations of oral transcripts, justifying data analysis.

More than one-fifth of the petitioners, 21.35 per cent or 76 out of 356 cases, reported, 'force was used' and, or alcohol and drugs were part of the sexual experience when they became pregnant.[56] The amount of force a man used to induce a woman to yield is not patently clear. Table 5.10 illustrates the breakdown of accepted and rejected cases in which no force was reported, force was an issue, or women found themselves in a compromising situation. The 'unclear' category is largely derived from the rejected petitions. Either the woman had not answered the question satisfactorily or her application never reached the stage of the examination process. Many transcripts simply recounted the ways in which men took advantage of women. To put it bluntly, these were simple cases of abuse of power, in terms of class, sheer physical overpowering strength, or deceitfulness on the part of the perpetrator.

Included in the 'no force' category are cases in which the father of the child was engaged, married to someone else, or a widower. In some petitions, women reported they were 'insensate' or out of their senses because they had been given some potent drug or alcohol. At such times, women reported fainting, claiming not to have known what had happened. Perhaps these were cases of rape. Clear-cut cases of 'force' include accounts of physical violence. That said, the following examples present a particular course of events leading to the pregnancy.

Table 5.10: All FH Petitions Reporting Force, 1842–92[57]

Category	**No Force Reported**	**Force Reported**	**Compromising Situation**	**Unclear**	**Total**
	N	N	N	N	N
Accepted	148	66	9	4	227
Rejected	51	10	0	68	129
Total	199	76	9	72	356
Percentage	55.90	21.35	2.53	20.22	

In an 1842 petition, the mother Elizabeth T. (aged 32) was much older than the average accepted petitioner age of 20–24 years. The father, William S., worked for Elizabeth's brother in his confectionery shop in Berkeley

Square, situated in fashionable St George's Hanover Square, off Regent Street. The father was described as a respectable young man. The petitioner and the father met frequently in the bakehouse in the course of a day's work. They had known each other for six months before he attempted 'by force to effect his purpose', at a time when the petitioner's brother, her protector, was away from the house.[58] She reported nobody was around when the 'father' raped her. Overtaken by shame, she told no one about the calculated act the man had perpetrated against her. When the subject found herself pregnant, she told the father, who left immediately. Her recommender and employer, Lady Brodie, said up to the time of this incident, 'she bore the most unexceptionable character and I could have no suspicion of familiarity'.[59] Lady Brodie purchased a subscription for Elizabeth's confinement at Westminster Hospital. Thereafter, Elizabeth found a 'situation' as a wet-nurse for a wealthy woman on Berkeley Square.[60] The committee accepted this petition.

In the case of Harriet G., the father was 30 years of age, the mother 18 years of age. The father, a fellow servant, proposed marriage. She refused because she believed she was too young. Rejected, he induced her to come into his bedroom, and there he raped her. Criminal conversation continued, reported the enquirer. They talked of marriage, but did nothing about it because of the fear they would not be happy with each other. After the woman discovered and reported she was pregnant, the father disappeared.[61] The committee accepted this petition.

Jane L. (aged 23), who worked as a domestic for an attorney, recounted she had known the father, a law clerk, for three years. He had promised marriage, and he told his employer he had promised marriage. 'Connection took place and not with her consent, he used violence. He had frequently solicited her before.'[62] She reported telling her master about the violence. 'Connection' was repeated several times thereafter. When she found herself pregnant, she told the father. He did not believe her and left. She paid all the expenses of the delivery from her savings. This of a case of an individual in a position of power, by virtue of class and occupation, taking advantage of one in a subordinate position. It could also have been a case of entrapment, or simply an example of a young woman seeking to marry up. Jane L. obviously hoped to marry; otherwise she would not have put her suitor off for almost three years. She, however, was unsuccessful in her bid. She got pregnant; the father left; and in 1851, where no magistrates, guardians, or laws could stop him.[63]

In another example of reported force, the woman submitted her petition twice. She claimed a soldier raped her. Anne H. (aged 24) worked as a domestic at a respectable Fitzroy Square home, and while on holiday with her cousins at Dover, an army town, she ran into trouble. Anne reported that one evening after a gathering with her friends and family members, who left the festivities, and she found herself alone with an officer. The transcriber did not mention the venue for the festivities. Neither was it clear why Anne had not left with the others. All we know from the transcript is, she remained in the company of the military man. Anne's account reflected her insecurity and fear of abandonment by her friends. 'They suddenly retired.'[64] The father locked the door of the room where they had been gathered for the party and 'effected his purpose by violence'.[65] Anne H. reported that he kept her against her will for several hours. The next day she learned her cousins were in collusion with the officer and had set her up. The main problem facing Anne H., in this case, was not the problem of caring for her infant. Rather it was her intense fear of what her own father would do, should he find what had happened.

The transcript reported: 'She lives in dread of the discovery of her present condition by her father, which would be visited with great severity upon her mother, for having kept the knowledge of it from him.'[66] Moreover, her wet-nurse blackmailed Anne H. Here we see the problem of baby-farming at its worst. If Anne H. could not keep up with the payments, the wet-nurse threatened to tell her father what had happened to his daughter. In closing, the transcriber noted: 'That this accumulation of distressing facts has impelled her to renew her application to the Foundling Hospital, wherein rests her only hope of rescue from her present despairing conditions.'[67] Although the police could attempt to pursue the father, the family could not pursue him because of the extreme shame visited upon them as a consequence of Anne's plight. Finally, by the time all of this had transpired, the father, a soldier, was off to India. Anne's petition was accepted.

In 1881, Elizabeth P. (aged 19) stood before the committee men. She worked as a general servant in Haverstock Hill, an area of large estates and villas. The father worked as a waiter in a village.[68] Elizabeth testified:

> When I first went there I found him employed as a waiter. After I had been there about six months he began to pay me particular attention, and very shortly after he seduced me in his bedroom. It was my duty to attend to his bedroom and one day when I went to perform my duties there he forcibly seduced me. I made every resistance at the time but did not complain to anyone. c.c. was repeated for about three months when I left. I then went home to my aunt.[69]

This was a case of a woman being placed in a compromising situation. Whether the father used force or not, he clearly used 'seduction', a word that carries many implications. Her former employer testified:

> There had been a clear attachment, one for the other. On one occasion,

> she saw the latter kiss the petitioner, and she thought it prudent that they should be parted. She did not wish to imply that the petitioner was generally light or frivolous in her behaviour.[70]

By 1881, laws had passed in favour of abandoned mothers. Therefore, Elizabeth P. took out a summons against the father, but the police could not find him. The committee accepted this case. Moreover, similar legal strategies pursued by other petitioners worked in their favour.

Categorized under the framework of a 'compromising situation' are the following possibilities. A young woman reported being alone at home, without parents, or employers; or perhaps, she happened to be out walking and an aggressive man paid her unsolicited attention. For example, in 1861 Harriet Q. reported 'he molested me, following me about the house'.[71] Are we to take her at her word, he removed her clothing, or had he attacked her? She fainted and did not know what had happened until she realized she was pregnant.[72] In such incidents, the woman may unwittingly have placed herself in this situation. Whether the woman wished to dramatize the lack of control she felt in the relationship or understood the committee may have been more receptive to her story is problematic. Table 5.11 shows that 8.57 per cent of young petitioners reported their pregnancies resulted from a compromising situation. By contrast, this was not the case for women over 30 years of age.[73]

Just how dangerous life could be sometimes for a young a woman in the age of Victoria is evident in the case of Sarah Jane H. (aged 15) who delivered her baby at Queen Charlotte's Lying-in Hospital around Christmas time. She had been 'seduced' at 14 years of age by a married man who disappeared after she announced her pregnancy. The assault, described as 'violent', was clearly a case of rape. When her mother learned what had happened to her daughter, she went to her local poor law guardians. They said they could do nothing and sent her to the magistrates' office. The police pursued the father, caught, tried and convicted him of 'criminal conversation with a minor'.[74] The magistrate sentenced the aggressor to four months' hard labour.[75] Around 1880, evidence shows the committee became increasingly sympathetic to minors, admitting the infants of young women aged 15–19, who clearly suffered from an assaulting aggressor.

Occasionally, allusions to incest crept into the petitions. One case involved a petitioner (aged 17) who lived with her parents. When cleaning her uncle's room one day, 'he took me on his knee and had c.c. with me in a chair. This was never repeated.'[76] Her uncle warned her not to tell her mother or anyone else what had happened. She reported being very frightened. The uncle said: 'I have done you no harm, and don't you tell your mother.'[77] This was an

Table 5.11: All FH Mothers' Ages vs Compromised Relationships, 1842–92[78]

Cohort	N	No Force Reported %	Force Reported %	Compromising Situation %	Unclear %
15–19	70	51.43	25.71	8.57	14.29
20–24	194	56.19	24.22	1.03	18.56
25–29	74	62.16	13.52	1.35	22.97
30–34	18	50.00	8.33	0.00	41.67
	356				

exceptional case, generally, the offending party in many incest cases proved to be a stepfather. For example, a transcript revealed the young woman had been 'unable to resist advances made by her [step] father'. This case was admitted.[79] The committee rejected other 'stepfather' cases. Ann C. G. (aged 17), a needlewoman, reported she met the father of her child on her way to work. She lived with her own father who was a bricklayer; and her mother knew about her situation.[80] None of this was true. The Foundling Hospital enquirer referred to her relationship as an involvement with her 'father-in-law', or stepfather. The enquirer noted his disgust at the circumstances surrounding the case. He charged the petitioner and her family with deception. Writing that he had learned from a 'respectable authority' that her parents were frauds, 'known to be imposters in the daily habit of practising their artifices upon the sympathies of the benevolent'.[81]

If any hint of past sexual improprieties came to the fore from the petitioner's background, or that of the child's father, the committee also looked askance at the application. For example, they rejected a petitioner because 'previous to her acquaintance with the father she had sexual intercourse, four years ago with a man who was married'.[82] Furthermore, it was the petitioner's second child by another man from Islington, aged 26, a butcher.[83] In the 1842 case of Jane O. (aged 26), general servant, c.c. occurred after the couple had been out for a walk in a 'house of accommodation'. At first, sexual intercourse occurred without her consent. Yet, they had known each other for almost a year. The father made every promise to marry; then 'she gave way' and continued lovemaking. Two months after Jane O. learned she was pregnant, the father departed for places unknown.[84] The committee accepted this petition.[85] By contrast, Jane P. (aged 20), another general servant, had her petition rejected. The father, a general dealer, was a married man who had had sexual intercourse with the young woman while his wife was in the country visiting their children who were away at boarding school. Committee men decided, although the married 'father' was the one who had broken his marriage vows, in their view, he was not as much at fault as the servant. The committee rejected this petition.[86]

The reasons women gave for not marrying the father, though he had proposed marriage, included a lack of faith in the father's ability to provide for the family; and taking matters into their own hands by 'deserting' the father. Consider the following examples. One young man courted a girl, visiting her every evening at her parents' house for over two years. Although he proposed marriage to Mary Jane G. many times, she refused to marry him 'because of the business of the acquaintance and the insufficiency of means for support'.[87] Petitioner Abigail B. (aged 24), who worked as a housemaid, reported she 'has every reason for believing that he [the father] is too indolent to maintain himself'.[88] She suggested he would not be able to support her or the child. Moreover, she could not trust him.[89] One couple, working as domestics, had a long-term relationship. After the father learned of the petitioner's pregnancy, he proposed; but the young woman was unwilling to marry him. She left her job and returned home to her mother. Perhaps to prove the sincerity of the relationship, the petitioner reported the father had given her ten shillings before he departed for Canada.[90]

In another case, the father of Caroline G.'s infant worked as a pharmacist; he had promised to provide for the child. While the petitioner lived on the little money she had saved while working as a laundress, the father still owed her £1.[91] At which point, the mother had to rely on friends and relatives for her confinement. In this early case, dated 1841, the question of support arose for Mary W. (aged 28), a general servant. The mother reported she had met the father at church. They were from Oldham, Lancashire. After a courtship of 20 months, the father proposed marriage. 'Connection' occurred, and three months after the first connection, she told the father she was pregnant. Mary W. urged the father to marry her 'in order that her Mother (who resides at Ryde Lane near Rippondale) might not know her misfortune'.[92] The father, an engineer, said he was out of work and going to London. He asked Mary to follow him. Upon arrival, she could not find him, although he had found work, lodgings and provided the name and address of his landlord. In London and pregnant, without a friend in the world with the exception of Mrs Smith, a relative of her mother, Mary resorted to deception and told Mrs Smith she was married and pregnant. It is probable that Smith understood the woman's situation; but said nothing. After settling in, the soon-to-be mother pawned her clothes and spent all her savings. Three weeks later, after the 'father' had not shown up, Mrs Smith became suspicious. Mary W. confessed to her. The women reported that they had tried in vain to find the father.[93]

Women met the fathers of their babies in their homes, at work, parties and on the streets of London. We know this, because, committee men attached a weight or measure to meeting places. In the process of investigating the circumstances surrounding a pregnancy, the committee asked whether the father had given the petitioner drugs, alcohol or even a cup of tea.[94] Women frequently admitted to such circumstances, while reporting on the difficulties they faced in these situations. Of the petitions surveyed, 3.4 per cent claimed their personal security had been compromised while under the influence of drugs or spirits of alcohol when they became pregnant. The petitions show how problems caused by intoxicating substances had not gone unnoticed by the committeemen. When they suspected that the father had used drugs or alcohol to seduce the young woman, they raised some specific questions. As a result, the men received some explicit accounts of such activity. For example, one petitioner reported, 'Just before leaving Mrs Bean's the Father seduced me, against my consent, on Hackney Downs. He rubbed a handkerchief over my face [,] when I became insensible and while in this state he seduced me.'[95] Sarah P. (aged 20) stated in her testimony that she knew she had been seeing a man who fathered four children, but he died of cholera in September. She alleged that the father of her child had drugged her, claiming she was in no way a consenting party. The committee observed that the mother was in a wretched state of health, but rejected her petition nonetheless.[96] Emma M. reported:

> When first acquainted with the Father I was living with my sister, Mrs Carter at 39 Almorah Road N. assisting in the housework. The Father visited at the house, and in this way I became acquainted with him. After a time, he wished me to walk out with him, which I did for about three months.[97]

The father invited Emma M. to have a cup of coffee. After they were seated in the shop and had ordered a coffee, the father gave the woman something else to drink. Unable to determine whether he had given her gin or brandy, she reported the drink 'rendered me partially insensible'.[98] The father promised to marry her several times. With the commitment to wed, 'criminal conversation' took place repeatedly. The committee rejected this petition.[99] Another transcript reported the following:

> Petitioner tells an unintelligible story about a glass of brandy and water of which she partook with the father from the effects of which she became

> insensible; but she was not aware the father had had intercourse with her until she found herself in the family way.[100]

The couple had been engaged for four months when the petitioner testified: 'He seduced me at my place when everyone was out of Town: criminal conversation was repeated: the first time under the influence of drink which he gave me.'[101] The committee rejected this petition.

One of the most suspect places to meet a man, of course, was at a party where people were imbibing in spirits, thus making women more vulnerable. Elizabeth C. met the father of her child after he had walked her home from a party. He set a date to see her again. Upon meeting a second time, 'criminal conversation' took place without a promise of marriage. The father was already married.[102] Inevitably, committee men rejected petitions such as these, without providing justifications (Table 5.12).

The following examples show intimate exchanges transpired for much less than a promise of marriage. Throughout these petitions, a cup of tea signified part of the social exchange system that caused many problems for young domestics. The degree to which a cup of tea or coffee implied a romantic interlude or an invitation for an exchange of sexual favours remains problematic. Whether these exchanges constituted prostitution is questionable. We can understand these events in two ways. The first way suggests a simple sharing of a customary English practice among friends, old or new. The second interpretation takes a more sinister reading of taking tea together. Was a shared cup of tea an overture to something more? Consider

Table 5.12 Profile of FH Petitioners Reporting Use of Drugs and Alcohol, 1850–9[103]

Category	**Category N = 12**	**%**
Accepted Foundling Hospital Petition	N = 10	82.9
Rejected Foundling Hospital Petition,	N = 2	17.1
Acquaintance	1–3 months	46.3
Decade	1850–9	34.1
Cohort	20–24	63.4
Mothers' address	West London	41.0
Mothers' occupation	General servant	50.0
Fathers' class	Class 3 – Highly skilled	58.3

the following examples. In the case of Eleanor F. (aged 20), tea drinking constituted part of her courting experience. She worked as a dressmaker and first saw the father from her window at work. The language in the petition here suggested something sinister. Why would a woman be peering out of her window at work if she were busy? When on a walk one day, she met the man that she had observed from the safety of her window. He was a solicitor, not of her class. There was, however, nothing clandestine about their relationship. Some observers reported they had seen them walking and talking together every week. This very public relationship tended to imply a commitment to a friendship, at least. After two months, the couple had sexual intercourse, after tea at the Saracen's Head. When the woman discovered her pregnancy, the father denied paternity; but he gave her some money for her confinement. After seven months, he left for Ireland, where he could find employment without having to leave the British Isles. The mother left London for the resort town of Bath; where she was confined.[104]

Such behavior, coupled with casual contacts, led young women into trouble, making them unsuitable candidates for the beneficence of the Foundling Hospital. Eliza P. (aged 21) first met the father for tea, and went out walking with him. After sharing a cup, they had 'criminal conversation'. They repeated c.c. twice. The father promised her marriage and then left. Although the mother delivered the infant at Queen Charlotte's Lying-in Hospital, her petition was rejected.[105] Another rejected petitioner, Jane J., reported she had had a liaison with a 'gentleman' in 'Tea Gardens', with her consent; 'c.c.' was repeated. The petitioner claimed she went into confinement as a married woman, living from her savings.[106] Again, the committee rejected this petition – perhaps the bold honesty of the woman attributed to its failure to pass the test of respectability. Emma B. (aged 22), worked as a general servant for a milliner in Chelsea. She reported that the father, a law clerk 'accosted me on Oxford Street saying he thought he knew me'.[107] The father 'asked me to take tea with him in Cliffords Inn which I did[.] [I]t was on this occasion that c.c. took place.'[108] The couple repeated 'c.c'. three times at the same place. When Emma realized she was pregnant, she remained at her place of employment for a month and then went into lodgings.

> When pregnant I ceased visiting him[.] [O]n my confinement I wrote to him and he sent two lawyers' clerks one of whom said he was Mr Rice. I was confined at Queen Charlottes Hospital. If relieved I propose going to service on the character of Mr Willis.[109]

Neither the petition transcript nor the enquirer's findings provided an explanation regarding the clerks. We can surmise that they, the clerks, gave her enough money to pay for the confinement. The committee rejected her request because the relationship consisted of a casual contact that resulted in a pregnancy, but it again signalled inequalities based on class and the role such standards played in creating an acceptable case.[110] Another petitioner, stopped by the father on the street, refused to take up the father's invitation. She confessed that it was inappropriate to 'walk out' with a man she had just met. After asking some questions about each other, the couple set a date to meet again. The petitioner asserted: 'He promised me marriage and one evening we went to the Sadlers Wells Theatre and after he took me to a house of ill fame after two months I discovered my pregnancy and told him when he promised fairly, but soon after deserted me. C.c. was continued until June.'[111] The committee rejected this petition as well.

The committee rejected bigamy cases, but sometimes they decided otherwise. An 1859 petition marked one exception. Amelia J. (aged 24) worked as a general servant. The petitioner stated that she had married a man and had children by him before she had discovered he was married. The petitioner learned about the deception through a letter from the bigamist's wife.[112] She was confined in the Lyme Regis workhouse in Dorsetshire. Amelia was fortunate. She came from a small town and her recommender, the pastor's wife, gave her a glowing letter of support. The committee men admitted this baby.[113]

The reception of money by the petitioner from the father was often a red flag; but this could be remediated, especially if the woman had gone to the magistrate. As a reminder, the Poor Law Amendment Act of 1844 shifted the venue for hearings relating to 'bastardy' from quarter sessions to the magistrate courts. The mother's objective in applying to the magistrate was to get financial support from the father. If successful, there would be no need to give up her baby. When women took the fathers of their children to court for affiliation proceedings, they experienced limited successes. Despite changes in the bastardy laws, mothers' claims for financial assistance from putative fathers were never assured. Evidence that the laws had turned more aggressive in pursuing an errant father appeared in Foundling Hospital petitions, when Foundling Hospital officials added a new question to their investigation. 'Did you go to the magistrate?' After 1844, but more importantly after 1872, petitions showed evidence of unwed mothers going before the magistrates before applying to the Foundling Hospital, although some women remained unsure of, or unwilling to pursue legal remedies. As the century progressed, the Foundling Hospital mothers' first recourse, or remedy for her situation (if she had enough money and support from employers, family and friends) was to seek help from the local magistrate. Failure in pursuit of the legal route led women to the Foundling Hospital.[114]

Whether the women received money for sexual services is difficult to determine, even among rejected petitions. Such evidence, quite unlike cases in which alcohol usage appeared, does not readily appear. There was, in fact, a group of women who testified that they had been victimized by having their money taken from them rather than receiving funds. To verify the truth, the committee relied on a private investigator to verify the testimonies. The detective went to the fathers' employers and parents and raised the issue with them. In some cases, it was quite likely that the fathers used the mothers' money to leave the country. On the other hand, if the father had given the petitioner money, she usually claimed it was for the child's welfare. Secretary John Twiddy reported Caroline G. applied not once, but twice for her infant's admission. The father of her child worked as a pharmacist. In the interview, the father promised, 'it was his intention to provide for the child'.[115] Even if, fathers had promised to pay, they were often unable or unwilling to keep their promises. Taking another example, the 'Petitioner lived on what little money she had saved together with what she earned as a laundress. The father promised to pay the expenses of the confinement, but only did so in part, as he stills owes them £1.'[116]

Consider the following examples relating to transfer of funds. Annie S. reported, 'He never gave me any money, although it was borrowed from me.'[117] Jane C. (aged 20) worked as a laundry maid. She had known the father for four years. She had met the father's parents, and the couple planned to marry. They set a date to make the final arrangements. In this case, the father, who worked as a footman, took £6 of the petitioner's hard-earned money and disappeared for parts unknown.[118] Jane W. (aged 23) had a similar experience; the father of her child absconded with £7, and she pressed charges against the hustler and won.[119] The committee accepted these cases.

Women sought help from the magistrates before applying to the Foundling Hospital, but the law was uncooperative to a disheartening degree, at least until the late 1870s. In 1848 petitioner Rachel M. (aged 28), a general servant who worked for a family in St George Hanover Square, wrote to the committee men explaining her desperate situation. She reported that she was willing to pay half of the costs of raising the child if the father would pay the balance. She received £12 in wages per year, but believed that she did not have enough resources to bring up her baby. She loved her child, but needed help. Rachel wrote that she begged the father, a saddle-maker, to give her money to support his offspring. He would not give her 'one penny'.[120] She went to the magistrates at Marlborough St to get a summons against the father. She even brought evidence of their relationship, but the adjudicators were not satisfied that she was 'deserving'.[121]

> I showed them [the magistrates] the letters he wrote to me they said they was no good unless I had a witness to prove [to] him the communication

took place. [T]herefore they could not assist me in my sorrowful case because there was not sufficient ground to work.[122]

The committee rejected Rachel M.'s petition.

Exchanges with police commissioners and reports from magistrate offices appeared in the files during the 1880s. Emily M. (aged 19) who worked as a housemaid in Maida Vale, North London, reported that she had taken a summons against the father at Hammersmith. They had known each other for over a year; the father left six months after the baby was born. Emily won her appeal, 3 s. 6 d. per week. This was a fair sum of money for child support, but not enough to pay for a private wet-nurse whose fee was about 7 s. a week. If the mother worked, she was likely to make between 4–5 s. per week, but, of course, she could not care for her child. After the father received the summons, he left London for unknown parts. The police put out a warrant for the father's arrest. Her petition was accepted.[123]

Committee members admitted another similar case, Alice A. (aged 22), a general servant who had been employed for two-and-a-half years. She met the father in April 1889. In August, 'he had c.c. with' her.[124] When she told the father, a police officer, she was pregnant, she never again saw him again. In December, she left her job and went to the police station. The station officer told her the man had left the force. The mother had no family on whom to rely. Her father had died when she was four years of age. Since her former employer was a member of the Croydon Board of Guardians, the guardian admitted her to the workhouse infirmary for the confinement. Until then, the mother had lived on her savings. After delivering her baby, she went back to work. She earned £14 a year and paid 5 s. a week for her baby who was with a wet-nurse.[125] The committee accepted this application.

In the 1880s, the horrors of the cases become more apparent, less glossed over, and no longer couched in subtle language. In 1881, Elizabeth W. (aged 23), who worked as a cook, testified that the 'father' broke into her room and raped her. She told the father she was pregnant, but he said he would rather go to jail than marry her or support the child. After her confinement at Queen Charlotte's Lying-in Hospital, she went to the police court and summoned the father. The magistrate dismissed the case for 'want of evidence'. The father denied paternity. His parents were farmers and lived in Caistre, Northamptonshire. The Foundling Hospital enquirer even made a trip to Northamptonshire to ask his parents what had happened; the putative father's parents 'declined to discuss it. Because the matter has been brought before a magistrate who did not see his way to grant an affiliation order. They were extremely sorry for the petitioner.'[126] They said she was a 'respectable young woman'. Nevertheless, his parents declined to give her 'pecuniary assistance'.[127]

In the 1890s, the committee asserted more energies in pursuit of help for mothers. Elena S. (aged 22), who worked as a cook, became involved with her employer's coachman.[128] She was able to hide her pregnancy from her employer until after her delivery. Then, she went to the West London Police Court, where magistrates dismissed her case. Next, she turned to the Foundling Hospital and received a summons for a hearing. During this time, the Foundling Hospital enquirer assisted Elena with legal charges against the father. When Elena applied to the West London Police Court again, the Foundling Hospital committee men sent their enquirer with her. The enquirer commented: 'While Pet was applying to this Hospital, and to Police Court, she left her situation because she could not explain her frequent absence, as she had not informed her mistress she had a child.'[129] Elena reported that she was destitute. The enquirer advised her to go back to her 'mistress' and tell her the truth. Following his advice, the woman permitted her return to work at her former salary of £16 per year. Before acceptance, the enquirer reported that Elena's employer:

> Gives 'pet' an excellent character, could not have been a better servant, had heard from her the story of her shame, knew she felt it deeply and had made great sacrifice and suffered much to conceal it, would do all she could for her.[130]

Recourse to the courts could also prove dangerous. Alice B. (aged 19), who worked as a general servant, reported that she met the father while he was working as a cab driver on his route from London Bridge to Salisbury. She rode along to keep him company. Criminal conversation occurred at his lodgings while on holiday. They shared private time until Alice B. told the father that she was pregnant. Then, he said that he did not want to hear anything about it. 'He told me I had a remedy, I could summons him.'[131] When Alice subpoenaed him at Marlborough Street Police, the father's new girlfriend threatened the petitioner; and said that, if she submitted a warrant against the father, she would put a knife in her. This obviously frightened the petitioner, so she dropped the legal action. When the Foundling Hospital enquirer went to the Marlborough Street Police Court, the officer informed him that the case had been dropped for lack of evidence. The hospital proved sympathetic to her situation.[132]

By law, magistrates asked the unwed mother whether the putative father of her baby had given her money.[133] If she had received a certain amount of money, how much had she received? In 1872, the Foundling Hospital committee began to ask specifically if the father had given the mother money in compliance with the Bastardy Amendment Act.[134] Legally, willingness to support served as an informal proposal of marriage. The reception of money by the petitioner, however, could also serve as a red flag for prostitution. For some Victorians, one of the criteria for prostitution rested upon the reception of financial assistance from a father outside the bonds of marriage. It was a rare petition, however, that gave clear evidence that a man had offered the woman cash for sexual privileges. More than 75 per cent of the Foundling Hospital women were employed at the time of the petition application. At least 9 per cent of the petitioners lived at home and worked with their parents. They would, therefore, be unlikely candidates for this sort of question. Many women stated bluntly: 'The father never gave me any money.'[135]

Later petitions suggest that court proceedings increased after passage of the 1886 'Saint Pancras Petition for the Maintenance of Deserted Women Bill'. Although intended to provide for married women, the bill also compelled the deserting husband to maintain his wife and children and shaped the lives of single mothers, as well. The legislation attempted to keep mothers, eligible for spousal support, from entering the workhouse. Instead, poor law records reveal a whole host of new problems created by the legislation.[136] The laws would not be completely sympathetic to unwed mothers until 1909; when fathers were forced to take responsibility, insofar as it was possible, for their offspring.[137] Up to then, the mother needed to provide witnesses against the putative father if she wished to pursue the legal route. If no witnesses could be provided, the putative father could not be subpoenaed. While no easy legal interpretation existed, the law presumed the woman's irresponsible nature. Appeals by unwed mothers to magistrates were often unsupported. Few had the personal or financial resources to pursue this path before applying to the Foundling Hospital.[138]

Of course, class and money considerations go hand in hand as part of the calculus of respectability. Consider its subtle manifestation in the case of Sarah S. (aged 29) who worked as a general servant for a woman in St George Hanover Square, an exclusive area of West London.[139] Sarah's landlady reported that she had been confined as a married woman under the name of Harrison. She had never seen the petitioner's husband and she was late in paying her rent. Her employer stated that the petitioner had not performed her domestic duties satisfactorily. She frequently was 'going and visiting'. Moreover, the petitioner 'dressed in a manner unbecoming to her station, the expense of which, in her opinion, must have been far beyond her means'. The cook, purportedly in charge at the household, reported that she had seen the petitioner talking with a 'gentleman at the door, and that this man was supposed to be the father'. Foundling Hospital secretary John Brownlow did a bit of detective work on his own and discovered that the father was a medical man and a member of a prominent family in Grosvenor Square, a 'place of high fashion'.[140] The report that the domestic had not completed her work and dressed in a manner beyond her station, offset whatever influence the father's professional credentials may have lent to the case. Perhaps, the committee believed this woman flaunted the social order. They, therefore, rejected this case.

An out-of-wedlock pregnancy could cause havoc in any household, wealthy or poor. Some petitions reflect the elite culture of the wealthy and provide rare glimpses into private lives when individuals explicitly transgress the lines of class. The following petition demonstrates this situation. An affluent North London family employed Louisa R. (aged 26) as a governess.[141] Her master's son, Charles, a midshipman in the navy had just returned from an assignment in India.[142] The petition suggested that the father, then 16, had been noticeably changed by his duty there. The committee attentively noted his arrival and departure schedule in the details of the petition. The transcriber reported the father of the child (less than 16 years of age) had been home from India for two months when the 'connection' occurred in Louisa R.'s bedroom. Although the father had been seriously ill, he managed to find his way there; and unfortunately, for Louisa, their bedroom doors connected to each other. On the night of the intrusion, Louisa had not bolted her door. The son never entered her room again. He left England for India in March. Louisa had not complained of his conduct. When she learned of her pregnancy in June, she told her employer.[143]

When the Foundling Hospital enquirer interviewed Louisa's employer, Harris senior provided the following details. Mr Harris, the master of this wealthy household, asserted that his son Charles, fathered the child. The petitioner had told him so. Although Harris assuredly doubted the governess' claims, he paid for her confinement, secured a wet-nurse for the infant, and another 'situation' with a wealthy family. Was it not convenient for Harris senior, the young man's father, to pin the blame for the woman's pregnancy on his son? After all, his son had returned to India and could in no way defend himself. Moreover, his son was sick, but apparently not too sick, for he was ostensibly healthy enough to enter the governess' room in the middle of the night and impregnate her. Of course, the pregnancy was the governess' fault, because she had not locked the door to her room before going to sleep. The committee paid attention to the arrival and departure day of the father, suggesting that maybe they thought that the governess had been involved with someone else, namely Harris Senior, a wealthy man. Such attention to details surrounding sexual intercourse indicates a growing interest among committee men to establish even firmer guidelines for admission. In a departure from practice, the transcriber recorded that the infant was 'unanimously admitted

3 November 1851'.[144] Few other petitions reveal details relating to the vote after this case.

Another case of an application arriving from an elite family is that of Alice L. In this 1871 petition, the domestic was not in trouble; it was the daughter of a wealthy family. Alice L. (aged 20) entered a secret liaison with the footman in her parents' house. She had known him for three years; they fell in love. When she told the young man she was 'in the family way', they ran away to Gravesend.[145] They probably intended to cross the English Channel via ferry to France. Alice's brother followed them and retrieved Alice L. She never saw the father of her child again. In this transcript, we 'hear' very little of Alice L.; apparently, another party spoke for her. Unlike the case of Sarah F., compelled to testify on her own behalf, the committee removed this obligation because her family had come to her defence. As the case demonstrates, the young woman was wealthy. Love and affection prevailed over class and family ties. Alice L.'s aborted flight highlights a brave and bold attempt. Perhaps, her case exemplifies a new sort of adventuresome and open young woman. Alice's case provides one of the truly romantic stories in the Foundling Hospital petitions. Yet shame and humiliation associated with having an illegitimate child, especially the baby of the footman, would have been devastating to the family. This justified admission of this particular infant. The same would not have been true, if the tables had been turned. If Alice L. had been the maid, and involved with a young man from this family, as in Louisa R.'s case, the uproar would not have been as harsh. The wealthy family would have denied responsibility and chalked it up to their son's profligacy and youthful vigour. The transcriber observed the petitioner appeared to be of a different class than her lover, and the relationship could hold no future. In the name of respectability, the family hid Alice L.'s folly behind a veil of secrecy within the walls of the Foundling Hospital estate. Such examples rarely occurred in the Foundling Hospital petitions.[146]

Many stories in the petition files are similar to each other. The unique cases stand out enough to warrant discussion. When intentions went awry, the women initially went into shock or action. The petitions reveal personal qualities that set Foundling Hospital petitioners apart from other women in similar circumstances. Some women believed that their characters had been ruined forever; others put up a fight. Perina P. could not believe that she had been abandoned and went into a state of despondency. The cook from Highgate was humiliated to the point of committing suicide. Sarah F. reluctantly disclosed required information about her child's father before the committee men, but she ultimately complied. She confessed that starvation was a greater fear than humiliation, and yet Sarah F. understood that to save her character, she needed to be relieved of her baby. Sarah wrote to Mr

Brownlow: 'The result of Saturday last determined my future course. The reception of my child has saved me from destruction.'[147]

Mothers usually cooperated with the Foundling Hospital enquirer's review of their credentials in order to hide their shame and protect their child. Eventually, all the women who made their way to the hospital's gate tried to exert some control over their future. Nonetheless, all petitioners understood that truth telling during the hearing process was requisite for acceptance. Differentiating among petitioners was a challenging task, because the committee had to chose among the petitions based on available slots. Thus, making their decision-making process doubly difficult. To highlight the percentages of admitted petitions versus hearings see Table 5.13. Between 1879 and 1907, the committee received an average of 149.17 enquiries per year, held an average of 90 'hearings' per year, accepted an average of 58.9 per cent of petitions for which hearings were held per year, and actually received 52.46 per cent of all infants per year (some mothers withdrew their petitions, and a small percentage of infants died before admission).

The committee attended to details surrounding the pregnancy, and whether or not the mother had given consent to sexual intercourse. Still, however, this information proved incomplete as they attempted to discern the circumstances surrounding each case. In search of more information, the committee also relied on other bits of information, including accounts from recommenders who knew the petitioner's 'character' before her 'fall'. Significantly, 82 per cent received strong recommendations from employers.[148] The committee also queried poor law guardians and magistrates regarding the respectability of women who requested public support. Thus, a web of connections relating to petitioners' stories unfolds with questions about who they worked for and who they knew.

Petitioners with strong recommendations from employers were most likely to be successful. These women were less likely to have been confined in a common lodging house or the workhouse because of the social connections they had established; these 'trusted' networks vouched for and protected both the social image and physical well-being of the unwed mother. Essentially, recommendations helped the committee members sift out the respectable from the non-respectable. Only petitions representing women of the highest character were successful. The men proved unwilling to bend their rules, even for a benefactor of the Foundling Hospital charity. For this reason, an analysis of the recommenders' roles contributes to broadening our understanding of the meaning of the word 'character' and the ways in which the petitioner's supporters served as negotiators on her behalf.

Table 5.13: FH Hearings vs Admissions, 1879–1907[149]

Year	Total Applications	Appearing before Committee N	Accepted N	Accepted %	Admitted N	Admitted versus Hearings %
1879	243	89	47	52.81	42	47.19
1880	256	102	45	44.12	46	45.10
1881	268	102	47	46.08	48	47.06
1882	245	110	56	41.82	50	45.45
1883	138	95	46	48.42	44	46.32
1884	202	72	64	88.89	46	63.89
1885	177	69	54	78.26	37	53.62
1886	152	58	48	82.76	28	48.28
1887	179	101	40	39.60	40	39.60
1888	187	120	48	40.00	57	47.50
1889	166	105	43	40.95	45	42.86
1890	181	117	43	36.75	50	42.74
1891	159	81	41	50.62	33	40.74
1892	130	80	35	43.75	28	35.00
1893	152	107	42	39.25	45	42.06
1894	150	85	49	57.65	42	49.41
1895	130	117	50	42.74	58	49.57
1896	135	100	55	55.00	55	55.00
1897	112	96	51	53.13	49	51.04
1898	113	79	62	78.48	49	62.03
1899	99	80	50	62.50	40	50.00
1900	95	85	58	68.24	49	57.65
1901	102	86	55	63.95	47	54.65
1902	95	84	58	69.05	49	58.33
1903	91	78	65	83.33	51	65.38
1904	91	80	56	70.00	45	56.25
1905	107	85	68	80.00	58	68.24
1906	96	88	58	65.91	51	57.95
1907	75	66	59	89.39	39	59.09
Averages	149.17	90 per year	51	58.90%	47	52.46 %

6

'If You Will Kindly Take Her from Me, You Will Save My Character': Framing Respectability

In 1856, a petitioner explained that she lived and worked as a maid for a lady. The butler of the house promised her marriage. She gave consent; and he fathered her child. After delivery, she realized her inability to maintain herself. In a state of desperation, she wrote: 'If you will kindly take her from me you will save my character for not one of my friends are aware of the fact, and I am very anxious to spare them such trouble.'[1] The plight of young servants living under the same roof, without constant supervision appeared in the press as a topic of concern during the age of Victoria. The 'domestic passport' system, guaranteeing respectability among servants, carried about as much weight, opined *The Saturday Review,* as the prototype of the international passport system then under consideration by Parliament.[2] This comment expresses the Victorian understanding of a servant's character, and, perhaps, some exasperation with the limited control employers had in this relationship. The journal proposed a training school for the English 'service class', including domestic workers such as cooks, house and laundry maids. Barring a certification process that guaranteed stellar reputations, character references circulated among like-minded individuals who wished to support their favourite servants.[3] The network, or web, of connections extended from training homes in West and North London to refuges for unwed mothers and destitute women. Complex linkages of names, addresses and shared problems appear in the records at the Foundling Hospital. Most names remain relatively obscure; but there are others that deserve consideration, including Susan Mayne. Her case attracted considerable attention from novelist Charles Dickens; of course, her petition provides an exceptional example of the intersection between the major questions of this study: What did society say the poor deserved? How did society parcel out the just desserts? Under what circumstances did the indigent receive this help?

Work experiences in the homes of wealthy employers, including the nobility, built up a certain type of relationship between the employer and employee. Unlike other young women who worked in the factories of the North or the East End, service in the homes of the wealthy prepared the respectable domestic to take steps into the rarefied atmosphere of the Foundling Hospital estate. The rules for admission of the born out-of-wedlock infant required the petitioner, at the conclusion of her hearing, to supply the committee with a list of individuals who could speak to her respectable qualities. Ideally, the mother responded with a list of trusted people or institutions with whom she had developed a personal relationship, who would, she hoped, speak on her behalf. She then returned to her home to await the committee's verdict. The secretary and enquirer corresponded and sometimes met with recommenders who promised to vouch for the petitioner's character. The recommendation process formed an integral part of the assessment. Committee men wanted to verify the petitioner's account, assess her true character, and determine who would be responsible for the mother's well-being, if they received her baby. In redressing an injustice done to the mother, the charity fully intended to prevent further damage to the mother's character by taking her infant from her.

Recommendations arrived in the form of private notes and letters from a variety of personal and professional connections, including those of a confidential nature and from institutions such as Queen Charlotte's Lying-in Hospital, Urania Cottage, or the workhouse guardians. Female employers corresponded on embossed-ivory-coloured notepaper, edged in black, denoting the seriousness with which they took the responsibility of writing a letter of recommendation to the Foundling Hospital for their domestic or their wet-nurse.[4] The petition survey identified 54 different personal, private and public institutional endorsements.[5] The most successful petitions received the full support of employers, the largest cohort of recommenders. For purposes of analysis, recommenders are grouped into five categories under personal and private recommenders and four other categories listed under institutional recommenders as shown respectively in Table 6.1 and Table 6.2 on page 149.

Table 6.1: Personal and Private Recommenders for Accepted FH Petitions, 1842–92[6]

Recommenders	**N**	**Recommenders %**
Employers	82	44.33
Family and friends	60	32.43
Neighbours	17	9.19
Titled and notable	2	1.08
Clerics	24	12.97
Total	185	100.00

Most importantly, Table 6.1 shows 44.33 per cent of accepted petitioners received support from their employers. Family and friends accounted for the second group, standing at 32.43 percent.[7] Some petitions contained more than one letter of recommendation, or maybe it retained the oral transcript of an interview by the hospital investigator. For the most part, however, employers fell into two categories, those who employed before and after pregnancy. In the former group, if the employer agreed to assist the unwed mother during her pregnancy, this added to the credibility of the case. The latter group, usually women, had employed the petitioner as a wet-nurse after her delivery. Few former employers wished to retain their domestics in their service, after learning of the pregnancy, because her presence could blight the household's reputation. Even fewer agreed to give time off, with a promise of return. Instead, such women lost their jobs. Furthermore, in most cases, maintaining an unmarried mother as a domestic would have created a highly disturbing scenario, upsetting the lady of the house, and casting suspicion on all males, including husband, brother, son or other male employees. Moreover, if the putative father were an outsider, he might pose a danger to other women in the household. If the pregnancy became public knowledge among friends and family, it cast the household into a suspicious light and even impugned its respectability. Fears that other young women living in the same household might be influenced by the errant domestic's behaviour also framed the young domestic as a threat. Unscrupulous employers had little to fear from the law, as those maids who tried to involve the courts usually discovered at their cost.[8]

While some employers demonstrated support, others including female employers proved reluctant to testify. Perhaps such women believed the petitioner had no 'moral probity', making her support hypocritical. On the other hand, the employer could have been dissatisfied with the petitioner's work habits and demeanour. London chronicler Edward Walford described Victorian women as insensitive to the needs of unfortunate women. 'Their own sex affix a kind of moral ticket-of-leave to them, which effectually prevents their regaining their position.'[9] For example, the response of Sarah L.'s employer to her pregnancy was not uncommon. The petitioner reported that 'her mistress discovered her pregnancy. She [Sarah L.] confessed and was immediately discharged.'[10] Mary W.'s employer informed the enquirer, that although she trusted her ability to do the job, she feared:

> Her moral character will not bear investigation she having contracted habits of intimacy with a young man who is now I am told in London. She left me in consequence of my perceiving she was embonpoint pregnant which circumstance she denied again and again. [H]owever I warranted in

> arriving at the conclusion from appearances at the time and from the fact of her coming to London two or three months ago instead of going to her Mother and Sisters who were ignorant of her leaving the neighbourhood or of knowing where she had gone.[11]

Another case provides an instance of an unsupportive employer, as well as demonstrating how the onus fell on the unwed mother, not the father. Petitioner Catherine C. (aged 29), a nurse, reported she could not tell her mistress what had happened 'from shame'.[12] When the petitioner discovered her pregnancy, she left her position in Shropshire to 'come up' to London where she took a new position. When she told the father what had happened, 'he said he would take care of me'.[13] He disappeared when she was about to deliver her infant; therefore, she took lodgings in Lisson Grove and then went to the Marylebone Workhouse for her confinement.[14]

Some employers reported their suspicions; others expressed surprise by the pregnancy. They even claimed the event had gone against all they knew about the woman. A household in North London employed Isabella M. (aged 19) from Scotland as a general servant. She began experiencing 'some unexpected medical difficulties'.[15] She was in labour, about to deliver her baby, when the employers called their doctor for help. The enquirer reported the employers had been unaware their domestic was pregnant. They thought Isabella M. sickly, but they did not know why and expressed surprise 'when her real condition was declared by Dr Claremont'.[16] Instead of permitting the petitioner to deliver her infant at their home, their doctor called a cab and escorted her to a more appropriate venue for her station in which to deliver her infant, St Pancras Workhouse.[17] Later, the petitioner admitted she had 'c.c.' with the father without a promise to marry. He used force, but she did not complain to anyone. The father, a hotel-keeper, aged 28, went off to Australia. The committee accepted this petition.[18]

The dynamic between employers and domestics often complicated a relationship that could be both personal and exploitative. Elizabeth C. (aged 19) worked as a general servant for a tripe cleaner and his wife.[19] She met John W., a footman, at her mistress' house on Baker Street while he was picking up an order for his employer. The father courted her for four months. Criminal connection took place in January. Two months later she found herself to be pregnant. When Elizabeth C. told the father she was pregnant, he said he would not look after her or the child. When the enquirer looked for the father, he could not be found. Supposedly, he went off to Gloucestershire, quite a distance from London. The terminology in the investigator's report suggests some doubt about Elizabeth C.'s version of events. He specifically noted the age difference between Elizabeth C.'s employers. 'Her master is about 24 and her mistress about four or five years older.'[20] Perhaps, the husband took liberties with the petitioner. On the one hand, the couple may have genuinely liked the girl, or more likely they needed her help. It was always difficult to find and train new and reliable help. On the other, countering the suspicions of the investigator, the transcriber recorded: 'Mrs Y., the petitioner's mistress, assisted the petitioner in her troubles and would not hesitate in taking her back if she should be relieved of her child.'[21] She paid for her confinement and provided her with enough money to see her through recovery. Medical doctor 'Mr Harris of Marsham Street laid her [delivered her baby] and her mistress has advanced about £4 to £5 to maintain her,' reported the enquirer.

Payment for both the confinement and the amount of money given to the petitioner would have been a considerable sum for a husband and wife who worked as tripe cleaners. It is difficult to imagine, however, that the tripe cleaner's wife, even if she were several years older than her husband as noted in the transcript, would be willing to pay for her husband's indiscretions. Nevertheless, Elizabeth's mistress willingly paid for some reason, which we cannot detect. Most probably, her mistress' support stemmed from the fact Elizabeth was a skilled worker and the mistress wished to have her freed of the child. Tripe cleaning was hard and messy work. Elizabeth's employers could not, however, maintain a proper business image and retain the services of an unwed mother with a child in tow. The committee accepted Elizabeth's child.[22]

Far from being supportive, some unscrupulous employers took advantage of their vulnerable help. An accepted petition dated 1880 leaves little to the imagination regarding exploitative employer–employee relationships. Anne N. (aged 19) worked as a general servant for a family in Kentish Town.[23] The married father, 30 years of age, worked as a tailor. His wife had just had a baby. At first glance, nothing appeared unusual in the transcript. The petitioner stated, 'I was there nearly three years and left on 1 April 1879'.[24] Then she reassured the committee that her employer had 'never taken any liberties with me, or led me to suppose he intended anything wrong'.[25] Nevertheless, the petitioner continued:

> About the end of Oct. 1878, I was hanging out the linen, which had been washed to dry in the parlour, standing on a pair of steps when he suddenly seized me, and violently seduced me. There were persons in the house, but he prevented me calling out by putting his hand before my mouth. I was afraid to tell anyone. 'C.c.' was twice repeated and on the last occasion Mrs Jones's mother witnessed my struggles to get away, and exclaimed: 'My God! John, what have you done to the girl?' When my condition became known to my mistress she sent me away.[26]

The case of Anne A. (aged 22) demonstrates the power of character references from an aristocrat. Lady Margaret Cocks of Eastenor Castle, Herefordshire, employed the petitioner as a 'lady's maid'. The young maid accompanied Lady Margaret on a trip to Paris. The petitioner did not mention the purpose of the trip. While there, the women stayed in a hotel. The courier's room was adjacent to Anne's bedroom. Anne said Louis Tamburini, the father, 'entered her room "unexpectedly". She made resistance but gave no alarm for fear of exposure.' Anne never told Lady Margaret what had happened and never saw the father again. She left Lady Margaret's employment when she was five months pregnant, staying with her grandmother in Malvern, Worcestershire. After delivering her baby, she returned to London to work for Lady Margaret at her mansion located on Montague and Portman Squares in Marylebone.[27] Lady Margaret, her employer, wrote the following generous letter of recommendation.

> Her moral character and conduct were irreproachable. She has since strongly expressed her contrition for her past fault and I hope and believe she is sincere. I believe also she was led into error by a continuation of art and deceit practised against her. She has been quite deserted by the father and has received no assistance.[28]

Anne A. also received a letter of recommendation from her grandmother who paid her expenses. Her employer and family had not abandoned her. Had the committee not been dealing with titled nobility, they would have been inclined to ask why the women were staying in a hotel and not with friends, and who would have been watching over the activities of the young lady's maid. Neither of these questions appeared in the petition transcript. If the petitioner, Anne A., had shown no remorse or regret, her petition would have been rejected, but according to the transcriber, Anne A. exhibited deep repentance.[29]

The wealthier the recommender, the better the chances the petition would be accepted. Elizabeth H. (aged 22) worked as a cook for a well-to-do family. Her former mistress testified that Elizabeth was from the countryside and had come to London to find a situation. She had conducted herself 'with propriety', when she met a stonemason who promised to marry her. After he had learned she was pregnant, he departed for America. Elizabeth had the good fortune to deliver her infant at Queen Charlotte's Lying-in Hospital through a subscription from generous family. From there, she went to the home of another rich family where she served as a wet-nurse. Her petition was accepted.[30]

Occasionally, employers' recommendations united the committee in favour of approval. Ann W.'s (aged 15) petition had failed the first time around, but when her employer wrote a glowing letter of recommendation, the committee reversed its decision.[31] Ann W., an orphan, worked as a general servant. Her relatives lived in nearby Paddington and expected to keep an eye on her. The 18 year old father of her child, also orphaned, worked at a messy and physically demanding job in the same household as a pot washer. Their employer, Mr D., had taken the young people in under his wing. He had known their respective parents as former servants of upstanding character. Offering testimony on behalf of Ann W., Mr D, taking the side of the chap, stated he could not fire the young man for impregnating Ann because this would place a 'blot upon his character; and to dismiss him would be, he feared, exposing him to ruin'.[32] Since the young father had a job, Ann appealed to him for assistance. He said he could provide nothing. When the young man learned Ann was going to a magistrate, he suddenly disappeared. Ann's recommender, Mr D., confirmed Ann W. had no adequate means of support. The committee accepted Ann W.'s petition.[33]

Female recommenders, who employed the petitioner before her pregnancy, were usually willing to write recommendations, although not always. Employers frequently spoke directly to the issue of character and most obviously wished to assure the committee men of the mother's virtuosity. Women recommenders often reported on circumstances surrounding the pregnancy, including the identity of the father, and the nature and habits of their employee. The well-to-do often indicated they hoped to retain the petitioner as a trusted servant. If they could not guarantee future employment for the petitioner, they promised to find a suitable situation for her.[34] Occasionally recommenders questioned the mother's decision to appeal to the Foundling Hospital. Lady Knatchbull wrote:

> I cannot tell who had been advising Emma to part with her baby. I do not myself at all approve of her casting it off like that. I really do believe she is a fit person to receive the benefits of the Charity.[35]

References from wealthy women, who employed the petitioner as a wet nurse after confinement, were also enfolded within the petition packet.[36] Commonly, they located the petitioner's name on a list of wet-nurses supplied by Queen Charlotte's Lying-in Hospital. The maternity hospital served as a 'finding service' for wealthy mothers seeking 'respectable wet-nurses'.[37] The recommended mothers wet-nursed the babies of these genteel women. Doing so, obliged them to entrust their own, less fortunate infants, to a poorer wet-nurse or baby-farmer. Women who employed wet-nurses from Queen Charlotte's Lying-in Hospital, obviously understood the situation of their infant's surrogate mother. The secret, her employee had given birth to an illegitimate child, was part of the bargain kept between the wealthy and poor mothers. If the relationship proved positive between these women, help would be forthcoming. For example, in 1891 the Foundling Hospital enquirer affirmed her employer gave Elena S., a petitioner recommended by Queen Charlotte's Lying-in Hospital, an excellent character. The employer said Elena (aged 22) could not have been a better servant. She had heard from her the story of her shame, knew she felt it deeply, had made a great sacrifice and suffered much to conceal it. Therefore, the employer believed she had done all she possibly could have for Elena.[38]

The case of Margaret B. (aged 27) further demonstrates the contribution of employers and family members to the success of a petition. Margaret B.'s application stated her address as Brixton. The investigator learned the father had been working as a footman near Westbourne Park.[39] In this 1863 case, the committee discussed the putative father's reputation. The petitioner and father were in the house at the same time, under the supervision of the cook, an elderly person, who had 'neglected her duty'. According to the recommender, it was the cook's job to watch over younger employees, indicating the authority vested in the cook as a trusted senior-household employee. Further, the employer had already banned the 'unscrupulous' father from his house. The informant described the petitioner as 'timid and unable physically to struggle against him'. Thus, she 'yielded to his violence'.[40] The young woman's health had deteriorated so badly that she had to go to the doctor, 'who hinted at pregnancy'.

On close questioning, the woman admitted to what had happened on the day her employers were out of town. When employers pressed the father, he admitted paternity but refused to marry the petitioner. After his Westbourne Terrace employer fired him, he could not be found by authorities. This left the petitioner without recourse but to go to her family. Her brother, the closest family member living in London, received her 'kindly,' but he and his wife had a large family and could not support her.[41] Margaret B.'s employers took her back into service after she delivered her infant; she had placed the newborn at a 'baby farm'. Child care such as this sort cost as much as six shillings a week. There, the neonate along with several other babies would be cared under poor circumstances. Not surprisingly the infant had died at three months of age before the committee made their decision. Burial expenses of £1 10 shillings then fell upon the mother's shoulders.[42]

In many cases, the whole family bore the shame. Petitioners' parents believed that maintaining at least a veneer of respectability within the community, made it imperative to maintain silence about their daughter's condition. The pressure to protect one's daughter pressed down hard on rich and poor alike. The utter mortification of such an event generally prompted a variety of strategies, including the departure of the offending daughter, or the illegitimate baby immediately after birth. A lone mother reported: 'I have never seen my child. I lost my senses after my confinement.'[43] In 1888, another petitioner's father, upon learning of her situation, gave her £10, told her to leave, and 'never to send or to write'.[44] Some petitioners stated they could not tell family members or friends what had happened to them. Others had no choice but to share their problems. Most Foundling Hospital mothers and their families believed their daughters had impeccable characters, and with the exception of this one fall they were deserving of assistance. Consequently, family members and friends formed a considerable percentage (26.4 per cent) of recommender.[45]

Annie J. (aged 27) worked as a maid by helping her mother with the daily chores at their lodging house. Her mother's letter verified what had happened. 'Sir, I beg to acknowledge the receipt of your letter in reference to my daughter,' wrote Annie's mother.[46] Who then explained how she had taken in this man with an Irish surname, Thomas C., as a lodger. The petitioner's mother continued:

> To my utter astonishment he seduced my daughter [...][A]s soon as she told me what had occurred, I ordered him out of my house he had promised her marriage but as soon as she pressed him to fulfil his promise he under some pretence declined to do so but tried every means to induce her to go and live with him as his wife but she stoutly refused to do so. I then sent her to an Aunt in the country however he followed her there.[47]

Even though they were business partners, this mother's anxiety regarding her daughter's ill-fated affair was so great she sent her daughter out of town. Thereafter, the petitioner's mother sold her shop and moved up to London.[48]

Annie J. found a situation in Uxbridge, a small town northwest of the City, where she contracted rheumatic fever. With the help of the rector's wife at St Peters, Wolverhampton, Annie J. was admitted to the Home for Deserted Mothers at 35 Great Coram Street, also known as Mrs Gurney's Home, situated only a block from the Foundling Hospital. There she almost died. The matron, Mrs Jeffcock, reaffirmed the petitioner's account. The girl was left alone in her mother's house with a lodger, attributing the 'fall' to those unfortunate circumstances. Annie's Uxbridge employer verified the petitioner was 'a good and dutiful girl who always had the best characteristics until this sad fall. And I do believe that she has proposed in her heart to do always what is right for her life to come.'[49]

Florence E. (aged 19 years) lived with her parents. She became involved with a valet from Lord March's household in Chichester.[50] When her parents learned she was pregnant, they sent Florence to her sister's house in Harlesden, North London. Somebody in the family had enough money to provide a subscription ticket to Queen Charlotte's Lying-in Hospital. After her confinement, she returned to her sister's home; where her family helped to pay for infant care. Her parents were so supportive that they rented their 'furnished house in Brighton' in order to cover the expenses of this baby. The parents then moved out of their neighbourhood into a smaller apartment.[51] In short, this was not only a matter of pride, but an economic reality as well.

In the case of Catherine W. (aged 25), the woman's father testified for her. Catherine worked in the family business as a shoe binder. Her role in the family economy was essential to the family as a whole. Her father wrote a long letter to the Foundling Hospital. He said he had taken the putative father into his house as a lodger. The father began to court Catherine and 'promised her marriage'. He reassuringly told Catherine he had published the banns of marriage. Catherine's father said his daughter was easy prey, even though she was already 25 years of age. After Catherine had become pregnant, her irate father called the sire of her child a 'villain'. When asked for child support, the putative father replied: 'He would do no more than the law compelled him.' This proved to be absolutely nothing under the law, and because the father had absconded. The petitioner's father closed his letter with a plea:

> I trust gentlemen, you will make all due allowances for a father's feelings for his child, considering it my bounden duty, where I think there is a glimmer of hope to benefit my child, and to see her reinstated in society again.[52]

The committee accepted Catherine's plea based on family and employer support; as well as her attempt to hide her condition. Friends also helped petitioners in a variety of ways. A wet-nurse Ann F. (aged 21) reported she had known the father of her child for many years. After several years of separation, they renewed their friendship as a romantic liaison. The father, who worked as a gentleman's servant, had promised marriage. 'C[riminal].C[onversation] took place at a friend's house in Bishopsgate, and was never repeated.' Ann's recommender, whose husband was a reader at the synagogue and teacher of German and Hebrew, spoke well of her. The committee accepted this baby.[53]

Elizabeth C. (aged 23) worked as a needlewoman who found herself pregnant and with a partner willing to marry her. After the banns of marriage had been read at St Andrew's Church in Holborn, the father of her child died. The mother held the death certificate to verify her statement. Elizabeth C. also had a network of friends who could help in her desperation. She reported, 'I went to hide my shame to Mrs and Mr Munroe, Southall, Greenford,

Middlesex', (Southall was a small town located about 12 miles west of Shepherd's Bush).[54]

Another friend helped Anne N. who delivered her baby in the Islington Workhouse. She had strong recommendations from friends, neighbours and her current employer. A letter from a clerk at the British Museum wrote on museum stationery:

> The bearer of this note is a poor unfortunate girl, who is deserving of the sympathy of those that can possibly help her. She is a workhouse girl, unacquainted with the ways of this world[;] in fact she is most ignorant about those affairs which many boys and girls know at an early age.[55]

Anne N.'s parents may have abandoned her as an infant. Or, her parents may have died, or were too poor to maintain her. Whatever the reason, a poor law asylum and school sheltered and educated her. She was not a young woman of the streets; but the blame for her pregnancy was placed on the inadequacies of her upbringing, namely lack of parental oversight. The recommender continued:

> Though her conduct may seem inexplicable, yet I believe that she had no idea of that which was done to her. The man took advantage of her simplicity. His wife was upstairs on account of her baby. The girl now knows the nature of her guilt, but at first she appeared scarcely cognisant of what had taken place.[56]

The note clearly states what had happened to Anne N. A neighbour, Mrs Binley, who heard about this petitioner's experience, took the girl in until she was ready to be confined; about a week before her labour and delivery she went into the Islington Workhouse. After her confinement, Anne returned to Mrs Binley who had agreed to employ the young woman as her servant, while paying a wet-nurse to care for the infant. Mrs Binley told the enquirer that if Anne N. were not relieved of her infant, then she would have to return to the workhouse. When the enquirer went to have a quiet word with the neighbours about Anne N.'s case, they spoke highly of her, and reported they were exceedingly angry with 'the man'.[57]

The committee accepted Anne's petition based on notes from employers, family, and friends, attesting to hospital efforts to measure whether the young woman proved worthy of a second chance. The elite wished to preserve and retain the character and services of their domestics or other deserving women. Families tried to preserve their reputations, as well as their daughters. Data suggests that the recommenders communicated their shared values with the committee, hoping they would consider the 'extenuating circumstances' that brought the young woman to the Foundling asylum on Guilford Street in the first place. The Foundling Hospital Board of Governors, committee men, recommenders, and the working women who applied agreed on what constituted a respectable character. Moreover, supporters clearly wished to assure the men that this was the petitioner's first fall, she was a reliable employee, a faithful daughter, and her character redeemable. Indeed, recommenders vouched for the petitioner's potential for redemption.

At least 12.97 per cent of accepted petitions contained support from clerics, aiding their chances considerably. Clerical support usually arrived from small towns outside of London. She may have moved to London, but in the meantime, she appealed to her hometown clergy for support. The case of Frances B., a housemaid (aged 26), who had worked at the same place for nine years provides such an example. Her petition was one of the few in which the transcriber specifically noted the banns of marriage, but she conceived the baby beforehand. This would not have posed a particular problem for her, if her fiancé had not died before their marriage. Upon learning of her pregnancy, Reverend Druce from St Mary's Ipswich was successful in obtaining a subscription letter to Queen Charlotte's Lying-in Hospital. When the hospital enquirer interviewed the vicar, he reported he had known both parents. They were members of his Sunday school class and he had met them at a temperance meeting. Druce volunteered that they were 'very respectable young people. He had not the least doubt but for the death of the father, by this time, they would have been married. The Vicar strongly wished 'to recommend Petitioner to the favorable consideration of the Committee.'[58]

Richard Croft, curate at St Matthew's, Westminster, attempted to save the 'character' of Ann H. (aged 23), a general servant. Ann had been in the workhouse for four months, entering two months before her baby was born. Croft wrote: 'I take advantage of your kind permission to lay before you a statement in reference to a poor girl named Ann H. who has brought a child in hope[s] of obtaining admission to the Foundling Hospital.' Ann's parents were dead. She received help from her sister, who worked as a general servant in the home of a doctor. She had no other assistance. Croft found her on the verge of starvation in a 'low lodging house and surrounded by vice in very miserable circumstances'. He advised her to take her baby to the Foundling Hospital, which she willingly did. Croft had inquired about her character and found there was 'no reason to suppose that she has been a prostitute'.[59] If committee men received her child, Croft promised he would take her to a 'penitentiary' immediately.[60] Apparently, Mr Brownlow responded in a rather strong fashion regarding Ann's stay in the workhouse, because Croft replied with the following rather pointed note:

> I was much grieved to find that there was no hope of admission for the child of Ann H. Of course I cannot pretend to remonstrate against the decision of the committee but I cannot help observing that the ground for refusal does appear rather strange for she only went into the workhouse to be confined. And if she had had one friend in the world no doubt she would not have gone there at all or at least would have left immediately.[61]

Reluctant to give up, Croft offered 'pecuniary payment', hoping this enticement would facilitate admission. He was not to be satisfied; the Foundling Hospital committee men promptly rebuffed him.[62]

Another unsuccessful case shows how a vicar attempted to shift all blame to the father. Harriet R.'s pastor, Reverend Spooner, the vicar of Edgbaston, tried to help. After baptizing the baby, Reverend Spooner contacted his brother in London regarding this case. He made arrangements for Harriet R. and the baby to travel to London. There, the London Spooners found Harriet a position as a wet-nurse with a family from respectable Westbourne Park in Bayswater. As her service neared an end, her employer simply wanted to see the young woman relieved of her infant and assured the governors that Harriet R. was 'a young woman of irreproachable character' who did not know the father of her child was married at the time.[63] An interviewee from Edgbaston stymied success when they revealed the father of Harriet R.'s child was a 'man with a wife who was still living', and had been sent to jail for bigamy in Warwickshire.[64] The petitioner had another child with this man, and she had continued a three-year relationship with him, a fatal flaw for admission. The Foundling Hospital required the pregnancy be the mother's first. Even a clergyman could not help Harriet R. (aged 24) who had previously worked as 'housekeeper'. The blessings and support of a clergyman could in no way clear a clouded character. The committee rejected this petition.[65]

If an expectant mother neither had employers nor family members upon whom she could rely, she occasionally subjected herself to the painful choice of seeking admission to a penitentiary, an unwed mothers' home, or worse, a poor law infirmary. Given the lesser of two evils, some mothers chose to enter 'reform houses' as truly penitent women. In turn, the Foundling Hospital relied on such charitable institutions, which were described as 'simply bewildering in number and variety' in the 840-page London charity register.[66] Spatial proximity between certain charities and the suggestive names aided petitioners and the public in discerning the purpose of a wide array of institutions. These same operations served as recommenders for petitioners and included unwed mothers' homes, respectable maternity charities, poor law guardians and magistrates, who, like the personal recommenders, proved helpful to both the committee men and the petitioner because they attested to her respectable character. The institutions also reassured the inquirers of the mother's resourcefulness, seeking help from respectable charities before applying to the Foundling. Petitions receiving support from large institutions accounted for 18.1 per cent of accepted petitions as shown in Table 6.2.[67]

Unwed mothers achieved considerable success at the Foundling Hospital if they applied to a penitentiary or unwed mothers' home beforehand. The historical origins of mother's homes and their attendant policies had roots in the first home for fallen women, the Magdalen Hospital, opened by Foundling Hospital governor Jonas Hanway in 1758. According to Hanway:

> Nothing shall be omitted which can promote the great ends of preserving life, of rendering that life useful, and of recovering those who are now lost to the community.[68]

Following in Hanway's footsteps, men opened and staffed the first Anglican home for penitents in London in 1806.[69] The Westminster and Northwest London Female Asylum opened its doors in 1837 in poverty-stricken St Pancras. The Asylum's ninth annual report stated the institution maintained around 20 women a year.[70] It aimed to reform and place women in a respectable job or situation, meaning place of employment, which would restore their character. The Asylum secured new jobs for about 40 percent of the women, restored the remainder to friends; or the women left on their own accord.[71] A similar endeavour, founded in 1857, the London Female Preventive and Reformatory Institution, aided 'friendless young women and girls' and aimed to rescue women from the streets, parks, police, courts, hospitals, infirmaries and 'other places by day and night' also served unwed mothers.[72]

Thus, many women who petitioned the Foundling Hospital had already experienced some type of investigative and evaluative process at a maternity

Table 6.2: FH Institutional Recommenders, 1842–92[73]

Recommenders	**N**	**Recommenders %**
Mothers' homes	25	59.52
Doctor, midwife	11	26.19
Board of guardians and local magistrates	4	9.53
Charity Organisation Society	2	4.76
Total	42	100.00

or reform home before making an application. Between 1842 and 1892, no fewer than ten such homes appeared in the Foundling Hospital petitions, including: St Mary Magdalene Home, Urania Cottage, Queen Charlotte's Row Female Reformatory, Mrs Gurney's Home, The Women's Home, The Mother's Home at St James, The Society for the Protection of Women and Children, Canon Holland's Home, Winfred House, and the Girl's Friendly Society. Other London institutions with similar aims included the Home for Gentlewomen in Reduced Circumstances, and the Home of Hope for the Restoration of Fallen and the Protection of Friendless Young Women.[74] Generally, the institutional names indicated how society regarded unwed mothers – not better than whores or criminals who belonged in a reformatory, or helpless victims in need of protection. If a woman behaved properly at one of these homes, then, she could receive a good 'character' reference from her supervisor at the home. Since prospective employers had closely observed and screened the candidates before making an offer of employment as a wet-nurse, their chances for infant's acceptance at the Foundling increased.[75]

Institutions such as Mrs Gurney's Home, the London Female Preventive and Reformatory Institution, and the Londesborough Samaritan Fund aided Queen Charlotte's Lying-in Hospital in providing places for unwed mothers after delivery. Mrs Gurney went so far as to open a home for unwed mothers at 35 Great Coram Street, situated not far from the Foundling Hospital. Known as the 'Refuge for Deserted Mothers and Children', at least 11 per cent of the successful Foundling Hospital petitions came from this institution.[76] St Magdalene Home in Weymouth Street, not far from the Marylebone Workhouse, opened in 1865. This private venture also maintained a close association with Queen Charlotte's Lying-in Hospital. The home closed within two years, reopening in 1868 in Paddington, a middle-class community situated west of Marylebone.[77] In 1882, Mrs Charles Roundell established a home for single mothers and named it the Queen Charlotte's Home. Although this charity did not have financial ties with Queen Charlotte's Lying-in Hospital, it received women confined at Queen Charlotte's. Few would have difficulty in determining this charitable endeavour provided services for unwed mothers.[78]

An example of women who operated without bricks, mortar and an address, with nothing more than a Bible, included 'Ranyards Bible Women', founded by Mrs L. N. Ranyard in 1857. They worked as Anglican missionaries in London workhouses and infirmaries. In 1868, the women added a nursing branch to their initiative.[79] The nurses also frequently identified suitable candidates for Queen Charlotte's Lying-in Hospital, choosing young mothers whom they thought to be respectable. The Bible Women discovered whether the 'fall' had been the mother's first and offered destitute young mothers a place at the Refuge for Deserted Mothers and Children. Upon arrival, the young mothers received food, clothing and shelter. When strong enough, the matrons found employment for them and sent their infants out to be wet-nursed. Frequently, the Bible women placed young mothers in the homes of wealthy women seeking wet-nurses for their own infants.[80]

Near the end of the petition transcript, the Foundling Hospital transcriber consistently noted the place of confinement with a line or two: 'petitioner confined at Queen Charlotte's Lying-in Hospital; petitioner confined at Marylebone Workhouse; petitioner laid by Dr Marsham.' The medical notes also proved a determining factor and verified the respectability of the petition. Midwives and doctors reported on the health of the mother and whether or not this was a first pregnancy as this might have a bearing on her 'character'.[81] In some cases, medical attendants successfully argued the need for support based on the poor clinical condition of the mother. Most accepted Foundling Hospital petitioners delivered their babies in respectable venues. At least 23.3 per cent of all Foundling Hospital petitioners were under the care of doctors and midwives. Of the petitioners applying to the

Table 6.3: FH Survey of All Confinement Venues[82]

Confinement Venues	**N**	**Venue %**
Doctors and midwives	83	23.3
Family and friends	43	12.1
Lodgings, rented on own	84	23.6
Lying-in institutions	74	20.8
Workhouses	72	20.2
Total	356	100.0

Foundling Hospital, 20.8 per cent relied on lying-in homes for their confinements as shown in Table 6.3.[83]

The data in Table 6.4, showing the figures for accepted petitions, indicate that 28.2 per cent delivered their infants at a lying-in hospital; while 28.6 per cent of all accepted petitioners delivered their infants with the help of doctors or midwives. The more connected a woman, the more she could rely on her family and friends, so that close associates aided 15.9 per cent. Petitioners reporting they had delivered their infants in 'common lodgings', or they had saved enough money to rent a room for delivery, counted for 23.6 per cent. Some women who delivered their babies in a rented room, called upon a doctor or midwife, attached to a hospital such as St George's Hospital in the West End, for assistance.[84] In these cases, the respectable doctor proved essential for the petitioner's success.

The petition of Amelia R. (aged 19), who listed her occupation as a homemaker, illustrates the three-way relationship between the Foundling Hospital, confinement venues, and the petitioner. She maintained a small boarding house by 'letting' rooms to lodgers, a risky but ambitious enterprise for a young girl. An Italian opera singer took Amelia by surprise. He seduced her within days of arrival. She had not given consent, and he had not promised to marry her. When Amelia R. found herself pregnant, she went to the Home for Destitute Women on Marylebone Road. The matrons at the home wrote: 'The petitioner's conduct while at the Home is reported as being quite satisfactory. She is very penitent for her error thro' which she had endured much mental and bodily suffering.'[85] Educated, Amelia R. completed her own petition. The handwriting and signature matched. Amelia, however, had a disability, a 'bad leg'. If such a woman arrived with a disability, the committee tended to be more sympathetic. Her petition was successful. Later, after the hospital had received her infant, Amelia R. wrote frequent letters to Mr Brownlow regarding the well-being of her child.[86]

In another case, the Foundling Hospital enquirer had gone to the York Road Lying-in Hospital, south of the Thames in Lambeth, to check on the records of Elizabeth W. (aged 19), who had worked as a nurse. Elizabeth W., from Kent, had been in London less than three years. The details kept in the maternity registers corresponded to the petitioner's account. The hospital matron and the midwife affirmed her conduct as satisfactory. Unfortunately,

Table 6.4: Accepted FH Petition Confinement Sites[87]

Confinement	N	Venue %
Doctors and midwives	65	28.6
Family and friends	36	15.9
Lying-in institutions	64	28.2
Lodgings, rented own	11	4.8
Workhouses	51	22.5
Total	227	100.0

'her milk having failed her and the child refusing its food it has been absolutely necessary in order to preserve it to put it to a wet-nurse'.[88] The expense of five shillings per week for a wet nurse fell very heavily on the petitioner. If the petitioner could not pay, the baby would be returned to the mother. Since the mother could not supply the necessary breast milk, she could have resorted to infant formula, or farinaceous foods, and most likely watch her baby starve to death. Placing the child with the Foundling Hospital could literally save its life. Elizabeth's petition was successful.[89]

The enquirer solicited the following testimony from the midwife in the case of Clara H. (aged 19), who worked as a general servant and appeared overwhelmingly distraught because she had been 'seduced by her brother-in-law'.[90] Clara claimed he visited her while family members were at church services. After her relatives had learned Clara H. was pregnant, they moved her to another town. Clara's midwife reported: 'I have not the least doubt it was her first child, I never saw her before I was called to attend her in labour. She did not appear to be more than 18 years of age and so distressed that I felt quite interested in the poor girl's trial as by what I could learn she was sadly deceived. I am your obedient servant, E. A. Young, Midwife.'[91]

If the mother delivered her infant in a common lodging house, her chances for acceptance were limited because of this venue's association, as Henry Mayhew explained, with prostitution.[92] Committee men were also suspicious because such a place told no tales. Rarely could a mother provide a credible witness to the delivery of her infant. In most cases, recourse to lodgings reflected the desperate mother's intent to hide her shame.[93] For the most part, rejected petitioners could not rely on their families, employers, or respectable charities to provide a subscription to a lying-in institution. Few had money to pay for a doctor or midwife; thus, they fell on the poor laws.[94] Mothers confined in the workhouse had great needs, but necessity was not a legitimate requisite for help at the Foundling Hospital. Although accepted petitioners resorted to the workhouse, the inscription 'workhouse' on a petition served as a cautionary sign. The stigma associated with a birth there edged its way into the petition narrative. John Brownlow's sometimes-derisive notes tell us much. Phrases such as 'Child was born in Saint Martins' and 'This Child was born in Marylebone Workhouse, where she is *settled* no courtship or promise of marriage'. 'This Petitioner has another illegitimate child.' '*This* born in Lambeth workhouse.' In short, simply put, a 'Child born in Marylebone Workhouse' was enough to disqualify a petition before it went to the committee.[95] Upon Brownlow's retirement, accepted petitions from over 26 different workhouses increased. Obviously, his prejudice against such humble origins played out in candidate selection. Changes indicating a shift in confinement sites, suggests the committee moved from selecting petitions originating in the Metropolis to extra-metropolitan locations, where access to mothers' homes remained limited.[96] In these cases, excellent recommendations accompanied petitions from outside London.[97]

The Foundling Hospital accepted petitions from respectable establishments such as Queen Charlotte's Lying-in Hospital in Hammersmith, the General Lying-in Hospital on York Road, and Adelaide Hospital on Golden Square. If committee men rejected a case, in which the mother delivered at a lying-in home, there were extenuating circumstances. The committee men accepted 41 petitions, or 18 per cent, from Queen Charlotte's Lying-in Hospital. Table 6.5 demonstrates a rising trend of acceptances from Queen Charlotte's Lying-in Hospital, making it apparent that this hospital increasingly served as a stepping-stone for the admission.[99]

Table 6.5: Accepted FH Petitions – Queen Charlotte's by Decade, 1842–92[98]

Institutions		
Queen Charlotte's Lying-in Hospital		
Decade	**N**	**Petitioners %**
1842–9	3	7.33
1850–9	6	14.63
1860–9	7	17.07
1870–9	7	17.07
1880–92	18	43.90
Total	41	100.00

Table 6.6 provides a profile of the Foundling Hospital petitioners confined at Queen Charlotte's Lying-in Hospital. The data indicate the degree to which a respectable job and recommendation from an employer counted towards admission of an unwed mother to Queen Charlotte's Lying-in Hospital, and in turn, acceptance of her illegitimate child to the Foundling. Significantly, 70.7 per cent of petitioners, aged 15 to 19 years, who delivered at Queen Charlotte's Lying-in Hospital were younger than might be expected, with the youngest, albeit rarest cases appearing at 14 years of age. In this particular cohort, 97.6 per cent could sign their name. More mothers gave consent to sexual relations than had received a promise of marriage; but still the mother had received a promise to marry. Around 29.3 per cent admitted to having known the father of their child for more than nine months. More than 56 per cent listed their

Table 6.6: Queen Charlotte's Lying-in Hospital Mothers' Profile[100]

Description of Category	Mothers' Profile %
Mother's age 15–19 years	70.7
Mother could sign name	97.6
Mother gave consent to sexual relations	85.4
Length of acquaintance between mother and father longer than nine months	29.3
Mothers' address North or West London	56.1
Mothers' occupation – housemaid or general servant	51.2
Mother's recommender – employer	41.5
Mother received a promise of marriage	68.3
Father's occupation skilled labourer or better	41.5

addresses under the north or west London districts. At least 50 per cent listed their occupation as general servant, with 40 per cent receiving a recommendation from their employer. The youthfulness of the candidates, the strains of sustaining a child in poverty, and the possibility of another 'fall' amongst lower-ranked domestics, concerned hospital administrators. They believed these women would look for a partner who could support them, but as a consequence, the woman would again become pregnant. Significantly, the Foundling Hospital, on average, received only 50 infants per year, while Queen Charlotte's Lying-in Hospital had a much larger clientele. This suggests Queen Charlotte's recommended only the best cases to the Foundling Hospital.

Recommendations from poor law guardians or magistrates rarely supported petitions. Moreover, John Brownlow, as mentioned above, displayed reluctance to accept such petitions. For example, in 1854 a single mother Eve H. (aged 20), who was living in the Whitechapel Workhouse caught the attention of a member of the Whitechapel Board of Guardians, Thomas Craven. He wrote a long letter about her 'fine character', a remarkable outlay of sympathy on his part, in light of the responses exhibited by other colleagues to the plight of unmarried mothers.[101] Craven obviously believed she was somehow out of place and wanted to get 'the child into your hospital'.[102] Then he proposed to place the mother in 'another asylum whereby her character might be recovered'.[103] The guardian thought it most 'disadvantageous' to take a child away from its mother too early, but if he needed to comply with the rules of the Foundling Hospital, he would do so. The committee did not accept Craven's recommendation on Eve's behalf.[104]

Associating the workhouse with the Irish, the Foundling Hospital also appropriated practices relating to religion in workhouses, maintaining a strict and uniform set of spiritual standards that correlated with the Church of England. Clearly, the Irish Catholic community would have been in considerable need from the 1840s onward. In 1861 Roman Catholic men, women and children comprised 11.9 per cent of London workhouse inmates. They also lived in the areas least represented among accepted petitions, central, south and east London.[105] If the committee men had no desire to accommodate poor law guardians, they were even less responsive to Irish MPs, Mr John Kelly and Mr Patrick O'Brien, both interested in testing the full extent of Hospital administrative policies. Strong, direct language from a no nonsense sort of man, Foundling Hospital treasurer George Burrow Gregory, silenced Irish MPs when questioned regarding policies relating to Roman Catholics. At a second set of hearings on the Infant Life Protection Bill (1891), Gregory testified the Foundling Hospital would not indulge Roman Catholics.[106] In a follow-up question, Kelly and O'Brien queried Gregory again, and asked whether there were any Catholic children at the hospital. If so, were the children educated and schooled in Roman Catholicism and permitted to attend Holy Mass? Gregory replied:

> We should ask why she had not applied to a Catholic institution, and why the child had not been taken in. I may say we do not want Catholic children at all; we would rather be without them.[107]

Given the 'special relationship between the state, Church of England and the Foundling', O' Brien questioned Gregory again about whether the Foundling afforded Catholic children their religious rights.[108] The treasurer reiterated: 'As I said before, that we really do not want Roman Catholic children; we would rather they should go to their own institutions.'[109] By 'their own institutions', he meant orphanages and asylums operated by Roman Catholic men and women.[110] Hence, the ornament of the metropolis preferred to place responsibility for Catholic unwed mothers on the religious congregations. Since the hospital, purportedly, did not subscribe to a particular creed, the committee took no account that some foundlings might have been baptized as Roman Catholics. In the general survey, one priest at Warwick Chapel and possibly, the Sisters of Charity of St Vincent de Paul at Carlisle Place, submitted recommendations. Significantly, the Sisters of Charity operated creches and homes for children across London, maintaining more-or-less, an open door policy for those in need.[111]

Assessing how many Catholic children might have been admitted raises more difficulties, although Irish surnames frequently appear in the petition bundles. Most destitute Irish Catholic mothers relied on, for example, St Patrick's Charity, Catholic boarding and poor law boarding schools, orphanages, hostels, family networks, and various other domiciles for women that appeared in London in the years following Catholic Emancipation in 1829.[112] Since the governors and committee refused to accommodate any religious creed, other than Anglicanism, there would be no Catholic Mass, catechism, first communion, or confirmation for children of Roman Catholic parentage. For a devout Catholic, this implied that the mother would jeopardize her own spiritual salvation as well as her infant's if the committee accepted the baby. Irish women applying for admission, then, faced even more difficult choices. Surnames, originating from Ireland, generally joined the 'rejected' bundles.

Victorians measured respectability by comparing their personal values with others. On the one hand, if a woman's behaviour and ethics matched those of her recommender, usually a person from amid the rising and respectable middle classes, then her chance for admission strengthened. On the other hand, the general profile of a rejected petitioner demonstrates how her character precluded this possibility. Many worked and lived as general servants in North London. The reported skill level of the fathers was lower than in the accepted group. They were less likely to have admited consent to sexual relations and had fewer promises of marriage. The mothers delivered their babies in the workhouse or lodgings. Finally, because of their low status work, they lacked credible recommendations from employers (Table 6.7).[113]

Furthermore, these women frequently submitted incomplete forms. Some failed to report their occupation accurately. Some could not prove abandonment by the father. In other cases, doubts relating to their respectability, cast a

Table 6.7: All FH Petitions, Mothers' Agency by Variables, 1842–92, 1842–59[114]

Categories	**Accepted Petitions 1842–92 %**	**Rejected Petitions 1842–59 %**
Reported consent	74.75	24.25
Promise to marry	82.14	17.86
Confinement in workhouse/lodgings	39.74	60.26
Employer as recommender	82.00	18.00

shadow on the petition. Others were questioned their ability to reform. These women probably never learned that the secretary dated and inscribed their petition with the word 'rejected' in large, scrawling, cursive writing. The 'rejected' petition joined a stack of about 150 ill-fated petitions for that year. As the secretary bundled them up, with a red grosgrain ribbon, and deposited the stack into a file drawer. The limited information supplied in the packet indicates that many rejected petitioners failed to advance to later stages of the process. Petitioners offered information relating to their pregnancy to the point at which they would have been asked to supply the name of the father or a respectable employer. For unsuccessful applicants, the largest category of supporters fell into the 'unknown–unlisted' class, standing at 71.3 per cent (Table 6.8). This clearly denotes a halt to the process by the committee men and required the secretary to send a rejection note. Other reasons for stopping the petitioning process stemmed from mothers' choices. Some withdrew their application because they preferred to keep their infants despite social disapproval. In other cases, the baby died, or the father returned. Conceivably, some could not withstand the humiliation of having their personal life investigated.[115] In sum, petitioners needed to prove three things for admission of their infants: (i) they had an employer, or someone else of note willing to write

Table 6.8: FH Rejected Petitioners' Recommenders[116]

Rejected Petitioners' Recommenders	N	Rejected Recommenders %
Clerics	1	0.7
Charles Dickens	1	0.7
Employers	18	14.0
Family and friends	6	4.7
Doctor, midwife	1	0.7
Mothers' home	3	2.3
Board of guardians and local magistrates	2	1.7
Neighbours	3	2.3
Titled, lady or lord	2	1.6
Unknown–unlisted	92	71.3
Total	129	100.0

a letter of support; (ii) they had not relied on public assistance more than was necessary; and (iii) they had not contracted venereal disease.

Although the selection process at the Foundling Hospital depended on her occupation, the question of promise and consent, the petitioner's recommender, and place where she delivered her infant, other factors could derail the petition. If critical character flaws appeared, the committee could not be persuaded otherwise, even if the recommender was as well-known and respected as Charles Dickens. By first exploring the relationship between Charles Dickens and the Founding Hospital and then tracing a sequence of events, we can better understand how charitable institutions, legal authorities, and private individuals worked to restore a woman's character in concert.

Some argue that Dickens's fictional world was not an accurate reflection of reality; others suggest he lived in a prison of his time. However, this reading of his literature, and activities particularly in relation to the Foundling Hospital challenges these claims. In 1822, Dickens's father moved his family from Kent to a house in Camden Town, and then to Bloomsbury, not far from the Foundling Hospital. His father went bankrupt; and magistrates sent him to debtors' prison at Marshalsea. The young man quit school at a young age. He worked at a 'blacking warehouse', where he earned six or seven shillings a week on the Strand, the main thoroughfare connecting the City and Westminster. After his father's release from debtors' prison, he returned to school and clerked at the Inns of Court for a year. Then he went to work for *The Mirror of Parliament*, a newspaper that recorded parliamentary debates, as an apprentice court reporter. After serving in the gallery of the House of Commons during the 1833–4 poor law debates, the novelist and commentator tested the New Poor Law legislation in the court of public opinion. Many references to this legislation appear along with Foundling Hospital personages in his literary and journalistic publications.

As a young boy, Dickens frequently walked around the perimeter of the Foundling Hospital grounds. We may envision the youth treading the pathways on the edge of the large property and asking his mother about the children he saw playing on the manicured lawn. He described the estate as 'commodious' and 'airy', with 'shady trees', and an 'incredible fish pond'.[117] If one could not visit the place, the account offered a chance to experience vicariously this unique domain, an example of a lived space, but also a representational space that orders relationships and links itself to the production of knowledge, including the written text or literature, signs, symbols, codes and interpersonal relationships. He first familiarized Victorians with the Foundling Hospital in his novels, the weekly journal *Household Words* and *All the Year Round*. Between 1838 and 1839, *Bentley's Miscellany* published *The Adventures of Oliver Twist, or the Parish Boy's Progress*.[118] Later novels such as *Little Dorrit*, *Bleak House* and *Our Mutual Friend* include references to the harshness of the New Poor Laws, the condition of unwed mothers, out-of-wedlock and abandoned children. The short story, *No Thoroughfare*, specifically explores complications arising from the admission of an infant at the Foundling.[119]

More specifically, Dickens protested the opprobrium associated with the condition of 'bastardy' and the Bastardy Amendments; the theme threads through *Oliver Twist* in examining the life of Oliver and his mother. He addresses the problem of workhouse births and introduces Mr Brownlow to his readers. The imagined Mr Brownlow maintains deeply held secrets, such as the petty theft; and only he has the power to redeem Oliver's reputation and secure his future. The real John Brownlow at the Foundling Hospital also kept secrets, had the power to restore an unwed mother's life to one of respectability and to assist her illegitimate child.[120] Whether Dickens used irony or praise to draw attention to the large estate on Guilford Street, Foundling Hospital petitioners would best recognize Mr Brownlow name as the man who admitted their baby to the institution, not the rescuer of Oliver.[121]

After publication of *Oliver Twist* in 1837–9, a friendship developed between Brownlow and Dickens.[122] Moreover, Dickens and his wife attended church services at the Foundling Hospital chapel. They rented the pew box next to the secretary of the Foundling Hospital, John Brownlow.[123] The gesture, on the part of the secretary acknowledged their status. They sat in front of the sanctuary, on the east side of the church, and immediately behind the Foundling Hospital Board of Governors.[124] He and his wife paid an annual pew rent for this honour.[125] According to the novelist in *Household Words*, administrators recruited 'the least conventional, most sensible, and naturally eloquent and earnest of preachers'.[126] He claimed: 'Sunday service was performed at its best with all the assistance of devotional music, yet free from the stage-playing of any *ism*, not forgetting schism'.[127] Having launched a relationship with the venerable institution, the following extended discussion of the Susan Mayne case is based on published and unpublished letters from him to the Foundling. Wherein, he takes an active role as a recommender in this particular case. Demonstrating how Victorians constructed respectability within well-defined parameters, it highlights the rigour with which the Foundling Hospital committeemen assessed petitions, ensuring that only women of the highest character succeeded. It also illustrates and exemplifies the inter-connectedness of charities that dealt with women's issues across London.

Dickens intervened on behalf of Susan Mayne, whose name appears in Dickens's published letters, to get her help at Urania Cottage, 'a home for homeless women', Queen Charlotte's Lying-in Hospital, the Foundling

Hospital, and a local magistrate.[128] In September 1855, Magistrate Hardwick at the Great Marlborough St Police Court in West London approached the well-known novelist seeking help for Mayne (aged 21).[129] The Hospital investigator, Mr Twiddy recorded that Hardwick had heard charges for drunkenness and prostitution brought against Mayne before.[130] Curiously, her case did not appear in the 'Police Log' in the *Times* dated 1 November 1854 to 15 February 1855; but it is also intriguing that the London police commissioner, Sir Richard Mayne, made it his business to reduce petty theft and crime on the streets of London.[131] Not that these two individuals were related, but it seems likely the press could censure itself on behalf of the head of the police force. Susan's case was even more unusual in the way it developed because of the considerable amount of support she received from the magistrate and his wife, Mrs Hardwick. The local judge had sentenced the literate domestic servant to one week in prison. In jail, she showed signs of repentance because she maintained sobriety; therefore, Hardwick released her on probation.[132] At the time, he asked Dickens for help in admitting her to the Burdett-Coutts Home for Destitute Females, or Urania Cottage in Shepherds Bush.[133]

Baroness Angela Burdett-Coutts, the exceedingly rich heiress to the Coutts banking fortune, was well known for her extensive philanthropic activities. She opened the house with the encouragement of Dickens in 1847.[134] It offered women an opportunity to begin anew, find suitable employment, or emigrate.[135] He served as almoner for the Home until 1855 and involved himself with daily operations. He dealt case-by-case with the petitions, frequently conferring with Burdett-Coutts.[136] Dickens memorialized Urania Cottage in *Household Words*, describing it as a 'Home for Homeless Women'.[137] He reported that the asylum had given hope to young women, placing them in jobs and saving them from again falling into sin.[138] Thus, with his first hand knowledge of daily operations, upon receiving the application form at the cottage for Susan Mayne, Dickens requested an interview with her and then relayed the details to Miss Burdett-Coutts.[139] According to Dickens:

> Mr Hardwick wrote to me the other day from Marlborough Street, about a girl (whom he had committed for seven days as a disorderly, but about whom the Police seemed to have been hasty and mistaken, it afterwards appeared), whom he was so anxious to get into the home that he was supporting her in the meanwhile at the Jailer's house [Hardwick's home] out of the poor box. The Jailer brought her here by my appointment. I was not so propitiated by her manner as Mr Hardwick was, and requested that the account she gave of herself should be closely enquired into. It turning out to be true when this was done, I did not feel justified in objecting to her; and Mrs Marchmont will fetch her, next Wednesday.[140]

Dickens achieved success in recommending Susan for admission to Urania Cottage. She remained there for a month. Sometime after her arrival, however, the matron, Mrs Marchmont, discovered that the 'unfortunate object' of Hardwick's sympathy was pregnant. Dickens promptly wrote to Hardwick:

> Our ladies have great apprehension that Susan Mayne is in the family way. On the other hand, our usual medical attendant at the Home is rather of the contrary opinion. A fortnight or so will probably decide the question; but if she should be in this state, it will be necessary for her to be taken away as soon as the fact is ascertained.[141]

The mission of Urania Cottage did not permit parturient women to stay, most likely out of fear that other women would begin to see this as a place as an alternative to the workhouse during pregnancy.

> In this case, I shall be obliged, most reluctantly to turn her upon your hands again. As the matter would necessarily be painful to Miss Coutts and Mrs Marchmont, the lady who superintends the Home is naturally uneasy about it, I have directed her, if her misgivings should be confirmed to write to Mr Welsh and ask him to remove the unfortunate object of your sympathy. If she should not be in the family-way after all (which I earnestly hope she may not be), then we need do nothing.[142]

Mayne's pregnancy forced Mrs Marchmont to ask her to leave. The matron sent the young woman to her mother, who lived near Leighton Buzzard, Buckinghamshire. After spending some time there, the young woman reappeared in London in an advanced stage of pregnancy. Apparently, both Mr and Mrs Hardwick retained their faith in Susan throughout her confinement because after returning to London, the Hardwicks continued to provide her with ten shillings per week for expenses and they paid for her lodgings. Hardwick withdrew the funds out of the poor box for her. According to the Foundling Hospital investigator Mr Twiddy, this money was under the magistrate's control.[143] Mayne's benefactors even provided a recommendation letter and paid a subscription to secure her admission to Queen Charlotte's Lying-in Hospital. If the governors and matrons believed the unwed mother respectable (after medical examinations, an interview, and close observation of her behaviour), they might encourage her to make out an application at the Foundling Hospital for her infant.

Understanding the strict rules by which the Foundling Hospital operated under Mr Brownlow, Hardwick appealed to Mrs Marchmont.[144] In a note to Mr Twiddy, enquirer at the Foundling, Marchmont observed that Mr

Hardwick 'was very desirous to benefit the poor girl'.[145] She also claimed that Susan had not been aware she was pregnant.[146] The matron's misgivings prompted her to write a note to Dickens, who was exhausted by his post as almoner and ready to resign his position at Urania Cottage before making his way towards Folkestone for a Channel crossing to France.[147] By the time Dickens had received the letter, he was about to cross the English Channel. One of the last things he attended to, before leaving, was to respond to her urgent request for help:

> As there is no form of the Foundling Hospital for me to sign in Susan M.'s behalf, I do not feel it right to address the Hospital authorities on the subject. But in case of you desiring to help with a spoken word, you have my full authority to ask for Mr Brownlow at the Institution and to tell him that we know the girl . . . [Illegible word] who is [illegible word] trying to recover herself, and that we can honestly recommend her application if any recommendation be ever desired. You can show Mr Brownlow this letter if you please, and explain to him how we come to know the case from Mr Hardwick at Marlborough Street having felt a strong compassion for the poor girl, and having carefully enquired into her statements.[148]

In short, Mayne's benefactors, the Hardwicks, Dickens and the prototypical social worker Marchmont, suggested a way to relieve Mayne of her illegitimate baby. Susan's initiative in the matter remains unclear. At some point, she agreed to petition the Foundling Hospital with the consequence that her 'character' came under further intense scrutiny. Her packet includes a statement from Queen Charlotte's Lying-in Hospital, wherein medical officers revealed another flaw. 'She had venereal disease upon her, but she denied that fact… [and] that she also declared that she did not know who the father of her child really was.'[149] The Queen Charlotte matron added that Susan's conduct was less than respectable while she domiciled there. In fact, her demeanour raised strong doubts, as to her ability to shake off the 'dissipated habits formerly contracted, and which were still evidently clinging to her'.[150] In addition to the medical complications, the Foundling Hospital enquirer had uncovered several disturbing elements in her past. Purportedly, Susan had been living with Mr Rogers, an American. Foreigners were always problematic in terms of the Foundling Hospital investigation. If the mother was English, and then, the father was Italian, German, French, American or Irish, the committee framed these men as unscrupulous characters who had taken advantage of the petitioner. Worse, in reconstructing Susan's story the committee discovered circumstances that offset their usual sympathy for an English woman seduced by a foreigner. She had been living with Rogers at 70

Gower Street, who, finding himself in financial straits, 'decamped carrying off the furniture, leaving the rent unpaid'.[151] After leaving London, the police published Mr Rogers' name in the newspaper for bankruptcy. Then her story took another twist, as Susan finally confessed to Foundling Hospital enquirer Mr Twiddy that Rogers was not the father of her child. Instead, she reported a medical student at Charing Cross Hospital, Mr Mitchell, held that distinction. Despite Charles Dickens's recommendation, Mr Twiddy doggedly focused on Susan's character, indicating the fate of her infant was not the issue. The governors denied the request for the admission of the hapless baby.[152]

For every woman who received the sorts of 'charitable' assistance offered to Susan M., there were thousands left with only the barest of support structures, namely the workhouse. Nevertheless, her story makes no mention of any interaction with the guardians of the poor. Therefore, we may assume she had no need to apply to the guardians of the poor for aid. If Susan M. was truly a prostitute, a streetwalker or regularly picked up by the police, then authorities would have taken harsher measures against her. Immediately, this raises more questions about her case. She was one of seven surveyed-Foundling Hospital petitioners who had delivered a baby at Queen Charlotte's Lying-in Hospital, to be rejected. Dickens admitted her to a home supported by the second wealthiest woman in Britain. Her Foundling Hospital recommendations arrived from a magistrate and Dickens, a hospital benefactor. Nonetheless, the Foundling Hospital committee denied her petition.

Throughout this narrative the voice of Susan Mayne, the woman about whom so many notables concerned themselves, is never heard. Something seems to be missing in this story that cannot be finished with the available information. Nonetheless, her case makes critical points by clearly highlighting the 'character test'. Venereal disease unquestionably disqualified her case. Such questions, not only surrounding the mothers' characters but also their medical conditions, weighed heavily on the Foundling Hospital committee minds. The men appear almost intransigent in this case, even when recommendations from highly respected individuals or institutions weighed in with recommendations on behalf of the mother. Perhaps, this case marks a transition from simply judging a mother's character to assisting her. Instead of placing the full burden on the woman, investigators started to make an effort to bring the law to bear on the disreputable father by taking her case to the magistrate. In short, however, the out-of-wedlock infant rendered the mother improvident in the eyes of the hospital committee and prevented her from challenging their judgement.

The women who wished to give up their infants and who met the stringent requirements for admission were the exception; they fit their lives into the Victorian calculus of respectability for women and the family. Many other petitions did not rise to this standard. Yet, the petitions indicate most mothers made rational choices in order to preserve their 'characters'.[153] The applicants acted to protect themselves. Despite the constraints of their situation, they knew why they had chosen to appeal to the Foundling Hospital; and could they generally explain their actions. The mothers worked and wrestled with meeting the requirements for their infants' admission and then giving up their babies. Although we may not be able to uncover the full implications of the mothers' decisions, their strategies demonstrate a constrained agency. The mother reached a crucial point in her personal life when 'something had to be done'. How many felt as did the petitioner who said: 'The whole [thing] seems some times a burden greater than I fear.'[154] Their life changing problems were untenable in the eyes of their families, and society. Further, their situation complicated their economic aspirations. One act smeared their character for life. Thus, they gave up their infants to retain their 'respectability', In this way, the mothers received the benefits of an elite Victorian charity. The day they relinquished the infant to the hospital marked a painful end filled with bitter regret and hope. In looking to the future, the restoration of their character permitted them to return to their former station in life, resume their duties in a decent job, and anticipate a respectable marriage.

7

'Dear Mr Brownlow, Will You Please Tell Me… '

The Foundling Hospital required more than a powerful recommendation to approve a petition. Despite the extensive acclaim of his writing, Dickens wielded only a limited amount of social and moral capital with this institution. Although his novels and the journal *Household Words* focused on problems facing unmarried mothers and children, and he also contributed proceeds of his works to the Foundling Hospital; his intervention could not rescue the character of a young woman if she had an infectious disease or demonstrated sexual improprieties beyond the first fall. That Dickens had an intimate first-hand perspective of the estate's day-to-day activities is patently clear, as he not only reflects on the poor laws, but also on the Foundling Hospital in his work. Apparently, the Foundling Hospital and its mission haunted Dickens until the end of his life. The frustrations of abandoning one's child to the nurse mother on receiving day are fictionalized in *No Thoroughfare*, which address Foundling Hospital rules that prohibited mothers from visiting their children without an appointment. Naturally, the hospital had not invited the mothers to chapel services. Some, reportedly tried to return to the chapel on Sundays to see if they could spot their child among the choristers. Dickens writes:

> Well! One day when we took Pet to church there to hear the music – because, as practical people, it is the business of our lives to show her everything that we can to please her – Mother [my usual name for Mrs Meagles] began to cry so, that it was necessary to take her out. 'What's the matter, Mother?'
>
> When I saw all those children ranged tier above tier, and appealing from the father none of them has ever known on earth, to the great Father of us all in Heaven, I thought, does any wretched mother ever come here, and look among those young faces, wondering which is the poor child she brought in to this forlorn world, never through all its life to know her love, her kiss, her face, her voice, even her name! Now that was practical in Mother and I told her so.[1]

Dickens published his novella, 'No Thoroughfare', in *The Christmas Stories from All the Year Round* in 1868.[2] In this narrative, he elaborated on the challenges of giving up an infant and the resulting mother's obsession. The account begins with a young mother standing at the porter's gates on Guilford Street waiting for a matron to exit on her way home from work. The anxious mother offered the worker two guineas for a piece of information – the name of her child. Those who knew the institutional rules recognized this transgression immediately; the young woman had overstepped her boundaries. Her relentless quest placed the Foundling Hospital worker under duress to the point she revealed the name 'Walter Wilding'. Years later the same woman appeared in the dining hall where the Foundling children were seated having lunch at very long tables after Sunday chapel services. Again, she bribed a matron to identify the child associated with the name, Walter Wilding. Twelve years had passed, when the desperate mother, who had since married and was now widowed, appeared at the door of Walter's wine company, Wilding and Company, located in the City. The mother applied for a position as housekeeper. The man she thought to be her son, Walter, accepted her into his home. Ultimately, she discovered the infant she had abandoned to the hospital had been adopted by other parents. The name, Walter Wilding, had been re-assigned. The search for the lost child, who, the mother thought to be living, tormented her and Dickens as well, obviously, or he would not have penned the story.[3]

Dickens' accounts of the Foundling Hospital surely fuelled the anxieties of labourers and domestics who could read and perhaps even write. Based on a general survey of the extensive collection of working-class autobiographies collated and documented by John Brunett and David Vincent at Brunel University, women's literacy is unique and different from male counterparts. In the accounts, we see stories of work and survival, but most do not reveal deeply personal perspectives.[4] While literacy, especially among women, proves difficult to measure until after passage of the 1870 Education Act, the Foundling Hospital papers give us a glimpse into this mode of personal communication. By counting and then measuring each mother's ability to sign her own name and assessing mothers' letters to Mr Brownlow, we can arrive at a clearer and more certain understanding of an increasingly valuable skill set for respectable domestic servants. Significantly, the petition form did not allocate a line or space for the mother's signature. Yet it appears someone asked her to sign at the bottom of the page. Some mothers placed an 'X' there; others tried to sign. The signatures show some writers as novices with decidedly unrefined and shaky handwriting, while others were more proficient. The ability to read, to sign one's name, or even to complete the application form, sets one petitioner apart from another, especially in light of the low educational expectations for working class women in the nineteenth century.

Table 7.1: All FH Mothers' Literacy Rates, 1842–92[5]

Literacy	N	Capability %
Independently completed petition	1	.30
Signed own name	301	88.70
Signed with an 'X'	54	11.00
Total	356	100.00

Table 7.1 shows 88.7 per cent of all petitioners capable of signing. By 1880, according to Table 7.2, virtually 100 per cent of the candidates surveyed could sign their name. Few signatures matched the handwriting on the remainder of the form, suggesting others may have been involved in this part of the process. The signatures on many forms appear to have been signed with the same style of handwriting, indicating a verbal assent to the veracity of the information provided on the form.[6]

Table 7.2: Percentage Change in FH Petitioners' Ability to Sign Name, 1860–92[7]

Literacy	1860–9 ability to sign name %	1870–9 ability to sign name %	1880–92 ability to sign name %
Signed with signature	96	95.7	100
Signed with an 'X'	4	4.3	0

Despite increasing reliance on professional recommendations and legal investigation, between the dates on which the mother submitted her application and the dates on which the Foundling Hospital received her baby ranged from 1.5 months in the 1860s to 2.2 months in the 1870s, as indicated in Table 7.3. The waiting ended in the nineteenth century with a letter via the postal service informing mothers whether the Foundling Hospital committee would accept her infant. On receiving day, she received the following instructions:

> Let this Paper be carefully kept, that it may be produced whenever an enquiry is made after the health of the Child, (which may be done on Mondays, between the Hours of Ten and Four) and also in case the Child should be claimed.[8]

Table 7.3: FH Application Process, Length of Time, 1842–92[9]

Decade	N	Mean time for application process
1842–9	97	1.7 months
1850–9	109	1.7 months
1860–9	50	2.2 months
1870–9	46	1.5 months
1880–92	54	2.1 months

The personal number served as the official identity marker for the child and assured parents who attempted to reclaim their child they were receiving their offspring.[10] The mother relinquished her parental rights and, in turn, the law absolved the child of its traditional responsibilities for the welfare of aging parents. Acting in *loci parentis,* the hospital governors retained legal guardianship over the foundling until he or she reached 21 years of age.[11]

In 1856, Foundling Hospital bylaws stipulated the child could not be over one year of age when the admission process started.[12] Committee men also stipulated the infant could not be younger than three months of age before admission, as newborns were less viable. In some cases, the babies died before admission. Table 7.4 shows the age of infants recorded on the petition fluctuated from 3.7 months to 4.5 months between 1842 and 1869; and then rose to over six months in the 1870s. The notable rise in ages most likely occurred because increasingly, mothers received guidance from women's charities who advised them to wait in order to improve their infant's viability.

Table 7.4: FH Infants' Age at Time of Mothers' Petition Application, 1842–92[13]

Decade	N	Infant's Age at Application Time
1842–9	97	4.5 months
1850–9	109	4.8 months
1860–9	50	3.7 months
1870–9	46	6.7 months
1880–92	54	6.2 months
	356	

The ability to sign one's own name is a minor achievement in comparison to the ability to express one's concerns in writing. Many mothers, who crossed the threshold of the Guilford Street gate and handed their baby over to the open arms of the waiting nurse mother, suffered from more than post-partum depression, they grieved the loss of their infant. This sorrow reveals itself in heartfelt requests for help from Mr Brownlow. Although emotional histories prove difficult to gauge in terms of a working-class mother's attachment to her infant, the freedom of expression, sense of liberation, and palliative experience that comes with being able to write about one's emotional state appears to have been highly valuable. Perhaps, this was most true because – as we should be reminded repeatedly, poor working-class mothers did not have time to keep a diary or regularly write letters to family, lovers and friends. They were working.[14]

Significantly, however, mothers' letters to Mr Brownlow provide rare glimpses into their hearts; and they emphasize agency along with the rational sacrifices she made on behalf of their infant. In sum, for women, the ability to write opened a door to access information about their child, whom they consciously chose to abandon. Indeed, for these women, literacy is a sign they valued the ability to read, write and speak for oneself, which created new possibilities for self-expression. By measuring and exploring the link between literacy as a form of self-expression and taking mothers' letters as a primary source, we will find heretofore-unknown insights to the hearts and minds of London maids. The notes date between 1857 and 1873. The secretary kept them on a spindle. Archivists tied up the letters with red ribbon; they were dusty with coal soot and unlikely to have been touched, as many stuck together until the 1990s. These letters concretize the realities facing the mothers and reveal their inner most concerns. Their communications arrived on irregular and misshapen pieces of paper, sometimes nothing more than a mere corner of a larger sheet, indicating scarcity of writing materials. Most importantly, the letters reveal the many turns of fate a Foundling Hospital mother could encounter.

Some mothers, when given the opportunity to give up their infant, refused the offer. For example, Mary L. (aged 28) received a favourable recommendation: 'I have known Mary L. this seven years and… she is in great distress and without means of supporting her child.'[15] When the time came to part from her infant, she declined. Her recommender wrote to the Foundling Hospital secretary: 'Mary L. presents her duty to the gentlemen of the foundling and feeling she can not part from her child she must respectfully decline their kindness.'[16] Some women delayed the admission process because of their reluctance to part with their infants, as in the case of Hannah R. (aged 31). The Foundling Hospital enquirer reported she willingly answered all the questions put to her. Yet, she was 'deeply distressed at the thought of parting with her child'. She told the enquirer she had put off her application from month-to-month in hopes of finding a way to support both her child and herself. In light of her failing health, the petitioner relinquished her infant who was then less than four months of age. Hannah fretfully anticipated the 'doom and miseries of the workhouse'. If she gave up her baby, she would be able to recover her lost 'situation'. No less important, she 'might become reconciled with her family', who had entirely 'discarded her'.[17]

The petitions indicate that several times a year an accepted baby died before its reception at the hospital. When Agatha A. found herself pregnant, she went to the St Mary Magdalene Home on Weymouth Street. As her confinement approached, she moved to Queen Charlotte's Lying-in Hospital for delivery. The matron arranged for her to enter the Institution for the Protection of Destitute Young Women after she delivered her baby at Queen Charlotte's. While waiting to hear whether the committee had accepted her petition, the baby became gravely ill. Sister Maria from St Mary Magdalene's wrote to Mr Brownlow for the petitioner. 'Sister Maria will be very glad to know if the reception of Agatha A.'s child can be put off for a time, it was to have been received on the 23rd but it is now in a precarious state.' Sister Maria said she did not expect the baby to live. Nonetheless, she reported, 'it will be a sad thing for the mother to part with it, not knowing whether it will live from one hour to the other'.[18]

Most women appeared extremely grateful for the opportunity the hospital had given them and their infant. For example: 'Sir, I beg to thank you for receiving my child and hope to have it safely installed in your valuable institution upon the date fixed in your letter and at the time named.'[19] Mothers who wrote within the first month after reception of their baby addressed the notes to 'Mr Brownlow'. In some cases, women expressed gratitude to the Foundling Hospital Board of Governors because the institution had given their children a chance to survive. For example, one mother wrote from Fitzroy Square: 'May I Sir, still ask one, favour, if you would kindly write to me, that I may know how she is I should indeed feel very grateful trusting you will pardon me.'[20] Another mother wrote: 'May God Spare and Bless my little Foundling is the prayer of his unhappy Mother.'[21] This short appeal reflects the mother's emotional attachment coupled with a desire to maintain a semblance of responsibility for her offspring.

Besides maintaining their respectability, mothers had other reasons to seek shelter for their infant, namely high infant mortality rates caused by epidemic diseases. Pernicious and contagious outbreaks of cholera prompted successful petitioners to write enquiring about the health of their child. If the infant died, the Foundling Hospital secretary informed the birth mother of its expiration. Upon hearing of the demise of her child, one mother responded in the following sophisticated and deeply spiritual way:

> I beg to acknowledge the receipt of your letter the 7th of June. I am truly grieved and pained to hear of the death of my dear little girl but in the midst of my grief I am consoled that that dear little spirit is happy forever. It has please[d] [G]od [*sic*] to take her to himself, and she is now spared from all her troubles and trials of this life.
>
> I do feel it very much but I shouldn't ought to sorrow over it since I was deprived of her presence. I can rest as[s]ured [*sic*] that she is now with Jesus. She has a new and happy home, I trust it will be the reason of often leading my thoughts to heaven where I know I have one so near and dear to me.
>
> I hope [G]od [*sic*] is working all these trials together affording everlasting good with many thanks Sir for all your kindness and attention to my dear little girl.
>
> I remain Sir your obedient servant Sarah T.[22]

The rules informed mothers who wished to enquire or visit that they needed to provide the information inscribed on the piece of parchment, which they had received in exchange for their infant. The slip of paper held the date of reception and the child's private letter. Few mothers, unlike Dickens' protagonist in *No Thoroughfare*, ever learned the names of their children. The parchment offered the only token of existence for the mother.[23] Letter after letter followed the same pattern. Mothers' poignantly referred to their lost children, not by their given name but as, my 'child', or my 'Dear Darling'. One mother wrote: 'Dear Mr Brownlow, Will you please tell me of the welfare of my child.'[24] Others categorized their babies by sex, asking: 'May I trouble you again to let me know how the Female Child F is, and if it is a healthy baby.' Another queried: 'Will you kindly inform me of the health of my child born Feb. 7th, 1869 Male (private letter B), entered the Foundling Hospital May 3rd, 1869.'[25]

On the other hand, some continued to refer to their infants by the names they had given them at baptism. For example:

> Just a line from Hannah D. To know how her dear child is going on her Name is Jessy May Margaret D. Who ent[e]r[e]d [*sic*] the Hospital July the 14th. Her private letter is K. Hannah D. will feel very much obliged to you sir for a reply, your obedient servant, Hannah D.[26]

A letter from Sarah P. expressed a mother's anxiety regarding her infant's new nurse mother or country mother. 'I do hope this woman is strong.'[27]

Occasionally, matrons from reformatories such as Allesley Reformatory in Coventry wrote on behalf of the mothers who left their infants with the Foundling Hospital.

> Would you kindly at your convenience write me a line, stating how the female infant admitted on the 7th January is, I copy the mark V. The mother, Ann F. is fretting about her, so I hope you will kindly excuse the liberty I have teken [*sic*] in troubling you so early. I remain your humble Servant, Charlotte E. W., Matron[28]

Employers sympathizing with their wet-nurses wrote as well:

> Harriet M. a young woman whose child was admitted into the Foundling Hospital, I think, at the beginning of November [of this year] is very anxious to know whether her child is well or no-If it is not contrary to rule would you kindly send me only one line in the enclosed envelope stating how the child is. I confess I feel many scruples in thus troubling you, but I am aware the young woman is very anxious to receive some tidings and I checked a friend making a similar application on her behalf two weeks ago since thinking it unreasonable that the enquiry should be made so shortly after the child had been admitted.[29]

Mothers expressed their emotional disposition and realistic fears about their infants' chances for in incomplete thoughts and sentences. 'It is a female child received in the Foundling the 21st of March 1859 on my paper the letter H.'[30] Clara H., whose cursive letters were formed by a very shaky hand, wrote: 'Will you be so kind as to tell me how my poor Child is though it is a child of shame I Still have got a Mother's love for it.'[31] Another chastened mother expressed hopes her son would be an obedient child. Although he was a friendless orphan, she prayed he would not end up 'like his unhappy Mother'.[32] Some of the regular correspondence arriving week-after-week reflected the rulings of the Foundling Hospital by-laws, which entitled mothers to enquire about the health of their child, nothing more. Not surprisingly, mothers of older foundlings continued to be concerned with their child's welfare and projected hopes and fears about their growth and progress. They wanted to know if their children were walking and talking like other children of the same age; some now childless women vicariously experienced the growth of their child. One, M.G. wrote:

> Sir, alltough [*sic*] I am only allowed, to ask after his health, I take the liberty to beg You, if You can inform me, if he can Walk and Speak, or if he is a

> backward or forward Child on the 6 of May he was 2 Years old, and I should like so mush [*sic*] to know, what kind of Child he is; those that saw him, thought him so peculiar.[33]

An average of eight women per week took advantage of the opportunity to visit the Foundling Hospital on Monday between the hours of 10 a.m. and 4 p.m. in the hopes of getting a glimpse of their child.[34] One woman wrote to the secretary apologizing for missing the appointed visiting hours. 'I was ten minutes too late and compelled to go to… [A] situation.... [at] the above address the same day,' Ann A.[35] One mother begged the secretary's pardon for taking the liberty of coming up with the following proposal, in which she offered to pay ten shillings a quarter to see her child three times a year.

> I hope you will pardon the liberty I have taken. I wish to know if I could see my child about three times a year if I was to Pay 10 Shillings a quarter in your hands… I should not wish to make myself known to my child as I know it would be against rules also unhappyness [*sic*] to the child. All I should wish would be for the child to be shown to me and for me to speak to her it is a female child received in the Foundling the 21 of March 1859 on my paper the letter H. I called last Monday to ask after the Child's Health and Should of spoken to you then but my courage failed me. Sir if this should not be alowed [*sic*] would you be kind enought [*sic*] to write to me. I am receiving good wages and have been in my place two years last [M]ay [*sic*]. [S]o I should feel most happy to give the trifle. Will you favour me by put[t]ing [*sic*] the answer in this envelope as I do not wish anyone to know [w]here [*sic*] the Letter comes from. With gratitude from your Humble Servant, Mary W.[36]

At the time, Mary W.'s child was about three years of age when she wrote her letter. Clearly, she confessed to her anxiety and hoped for relief from guilt, trying desperately to assuage her 'fall from grace'. Another mother writing to Brownlow stated her little boy was nine years of age:

> I hope the gentlemen will pardon this liberty but as the mother of a little boy name[d] John B. woich [who] [*sic*] is blind praying that you will grant me permis[s]hion [*sic*] to see him. [I]t is my husbands wish as well as my own. [I]t is truly hard a mother can n[e]iver [*sic*] forget [ou]ar [*sic*] first born. . . . My husband is a respfulabile [*sic*] man [.] [H]e [h]as been in [h]is master[']s servi[ce] [his master's service] [*sic*] 9 years and we can both get good c[h]ar[a]cters [*sic*]. I remain, Sir Your humble serv[a]int [*sic*], Anne B., 37 Ludgate Hill, Housekeeper.[37]

If a mother could not find her way to the chapel on Sunday morning to see her maturing child, she might be inclined to ask for material evidence such as a lock of hair or, later in the century, a photograph of her child.

> Clara H. is very anxious to know if her dear child is still living and in good health and whether it is now at the Hospital and if Mr Brownlow would be so kind as to let her know what name the child has and whether he would kindly have his likeness taken and send to Clara H. if she sent money to pay for it if so would be very thankfull [*sic*] and would pay for it as soon as she received it or would send the money before if he would be so kind as it is my earnest wish there is no number on the parchiment [*sic*] only the E – it was admitted March 22nd 1858.[38]

Most mothers, like Mary W., exhibited humility and deference in addressing the Foundling Hospital secretary.

> Will you at your convenience let me know if she still lives, and whether she is and has been well? I hope you will not attribute my long silence to indifference, my principal reason for not writing has been, the fear of counting too much on your generosity.[39]

From Kent Villa in Margate, one mother complained that she did not know her daughter was no longer living on the Foundling Hospital estate. She claimed deep disappointment 'when I found a stranger had taken her out of your Institution, as I had hoped to have taken her myself. Will you be so kind as to ease my mind by telling me where she is and with whom?'[40] Judging by her private letter and admission date, Amelia's child would have been 15 years of age at the time of the mother's query and serving her apprenticeship.[41] Others returned after many years abroad to find out what they could about their child they left behind. Some mothers had returned to London from as far away as Australia to see or get some information about their child.[42]

The emotional damage caused by separation was not limited to birth mothers. Nurse mothers also formed attachments to their surrogate children as a letter from the daughter of a former nurse attests:

> It is by my mother's request I am taking the grate [*sic*] liberty in writing to you asking you to favour her by letting her know how her little girl is Jane W. [A]lso if she may come in the country for a few weeks, my mother thinks it would improve her health and she would be greatly pleased in having her little company once again. Your humble servant, Mrs W. C.[43]

The nurse mothers also watched the infants die. Dr Piddock wrote:

> I ought to have written yesterday to tell you that the other little twin No. 20797 Margaret N. died on Saturday in a convulsion. The poor nurse is in great grief having lost her own infant the same evening from teething. I will post a receipt for the last payment on Friday.[44]

While nurse mothers could always return to the Foundling Hospital and visit their surrogate children and the foundlings permitted to return to their country mothers' homes, rules denied birth mothers this privilege. As witnessed, this did not mean the mother was unaffected by the trauma caused by the loss of her child. In describing the infant's arrival, Dickens wrote:

> Then they departed, and we saw the children. One was a boy; the other a girl. A parchment ticket inscribed with the figures 20,563 was sewn upon the shoulder strap of the male infant.[45]

Received A Blank Child

As soon as the baby arrived, the vicar baptized the infant while their wet-nurses or nurse mothers held it in their arms. The steward, matron, schoolmaster and head nurse witnessed the ceremonial blessing.[46] The secretary then renamed the new arrival, working through a list of names alphabetically. In the early years, the foundlings received names of notables drawn from history, fiction and contemporary life, including those of hospital governors. Problems arose when London society began to associate names affiliated with the hospital with the stigma of illegitimacy. Moreover, protests arose from several wealthy benefactors when mature foundlings appeared on their doorstep claiming descent. These naming complications forced the Foundling Hospital to change strategies by selecting forenames from the Bible and surnames from London street directories.[47]

From its earliest days, Jonas Hanway outlined and implemented wet nursing practices at the Foundling Hospital; this system continued into the nineteenth using the same countryside women from Kent and Surrey. The wet-nurses were more appropriately known as 'nurse mothers', or 'country mothers'. The names ascribed to these women suggests they not only served as food sources, but took on responsibilities for early childhood training. Records also indicate that the occupation of nurse mother may have been passed down from mother to daughter. Regulations prohibited the lactating mother from maintaining more than one nursing infant, but she could have other foundlings living with her.[48] The wet-nurse took the infant to the countryside within 24 hours of the reception. The relative success of this arrangement made the Foundling Hospital a model for other institutions that provided infant care. Although these practices reduced infant mortality rates and proved costly, by 1801, the estate had enough funds from investments to compensate the nurse mothers.[49] The institution enforced the strict rules and regulations for the surrogate mothers, by placing them under the supervision of an 'Inspectress of Nursemothers'. She travelled throughout the countryside visiting home-by-home to ensure the safety of the infants. The inspectress also recruited wet-nurses, who needed to be certified as healthy and free of syphilis. The 'nurse supervisor' resided within a three-mile radius of the homes of her charges in order to provide close supervision of residences and nursing practices. She also oversaw the treatment and health of infants and children, making sure that children received their proper vaccinations. The inspectress communicated in writing to the secretary about health difficulties or problems with the infants or nurse mothers. She was responsible for maintaining the security of the Foundling Hospital's copy of the parchment and private number, the only forms of identification provided for the infant upon admission to the Foundling.[50] The number of cases supervised by the matron determined her salary. She received 10s. 6d. annually for each nurse mother and child under her supervision.[51]

As pay mistress, the inspectress certified the women who took in infants could not be on parish relief because the stigma would cast them as disreputable members of the community, and they could also be accused of 'double-dipping', so to speak. The hospital paid nurse mothers, who traveled up to London to pick up an infant, a handsome four shillings for transportation and expenses. She also received six pence a day or £1 2s. per month for nursing the infant. If the nurse mother proved reliable, she received a bonus of ten shillings at the end of the year. The Hospital paid nurse mothers an additional 14–18 shillings for the second to fifth year of the child's life.[52] By 1870 they received £1 2s. 2d. per month, plus a £1 5s. gratuity at the end of the first and third years of the child's life.[53]

Nineteenth-century investigators found infant feeding practices and the reward system offered to the nurse mothers resulted in higher infant and child survival rates than at other institutions. Nonetheless, wet-nursing and toddler care at the Foundling Hospital was not as successful as managers would have liked others to believe. According to an 'in-house admissions register,' 26 per cent of the foundlings died in 1842.[54] In the cholera year of 1848, 17 per cent died; the lower percentages most likely occurred because small children were removed from London to Kent and Surrey and the Foundling Hospital received its water supply from a source in North London. In 1856 and 1866, however, the foundlings fared little better than other newborns and children under five years of age living in St George in the East. The loss of foundlings in those years amounted to 46 per cent and 42 per cent respectively. In 1858 in St George in the East, 53.29 per cent of all children under five years of age died. In 1866, 47.45 per cent of all children under five years of age died.[55] Up until the 1890s, the hospital, like other domiciliary institutions, struggled desperately to preserve the foundlings. Table 7.5 shows an average of 33 per cent of infants and children admitted at the Foundling Hospital died between 1842 and 1867.

Mortality rates for infants and children remained high for the next quarter of a century; those figures for 1868–92 fell by 30 per cent. A perceptible decline in the rates did not occur until 1893 when only 10 per cent died, but

Table 7. 5: Mortality Rates among FH Admissions, 1842–93[56]

Admission Yr	**Admitted N**	**Died N**	**Mortality %**	**Admission Yr**	**Admitted N**	**Died N**	**Mortality %**
1842	38	10	26	1868	63	26	41
1843	47	10	21	1869	44	13	30
1844	39	12	31	1870	39	16	41
1845	57	20	35	1871	51	20	39
1846	36	15	42	1872	43	13	30
1847	38	16	42	1873	32	7	22
1848	30	5	17	1874	65	17	26
1849	21	5	24	1875	32	9	28
1850	30	14	47	1876	39	17	44
1851	37	10	27	1877	31	15	48
1852	48	11	23	1878	47	12	26
1853	45	14	31	1879	42	17	40
1854	29	8	28	1880	46	19	41
1855	32	14	44	1881	48	12	25
1856	37	17	46	1882	49	12	24
1857	44	13	30	1883	44	13	30
1858	53	21	40	1884	46	13	28
1859	57	18	32	1885	37	11	30
1860	46	13	28	1886	29	6	21
1861	22	6	27	1887	40	13	33
1862	49	14	29	1888	57	13	23
1863	41	13	32	1889	45	12	27
1864	36	19	53	1890	50	11	22
1865	58	17	29	1891	32	10	31
1866	71	30	42	1892	27	5	19
1867	60	26	43	1893	48	5	10
1842–67	1101	371	33% avg	1868–93	1126	337	30% avg

the figure might have been an anomaly because the preceding year 19 per cent had died. In 1871 at the Infant Life Protection Act hearings, George Burrow Gregory, MP and Foundling Hospital treasurer, testified about mortality rates at the Foundling Hospital. Gregory told the Select Committee on Protection of Infant Life the infant mortality rate stood at about 9.5 per cent for the years 1861 to 1870.[57] When Gregory returned to complete his testimony, he retracted this number and said the rate for infants under one year of age was 16 per cent.[58] According to Gregory's 'in-house register' report, prepared for public consumption, mortality fluctuated from a low of 7 percent in 1863 to a high of 31 percent in 1867, with an average of 16 percent per year.

Table 7.6: Reported FH Infants Received vs Infant Child Mortality, 1861–70[59]

Year	Infants Received	Reported Infant and Child Mortality N	Reported Infant and Child Mortality %
1861	22	2	9
1862	48	7	15
1863	41	3	7
1864	36	4	11
1865	58	11	19
1866	69	9	13
1867	61	19	31
1868	63	12	19
1869	44	7	16
1870	40	3	8
Total	482	77	16 % avg

Table 7.7 indicates, however, that overall mortality rates at the asylum remained significantly higher than Gregory suggested. Even so, fewer foundlings died at the Foundling than those children who remained with their parents in St George in the East, where the infant and child mortality rates ranked among the highest in the metropolis.

Though Hanway was responsible for the Foundling's wet-nursing practices, he opposed leaving the children under the nurse mothers' tutelage for too

Table 7.7: Actual FH Infants Received vs Infant and Child Mortality, 1861–70[60]

Year	Infants Received	Total Infant and Child Mortality N	Total Infant and Child Mortality %
1861	22	6	27
1862	49	14	29
1863	41	13	32
1864	36	19	53
1865	58	17	29
1866	71	30	42
1867	60	26	43
1868	63	26	41
1869	44	13	30
1870	39	16	41
Total	483	180	37 % avg

long. As a man who reflected the assumptions of his age, he contended if children remained with nurse mothers past their toddler years, they would not receive a proper Christian education because of their station in life and she lacked technical skills required to prepare children for apprenticeships. Therefore, at the age of five, nurse mothers relinquished their charges to the London estate. After children had arrived there, they received an extensive education. They learned to read the Bible and their catechism, as well as other amusing tracts. Hanway ensured boys could read, because he believed they possessed rational skills. He also insisted that boys should learn to write. Girls, he thought, were unlikely to benefit from such training, reflecting common gender biases. He warned against teaching girls to write because, in essence, the skill provided a medium of self-expression thought to be inappropriate for females. Hanway wanted children to learn to read with an objectivity, most significantly, so they would not fall prey to Roman Catholicism.[61] Hanway's eighteenth-century safeguards continued into the nineteenth century and meant Foundling Hospital children had little interaction with the outside world. As time progressed, the governors took on a far more protective attitude towards the children. Nonetheless, the institution aimed to teach and train the children to become faithful Anglicans with the requisite skills for life in London or the empire.[62]

Clock, calendar and high walls ruled daily life at the Foundling Hospital in a monastic fashion. When children returned to London, they began their formal education. A regular schedule of study and sleep structured their day. They rose at 6 a.m. in the summer and dawn in the winter. Older children aided the younger foundlings in washing and dressing. Twice a week the children received cold baths.[63] Girls helped to clean their rooms and the hallways, and the boys pumped water for the buildings. Some children worked in the kitchens. Cooks served breakfast at 7.30 a.m., lunch at 1 p.m., and dinner at 6 p.m. Students went to class in the morning and after lunch, remained there until 5 p.m. in the summer and dusk in the winter. Occasionally, matrons permitted them to go outdoors to play. At 8 p.m., the foundlings went to bed.[64] On Saturdays, students had a half-day off; and two or three times a year the boys were permitted to take an excursion to Primrose Hill, but the girls were at all times kept within the hospital walls.[65] Interestingly, Victorians believed that confining the foundlings behind the brick walls prevented the children them from attaining the normal height and size of adult men or women. The confinement, Edward Walford noted, tended to stunt the growth of the children.[66]

Inadequate nutrition may have been more responsible for the small frames than the limited social space in which they grew to young adulthood. Their diet included staples of bread and cheese, three meat meals, and one serving of suet pudding each week. The dietary made no mention of fruit or vegetables in 1810. The menu remained much the same throughout the nineteenth century, with the addition of potatoes and mutton in 1828. Medical doctors recommended 'good white bread' should be substituted for 'bread', presumably wholemeal bread then available to the working classes. Medical officers dropped oatmeal from the choices because it was 'deficient in nutriment'. Nonetheless, these same individuals believed oatmeal was good enough for paupers in the workhouse where it was the staple food.[67] Undoubtedly, they based their recommendations on scientific studies reflecting changing food tastes among the rising middle classes.

In 1840, a committee formed to re-examine the general accommodations and daily regimen of the foundlings. The reviewers recommended annual holidays should be observed and a 'Drill Master' should be appointed for improving the physique of the boys and girls.[68] Upon Brownlow's accession to the office of secretary, he made several changes in the educational system. Whereas boys were trained as tailors and girls in needlework, since children tailored their own uniforms, the new administrator discontinued this practical curriculum. Instead, reading, writing, mathematics and musical training received emphasis. The Foundling Hospital began to employ a full-time bandmaster and a drawing instructor. He brought girls' education up to par with boys. Several young women won academic distinctions, demonstrating their preparedness for college level work. Other girls were sent to the Foundling Hospital's own School of Domestic Economy.[69]

Not all children were healthy and normal. The Foundling Hospital accepted some children with disabilities, although it was not its original intent. The governors acknowledged because of the 'state of their mental or physical developments' a few children were unable to maintain themselves. Brownlow described the individuals with disabilities, 12 in all under his care, in the following way:

> They grow up as *objects out of sight*, which would, under other circumstances, become the fitting inmates of institutions appropriated to special cases. These individuals were 'idiotic, deformed, blind or otherwise unfit for labour'.[70]

Brownlow reported that in former years, many more individuals with disabilities had been supported by the hospital. Yet the institution, he argued, was ill-equipped to provide life-long care for any foundling, not to mention those with long-term needs. Therefore, he established a separate fund to serve the requirements of the mentally and physically challenged, the 'Benevolent Fund of the Foundling Hospital for Adults'. This innovation relieved the hospital of this burden.[71] The attention given to children and adults with disabilities during this era reflects well on the Foundling Hospital.

The secretary minimized this even more hidden mission of the Foundling Hospital in order to maintain a level of respectability that attracted wealthy and powerful individuals to Sunday services.[72] Confirmation day, however, was an exceptional celebration in the nineteenth century. Young graduates of the Foundling Hospital programme, who had been 'preserved' by the good graces of the governors, returned to give thanks.[73] Announcements for these affairs appeared in *The Times*:

> On Sunday next several young persons brought us in this hospital, who have recently come of age, will attend Divine service to the chapel, to return thanks to Almighty God for their preservation and education by means of the charity. The sermon in the morning will be preached by the Rev. W. P. Pearce, late preacher to Melbourne Cathedral, and the services commence at 11 and 3.30.[74]

After Confirmation, the protection of the hospital extended well beyond its walls when foundlings left the confines for apprenticeships. Finding places for young adults as they neared their majority was part of the secretary's responsibilities. Generally, the governors placed about 30 foundlings a year. They located positions with tradesmen or in wealthy households as domestic servants. Administrators actively protected the foundlings, making sure the apprentice master and mistress agreed to the terms, including wages and length of service.[75] They also kept an eye on the progress of their wards until they completed their apprenticeship. At the end of their programmes, the hospital gave the foundlings a financial reward, a 'handsome five guineas' for exceptional behaviour.[76] The clergyman distributed the gifts as part of Easter Sunday church services.[77] At this time, governors gave departing foundlings a parchment that identified their origins with the Hospital, stating: 'Be not ashamed that you were bred in this hospital. Own it: and say, that it was thought the good Providence of Almighty God, by which you were taken Care of. Bless him for it.'[78]

In terms of post-Foundling Hospital employment, the community identified the Foundling Hospital with music and musical training. Each year several men, 79 for the years 1842 to 1864, joined the military as instrumentalists. They played in military bands, including the Coldstream Guards, Marine Band, 74th Highlanders, and the Band of the 7th Hussars upon completion of their training. Four boys went into the military or navy at 15 years of age (1842–64).[79] Thirteen went to the Royal Navy. The Hospital found apprenticeships for 73 per cent. According to Table 7.8, a minor trend appeared in terms of young women sent to homes as domestic servants, as numbers rose and fell. Interestingly, the hospital placed the greatest numbers of young women as domestics a year or two before and for several years after the publication of *Little Dorrit* by Dickens in 1857.

After the women had entrusted their children to the Foundling Hospital, most mothers simply disappeared, never saw their infants again, and started their lives anew. Some, however, applied for the restoration of their children. Regulations prohibited any communication between the mother and her child during the apprenticeship period, unless both parent and child approved of this correspondence. The hospital also feared the birth mother would return after her child had matured, and upon finding her child self-supporting, garnish some of her foundling's wages. Birth mothers reclaimed about 3 per cent of the foundlings as shown in Table 7.9. This occurred only after the mother proved to the secretary that she had been suitably redeemed and was living a respectable lifestyle, and she could in no way stand to benefit materially from the restoration of her child. Occasionally committee men refused to release a child.[80] If a mother were to apply for reclamation, the hospital preferred this to occur before the child reached ten years of age; this was an effort to protect the foundling from an exploitative mother.[81] The secretary did not keep a record of the annual requests for restoration of foundlings. We only know how foundlings many the hospital restored to mothers. Over the study's 50-year

Table 7.8: FH Military and Domestic Service Appointments, 1842–64[82]

Admission Yr	Military N	Sea N	Apprenticed N	Service N	Total per year
1842	3	0	23	0	26
1843	4	0	30	0	34
1844	2	0	21	0	23
1845	6	0	29	0	35
1846	3	0	17	0	20
1847	5	0	14	0	19
1848	4	2	16	3	35
1849	4	0	11	0	25
1850	3	0	10	0	13
1851	4	2	18	0	24
1852	2	0	28	0	30
1853	0	1	25	3	29
1854	3	2	11	2	18
1855	3	3	9	2	17
1856	1	2	12	5	20
1857	4	0	22	3	29
1858	5	1	21	3	30
1859	0	0	30	6	36
1860	2	0	17	5	24
1861	1	0	12	1	14
1862	9	0	18	4	31
1863	9	0	15	0	24
1864	2	0	12	0	14
Total	79	13	421	37	570

span, the number of children restored to parents rose from 0 to 15 per cent in 1892, as the century neared its end.

The Foundling Hospital was not in the business of serving as an adoption agency, but people enquired nonetheless. One couple wrote: 'Having no

Table 7.9: FH Register, Admissions vs Restorations, 1842–92[83]

Admission Yr	**Admitted N**	**Restored N**	**Restored %**
1842	38	2	5
1843	47	3	6
1844	39	0	0
1845	57	1	2
1846	36	1	3
1847	38	3	8
1848	30	0	0
1849	21	1	5
1850	30	1	3
1851	37	1	3
1852	48	0	0
1853	45	2	4
1854	29	2	7
1855	32	1	3
1856	37	1	3
1857	44	1	2
1858	53	2	4
1859	57	2	4
1860	46	2	4
1861	22	2	9
1862	49	2	4
1863	41	3	7
1864	36	2	6
1865	58	3	5
1866	71	3	4

1867	60	3	5
1868	63	3	5
1869	44	3	7
1870	39	1	3
1871	51	0	0
1872	43	1	2
1873	32	1	3
1874	65	1	2
1875	32	2	6
1876	39	2	5
1877	31	0	0
1878	47	0	0
1879	42	0	0
1880	46	0	0
1881	48	2	4
1882	49	3	6
1883	44	5	11
1884	46	0	0
1885	37	0	0
1886	29	0	0
1887	40	2	5
1888	57	1	2
1889	45	0	0
1890	50	0	0
1891	32	2	6
1892	27	4	15
Totals	2179	77	3.5 % avg

children of our own, it is our wish to adopt a child and if permitted to take one from your institution.'[84] The couple owned and operated the Spring Hill Academy, a respectable school. Indeed, their reputations were impeccable. Secretary Brownlow must have replied in a sharp tone, because the couple responded in the following way:

> I am sorry we made a mistake in our ideas of the Foundling Hospital. We thought you received only those children found as they sometimes are in infancy, *totally* deserted *and disowned*. Would you be kind enough to inform me of whether there is any institution in London or elsewhere for the reception of such children?[85]

The Foundling Hospital occupied an ambiguous place in Victorian society. Its public image as a refuge for 'foundling' children persisted; while little mention of the mother emanated directly from the institution. Victorian society 'blanked' the respectable mothers from their minds in many more ways than their children. For most, it is easier to love and care for an infant, child, and even a tendentious teen. It is much more difficult to accept unconditional responsibility for adult problems. Which is why Charles Dickens should have titled one of his essays 'On Child Abandonment by Blank Mothers'. Training and education made it possible to reframe the heritage of the children. They were born at the Hospital. Thus, the institution erased not only the identities of the children but that also of the mothers. The application process, although not hidden from public view, demanded the mothers become blanks in their children's lives. They, of course, made this choice. The mother approached the gate on Guilford Street, pulled the bell, and requested a petition from the porter. If the committee accepted the petition, the Foundling Hospital restored the character of the fallen woman by erasing the most outward sign of her personal flaw, her child, by taking in on the '*Blank* day of *blank*... a *blank* child'.[86] That event marked one of personal triumph and sorrow for the mothers. By virtue of being a woman, she experienced the constraints of biology and society. The emotional state of motherhood, the desire to see one's child grow up, and the quest for understanding revealed in the letters to Mr Brownlow by women who made difficult choices, points to many complexities in their lives. This act, making application to the London Foundling Hospital, demonstrates a desire to exercise the power of choice in their own lives despite dire consequences. The women responded to the legal burdens placed upon them by the poor laws, legislation targeting children born out of wedlock, and a calculus of respectability. Their actions were a function of one of these factors. Further, when considering the alternatives, from self-induced abortion, infanticide, abandonment on the streets of London, sending one's infant to a baby farmer in order to continue working, the Foundling Hospital, one among many, offered the best for the duo's future. As they left the estate, without their babe in arms, the mothers knew full well that their child would receive adequate food, clothing, shelter, medical attention, an education, and preparation for adulthood.

Conclusion

During the nineteenth century the Foundling Hospital, situated in Bloomsbury among the town homes of London's West End, reshaped Britain's attitude towards charitable giving by serving as the ornament of the metropolis. It provided a model for other Victorian charities and even for poor law administrators rationalizing charitable donations based on a calculus of respectability. This equation assessed the mother's character; because respectable society wished to avoid the practice of indiscriminate almsgiving to the undeserving poor. This relates directly to the central question of this book. What did society say the poor deserved? This query underpins every chapter and case study explored in this work. To do this, *Victorian Women* examined social values, space and time to find answers; each analytical framework illustrated the rules by which a young Victorian woman's reputation would be judged and by which she would receive her just desserts.

During the poor law debates, repeated rude comments and questions relating to unwed mothers appeared; letting the public know just how low the mother without a father for her children ranked in society. This national conversation resulted in 1834 legislation that rolled back protections for mothers and their children; and it relieved fathers of traditional paternal responsibilities that had been in place since the reign of Elizabeth. Passage of the New Poor Laws profoundly increased a mother's responsibilities for her born-out-of-wedlock child. Once pregnant and cognizant of the ramifications of the jeopardy in which she found herself, a young woman made decisions regarding her own life and that of her soon-to-be-born baby. She struggled under the stigma imposed by society-at-large and the new social and political regimen, not only because she had broken the rules of traditional behaviour, but also because she could fall on the 'rates' by relying on the workhouse infirmary for her confinement. Only select women chose, as a last resort, to abandon their infants to the 'ornament of the metropolis', London's model charity. Letters and petitions received by the Foundling Hospital lucidly illustrate their survival strategies and draw attention to the interwoven personal narratives playing out across London's extremely diverse social and geo-political landscape.

The petitioning process at the hospital defined the requisite credentials for the respectable unwed mother who sought support of the committee men.

The calculus of respectability required the mother be willing to complete an application form; she had to be willing to go to court – not only the court held in the offices of the central building of the London Foundling Hospital, but later, as the century progressed, to the magistrates' court. Although we have no known first-hand accounts of how she felt after her grilling experience, we may surmise that she suffered humiliation and shame as they stood before the committee and answered the following questions: Where did you meet the father? Where were you working? Did you receive a promise of marriage? Did you give consent? How long had you known the father before criminal conversation occurred? Under what circumstances did criminal conversation occur? Did he give you drugs or alcohol? Did you tell anyone? Where were you confined? Can you provide witnesses? Do you have recommenders? Ultimately, they asked: If relieved of your infant, will you be able to return to supporting yourself in a respectable position?

Five cases illustrating the workings of the calculus of respectability include: Mary Griffiths, Susan Mayne, Elizabeth M., the waitress in the vegetarian restaurant, Sarah F. and Barbara F. Last on the list, but first among informal petitions, one that could be cast as 'everywoman's appeal' appears in the case of Barbara F., forming the anti-model. Her case outlined parameters, as defined by the Foundling Hospital governors and committee men that almost immediately disqualified her petition. Barbara could not meet the profile because she was 32 years of age, married, with five children, more or less abandoned by her husband. Unfortunately, she got pregnant through an affair that lasted but one night. She could not identify the father. Living on Gower Street, she went to St Pancras Workhouse for delivery of her infant. After two weeks at the infirmary, she began a search for help – walking just a few blocks south to the London Foundling Hospital. In order to draw attention to her case, she wrote a letter to Secretary Brownlow, seeking his direct intervention. Of course, the committee rejected her case.

The highly publicized child murder case of Mary Griffiths, a young woman from Wales who searched London for help with a sick infant in her arms, highlights a web of aid for the destitute: St Marylebone Workhouse, friends, employers, the Gladstone Home, Foundling Hospital and then the place of last resort, the Sisters of Charity of St Vincent de Paul at Carlisle Place. By now, the sheer desperation of many young women facing similar circumstances becomes quite evident. Not receiving satisfaction from her options, she went to Hyde Park with the babe in arms and laid her infant in the Serpentine, where it died. The courts tried Griffiths for child murder.

We can hear the silent scream of desperation in the Griffiths case, if only indirectly. Yet, we can follow the actions of Foundling Hospital women as though they had written about the events in their diaries. There is one case, in which we really cannot hear a voice, that of 'petitioner' Susan Mayne. Charles Dickens, the London Magistrate Hardwicke, and even the second wealthiest woman in Britain at the time, Baroness Angela Burdett-Coutts, supported her in time of need. Instead of her wishes, we read about the philanthropic initiatives of others who had her best interests at heart. Her case offers a sharply focused example of the stringent parameters and social power of respectable Victorian values. While notable recommenders could help a case, the woman herself had to meet the standards set by the committee at the Foundling. Finally, Mayne's primary role in the narrative showcases Dickens's intimate familiarity with the walled institute on Guilford Street illustrates the limits of his social power and the influence of the calculus of respectability.

Every transcript began with this seminal phrase: 'When first acquainted with the father I was a… general servant.' Elizabeth M., aged 22, worked as a waitress in a vegetarian restaurant in the City. Perhaps, we could claim this as a most typical case. She met the father of her child while passing on the street. She received a promise to marry before giving consent to 'criminal conversation'. Upon discovering she had become pregnant, the father left for America. Fortunately, Elizabeth found support through Miss Pye's Home for Unwed Mothers. Her petition was accepted. On the other hand, the petition in which we most clearly hear the voice of the mother originates with a governess. Sarah F. asked point-blank, 'is my own name really required' in one of her detailed and somewhat fabricated letters. Atypical by comparison, she was the mother who had broken most of the rules for the admission process. Nonetheless, the committee took pity on her, most likely because of her ability to read, write, and teach, skills that would permit her to, if relieved of her infant, return to a life of respectability. Of the 356 petitions explored in this analysis, Sarah's represents the only accepted case discovered in the dusty sooty stacks and stacks of petitions held in protective custody of the London Metropolitan Archives for the Thomas Coram Foundation, in which the petitioner circumvented the system and had her infant admitted. Her case proves that intellect, education, and ability to defend oneself were invaluable. By contrast, few women could muster the courage and wherewithal to meet the criteria of this esteemed institution as evidenced by the halted progress of the rejected petitions. Those who were not able to take their infants to the Foundling Hospital on receiving day clearly represented the widest majority of lone mothers struggling to survive the vagaries of life in Victorian Britain and warrant further measured investigation. In closing, consider the perspective offered by Margaret Atwood's 1985 conclusion to *The Handmaid's Tale*: 'As all historians know, the past is a great darkness, and filled with echoes. Voices may reach us from it; but what they say to us is imbued with the obscurity of the matrix out of which they come; and try as we may, we cannot always decipher them precisely in the clearer light of our own day.'

Appendices

Appendix 1: Probability Defined

Probability is: the likelihood of an event happening twice in a row (given it has a chance to happen twice) [P(E)] x [P(E)]. Statisticians use the 5 per cent convention to test the likelihood of an event occurring. Statisticians begin with the test of an event that they do not wish to occur, usually based on one in 20 odds or 19:1 against an event occurring. Only 5 per cent in the end will have the probability of occurring in this particularly way. Putting the statement another way, we can say that we are 95 per cent sure that the event will not occur in the end. The 5 per cent convention is 'low enough', and we can either ignore the event, or look for another event that we wish to occur.[1]

Using the Chi-square test produces a 'P-value'. The 'P-value' describes the certainty with which a statement can be made, or the probability of an event occurring. The Chi-square measurement describes the degree to which a hypothetical statement is true. Significance at .05, .01, .001, determines the degree to which cases are similar or dissimilar.

Probability Table
1.0 = Certainty that populations are exactly alike
.05 = Impossible that populations are exactly alike
.5 = Indeterminate whether populations are similar or dissimilar
>.5 = Likely that populations are similar
<.5 = Unlikely that populations are similar

Appendix 2: Foundling Hospital Petition Form

To the Mothers of such Children as are fit objects to receive the advantages of this institution:

The Committee of Governors meet every Saturday Morning at Ten o'clock at the Foundling Hospital, to receive and deliberate on Petitions praying for the admission of Children. Children can only be received into this Hospital upon personal application of the Mothers. Petitions must set forth the true State of the Mother's Case; for if any deception is used the Petition will be rejected, and the Child will not be received into the Hospital. No application can be received previous to the birth of the Child, or should the child be above Twelve Months old. No person need apply, unless she shall have previously borne a good Character for Virtue, sobriety, and Honesty. N.B. The above paragraph was changed in 1856 to the following:

No Child can be admitted unless the Committee is satisfied, after due enquiry, of the previous good character, and present necessity of the Mother, and that the Father of the child has deserted it and the Mother, and that the reception of the Child will in all probability, be the means of replacing the Mother in the course of virtue, and the way of an honest livelihood. Persons who present Petitions to the Committee, must not previously apply to any Governor, or to any Officer or Servant belonging to the Hospital on the subject, on any pretense whatever; but they themselves must attend on Saturday Morning at the Hospital at Ten o' Clock, with their Petitions; all of which will be considered in rotation, whilst the Petitioners are expected to remain in attendance.

No Money is ever received for the admission of Children, nor any Fee or Perquisite allowed to be taken by any Officer of the Hospital, on pain of dismissal; and indeed any Person, who shall be known to offer the same, will subject her Petition to rejection; the Officers and Servants of the Hospital having been instructed to acquaint the Committee whenever any such offer is made. The Children of married Women and widows are not admissible into this Hospital. The Petition on the Half-sheet of this Paper is to be filled up with attention on the following Plan, the blanks being numbered as a guidance. Blank mark (1) Insert the name of Petitioner. (2) Place of Residence (2) Petitioner's Age. (4 and 5) Day and Month on which the Child was born. (6) Male or Female. (7) Father's Name. (8) His Trade. (9) Place of Residence when first acquainted with Petitioner. (10 and 11) When the Mother last saw him. (12) What is become of him. NOTE. Petitioners are required to attend the Committee every Saturday Morning, at Half-Past Nine o'clock, until their petitions are disposed of.[2]

Appendix 3: Foundling Hospital Petition Form – insert[3]

The petition of *(name)* of (address) humbly shewth:

That your petitioner is a (widow or spinster) ( ) years of age, and was on the ( ) day of ( ) delivered of a (*male or female child*), which is wholly dependent on your petitioner for its support being deserted by the father. That (*father's name*) is the father of the said child, and was, when your petitioner became acquainted with him, a (*trade*), at (*father's residence when acquaintance began*), and your petitioner last saw him on the ( ) day of ( ), and believes he is now (*what has become of him*). Your petitioner therefore humbly prays that you will be pleased to receive the said child.

Appendix 4: 1880–92 Petitions held by Thomas Coram Foundation in 1992–3 until transfer to London Metropolitan Archives.

Year	Personal Numbers	Year	Personal Numbers	Year	Personal Numbers
1880	21,767–21,812	1886	22,038–22,067	1892	22,294–22,322
1881	21,813–21,864	1887	22,068–22,111	Missing Petitions	
1882	21,865–21,912	1888	22,112–22,169	1882	21,190
1883	21,913–21,957	1889	22,170–22,209	1883	21,925
1884	21,958–21,999	1890	22,210–22,262	1886	22,064
1885	22,000–22,037	1891	22,263–22,293	1887	22,109

Appendix 5: Foundling Hospital Consent and Promise to Marry Codes, 1842–92

Yes	01
No	02
Drugs or alcohol involved	03
Force	04
Seduced by surprise while cleaning kitchen/bedroom as part of professional duty	05
Locked in man's bedroom by surprise	06
Alone in relatives' or employers' home, left unprotected	07
Alone in parents' home	08
Violently raped and assaulted	09
Seduced, fainted/resisted	10
Unclear as to circumstances of pregnancy	11
Young girl fainted, did not know what was happening to her	12
Uncle	13
Attacked suddenly while on walk	14
Took liberties, did not complain	15, 16
Married man, claimed to know	17
Married man, claimed not to know	18
Deserted married mother	19
Widow	20

Appendix 6: Promise to Marry Codes, 1842–92

Yes	01	Married	03
No promise	02	Engaged to another	04

Appendix 7: Foundling Hospital Recommenders, 1842–92

Mary Magdalene Home	Friends	Non-relative who raised petitioner	Nobility
Mrs Gurney's Home, Great Coram St	Family doctor, midwife	Clergyman, clergyman's wife, family minister, clergyman from female reformatory	Clergy member on staff at Clerkenwell house of detention
Family members, mother, father, sister, brother, stepmother	Charity Organisation Society	South London Institution for the Protection and Reformation of Females and for the Suppression and Prevention of Vice	Miss Maude Stanley
Employer	Solicitor	Whitechapel Guardian	Canon Holland's Home
Christ's Church School for Young Ladies	Foundling Hospital official	Charles Dickens	Girls' Friendly Society
Priest from Warwick St Chapel	Townspeople	St Matthews, Westminster	Queen Charlotte's Row Female Reformatory
Private investigator – 'T. Jolly Death, Cheapside'	Foundling Hospital investigator	London Missionary Society	Neighbours
St James' Home Mothers' Home, Hammersmith	Women's Home, 6 Seymour St	Society for the Protection of Women and Children	Sunday school teacher

Appendix 8: Foundling Hospital Petitioners' Occupations, 1842–92

Kitchen maid	Cook	Parents' employee	General servant
Lived with parents	Wet nurse	Nurse	Lady's companion
Governess	Bar maid	Mother's helper	Chambermaid
Nanny, nursemaid	Laundry maid	Needle woman	Shoe binder
Baker	Upholsterer	Nursery school operator	Cap maker
Dressmaker	Ladies maid	Shop clerk, assistant	Fancy boxmaker
Housemaid	Milliner	Waitress	Caretaker for elderly
Cloakmaker	Lodging house maid	Language instructor	Tailoress

Appendix 9: Foundling Hospital Mothers' Literacy, 1842–92

Yes – could sign name	01
No – could not sign name – 'X' marked sign	02
Teacher/governess	03
Could sign name, but could not fill out form	04, 05
Could read, fill in form and sign form	06

Appendix 10: Foundling Hospital Confinement Venues, 1842–92

Queen Charlotte's Lying-in Hospital	Family home	Poplar midwife	Marylebone Workhouse Infirmary	Islington Workhouse
St Olave's Workhouse, Southwark	In-laws' home	Wandsworth Infirmary	General Lying-in Hospital, York Road	Chelsea Workhouse Infirmary
Kensington Workhouse Infirmary	Homerton Workhouse Infirmary	Oxford midwife	Manchester St midwife	Tunbridge Wells Workhouse
Islington midwife	Bennet St, Blackfriars	East Ham midwife	Dartford Workhouse	Fulham Road Workhouse Infirmary
Mrs Thompon's Home, Winfred House	Wray Crescent	Employers' domicile	St Luke's Workhouse Infirmary, Holborn	'Rented room'
St Giles midwife	Vauxhall midwife	Lewes Union Workhouse	Lewisham Union Workhouse	Camberwell midwife
Notting Hill doctor	Soho Square doctor	Hackney midwife	Southall, Middlesex doctor	Lyme Regis Workhouse
Stepney midwife	Saint George Hanover Square boarding house	Brompton Workhouse	Brompton Road doctor	Surrey doctor
Holborn midwife, Mrs Beddell	Shoreditch midwife	Saint George in the East midwife, Mrs Hinton	Clerkenwell doctor	Paddington doctor
Clerkenwell Workhouse	Finsbury doctor	St George Hanover Square midwife	Birmingham midwife	Lambeth doctor

Strand surgeon	Kent midwife	Lambeth Infirmary	Midwife Tottenham	St James Workhouse
Poland St Westminster Union	Fulham midwife	Tavistock midwife	Bournemouth midwife	Mrs Hampson's home
Tollington, Wray Crescent	St George's, Southwark Union	Clapham midwife	Marylebone midwife	Newington Workhouse
Grandmother's house	Hammersmith Workhouse	Camberwell Workhouse	Bayswater midwife	Holborn doctor
Lodging house	St Margaret's Workhouse, Westminster	Hampstead lodging house	Maidenhead, Berkshire midwife	Whitechapel doctor
St Saviour's Hospital, Osnaburgh	Bermondsey Workhouse	St George Hanover Square Workhouse	Hampshire midwife	Marylebone doctor
St James Home for Unwed Mothers, Hammersmith	Charing Cross Road Hospital doctor	Holborn Union Workhouse	St Pancras, Gray's Inn Road, surgeon	Finsbury doctor
Marylebone Road Mothers' Home	Friend's house	Strand Union	Bloomsbury doctor	Tottenham surgeon
King's College Hospital	Shoreditch Workhouse	Whitechapel Union	Strand midwife	City surgeon
Hanwell Lunatic Asylum	Stepney Union Workhouse	St Martin's Workhouse	Cubitt Town midwife	Islington doctor
Adelaide Hospital, Golden Square	Lambeth Workhouse	Hackney Union Workhouse	Lodgings	Unknown

Appendix 11: Places to which Fathers Absconded, 1842–92

England, Scotland and Wales	**England, Scotland and Wales**	**Abroad**	**Other Circumstances**
London	Surrey	South Africa	Prison
Scotland	Rural England	Tasmania	At sea
Yorkshire	Bristol	China	Died
Devonshire	Warwickshire	Crimea	Joined army
Plymouth	Cambridgeshire	India	Hospital
Newcastle on Tyne	Northampton	Canada and United States	Windsor cavalry barracks
Rickmansworth	Norfolk	Hungary	Discharged from service
Wales	Wolvertonhampton	Australia	Woolwich Dockyard
Guernsey	Lancashire	Italy	Joined navy
Essex	Chichester	France	Railway service
Sussex	Hampshire	Ireland	Unknown

Appendix 12: Statutes Relating to Women, Infants and Children

18 Eliz. 1 c.3, Poor Laws
12 Car. II c. 24, Tenures Abolition Act
2 Geo. 3 c. 22, Poor Act
7 Geo. 3 c. 39, An Act for Better Regulation of Parish Poor Children
13 Geo. 3 c. 82, Lying-in Hospitals Act
11 Geo. 4 c. 30, Census Act
4 & 5 Will. 4 c. 76, s. 1–109, New Poor Law
2 & 3 Vict. c. 54, Custody of Infants Act
7 Will. 4 & Vict. c. 22, Births and Deaths Registration Act
2 & 3 Vict. c. 85, Bastard Children Act
7 & 8 Vict. c. 101, s. 40, Poor Law Amendment Act
10 & 11 Vict. c. 109, Poor Law Board Act
20 & 21 Vict. c. 85, Matrimonial Causes Act
24 & 25 Vict. c. 100, s. 50–1, Offences against the Person Act
30 & 31 Vict. c. 6, Metropolitan Asylums Act
34 & 35 Vict. c. 70, Local Government Board Act
35 Vict. c. 109, s. 1–10, Bastardy Laws Amendment Act
35 & 36 Vict. c. 38, Infant Life Protection Act
36 & 37 Vict. c. 12, Custody of Infants Act
48 & 49 Vict. c. 69, Criminal Law Amendment Act
49 & 50 Vict. c.27, Guardianship and Custody of Infants
52 & 53 Vict. c. 56, Register of Deserted Children pursuant to Poor Law Act
60 & 61 Vict. c. 57, Infant Life Protection Act
8 Edw. 7 c. 27, Married Women's Property Act
8 Edw. 7 c. 67, Children Act
9 Edw. 7 c. 13, Local Education Authorities (Medical Treatment Act)

Notes

Introduction

1 Foundling Hospital Secretary's Correspondence, A/FH/A/06/1 – 116/4, 1859, London Metropolitan Archives L[ondon] M[etropolitan] A[rchives].
2 Foundling Hospital Secretary's Correspondence, A/FH/A/06/1 – 116/4, 1859, LMA.
3 Foundling Hospital Secretary's Correspondence, A/FH/A/06/1 – 116/4, 1859, LMA.
4 Foundling Hospital Secretary's Correspondence, A/FH/A/06/1 – 116/4, 1859, LMA.
5 John Tosh, 'The Strengths and Weaknesses of Analytical History', in *The Pursuit of History* 4th edn (Harlow: Pearson Longman, 2006), p. 155.
6 Anthony Brundage, *The Making of the New Poor Laws: The Politics of Inquiry, Enactment, and Implementation, 1832–1839* (New Brunswick: Rutgers University Press, 1978); Ursula Henriques, 'Bastardy and the New Poor Law', *Past and Present* 37 (1967): 103–29, and Ursula Henriques, *Before the Welfare State: Social Administration in Early Industrial Britain* (London: Longman, 1979); Pat Thane, 'Women and the Poor Law in Victorian and Edwardian England', *History Workshop Journal* 6 (1978): 31–2; Pat Thane, *The Foundations of the Welfare State* (1982; repr., London: Longman, 1993). For an introduction to the debate on outdoor relief, see also Mary MacKinnon's 1987 article 'English Poor Law Policy and the Crusade against Outrelief', *The Journal of Economic History* 47 (1987): 603–25. Other works consulted include Jose Harris, 'Enterprise and Welfare States: A Comparative Perspective', *Transactions of the Royal Historical Society* (1990): 175–95; Peter Mandler, ed., *The Uses of Charity: The Poor on Relief in the Nineteenth-Century Metropolis* (Philadelphia: University of Pennsylvania Press, 1990); Derek Fraser, ed. *The New Poor Law in the Nineteenth Century* (New York: St Martin's, 1976); Peter Dunkley, *The Crisis of the Old Poor Law in England, 1795–1834: An Interpretive Essay* (New York: Garland, 1982); Nicholas C. Edsall, *The Anti-Poor Law Movement, 1834–1844* (Totowa, NJ: Rowan & Littlefield, Inc., 1971); John Knott, *Popular Opposition to the 1834 Poor Law* (New York: St Martin's Press, 1986); and Michael E. Rose, *The English Poor Law, 1780–1930* (New York: Barnes & Noble, Inc., 1971).
7 Gillian Pugh, *London's Forgotten Children: Thomas Coram and The Foundling Hospital* (2008; repr., Stroud, Gloucestershire: The History Press, 2010).
8 Ruth McClure, *Coram's Children* (New Haven: Yale University Press, 1981), p. 49. Alysa Levene, *Childcare, Health, and Mortality at the London Foundling Hospital* (New York: Manchester University Press, 2007). For a statistical overview of illegitimacy see Adrian Wilson, 'Illegitimacy and Its Implications in Mid-Eighteenth-Century London: The Evidence of the Foundling Hospital', *Continuity and Change* 4 (1988): 103–64.
9 Françoise Barret-Ducrocq, *Love in the Time of Victoria*, trans. John Howe, 2nd edn (London: Penguin Books, 1991), pp. 54–5.

10 John Gillis, 'Servants, Sexual Relations, and the Risks of Illegitimacy in London, 1801–1900', *Feminist Studies* 5 (1979): 142–73; Anna Clark, *Women's Silence, Men's Violence: Sexual Assault in England, 1770–1845* (London: Pandora Press, 1987). Simon R. S. Szreter, 'The Study of the Fertility Decline', in *Fertility, Class and Gender in Britain, 1860–1940* (Cambridge: Cambridge University Press, 1996), pp. 9–66.

11 Jenny Bourne Taylor, 'Received a Blank Child': John Brownlow, Charles Dickens, and the London Foundling Hospital – Archives and Fictions', *Nineteenth Century Literature* 56 (2001): 293–363.

12 Mary Poovey dedicates a chapter to space as a context suitable for historical analysis of Victorian cultural formation. Mary Poovey, 'The Production of Abstract Space', in *Making a Social Body: British Cultural Formation, 1830–1864* (Chicago: Chicago University Press, 1995), pp. 25–54. Doreen Massey and Daphne Spain take a feminist view of social space and the issue of spatial boundaries. Doreen Massey, *Space, Place and Gender* (Cambridge: Polity Press, 1994b), pp. 6–7; Daphne Spain, *Gendered Spaces* (Chapel Hill: The University of North Carolina Press, 1992), pp. 11–14. For examples of the ways in which physical geography and demography are intertwined with historical studies see Mary Eschelbach Gregson, 'Population Dynamics in Rural Missouri, 1860–1880', *Social Science History* 21 (1997): 85–110. For other applications of this methodology to demographic history, see Susan Cotts Watkins, *From Provinces into Nations: Demographic Integration in Western Europe, 1870–1960* (Princeton: Princeton University Press, 1991).

13 Published in 1974, *The Production of Space* by Henri Lefebvre challenges previous conceptions of social, cultural and intellectual geographies. Lefebvre argues social class and economic relationships produce spatial constructions. Lefebvre has little to say about the relationship between space and gender. He observes that the nineteenth-century working class was pushed by 'capital' into slums at the edge of the city. Henri Lefebvre, *The Production of* Space, trans. Donald Nicholson-Smith (Oxford: Blackwell, 1991), pp. 62, 316.

14 Lefebvre, *The Production of Space*, pp. 33, 39. See for example David Feldman and Gareth Stedman Jones, eds, *Metropolis London: Histories and Representations since 1800* (London: Routledge, 1989).

15 Scholars such as Edward Said, Elazar Barkan, Antonia Finnane, and Thomas Prasch distinguish between 'us' and 'them'. According to Elazar Barkan: '"We" were the upper classes, perhaps the middling lot aspiring upward. Primarily men. The "Others" populated the British Empire, the East End of London, and even many social and geographic quarters closer to home.' Barkan concentrates on questions of race and gender, rather than space and values. See Edward Said, *Culture and Imperialism* (New York: Alfred A. Knopf, 1993); Elazar Barkan, 'Post Anti-Colonial Histories: Representing the Other in Imperial Britain', *Journal of British Studies* (1994): 180. See also Antonia Finnane, 'The Origins of Prejudice: The Malintegration of Subei in Late Imperial China', *Comparative Studies in Society and History* 35 (1993): 214 and Thomas Prasch, 'Orientalism's Other, Other Orientalisms: Women in the Scheme of Empire', *Journal of Women's History* 7 (1995): 175–88.

16 Ellen Ross, 'Survival Networks: Women's Neighbourhood Sharing in London before World War I', *History Workshop Journal* 15 (1983): 4–27. Susan Cotts Watkins argues from a demographic vantage that state formation, market integration and nation building increasingly drew communities such as London into national and ultimately international

networks. In places where a community is integrated into a larger network, diversity in fertility, infant mortality and marriage patterns decrease. Cotts Watkins, *From Provinces into Nations: Demographic Integration in Western Europe, 1870–1960*, pp. 4–5.

17 Linda Colley, *Britons: the Forging of the Nation, 1707–1837* (New Haven: Yale University Press, 1992); Francis W. Sheppard, 'London and the Nation in the Nineteenth Century', *Transactions of the Royal Historical Society*, 5th Series, vol. 35 (London: Royal Historical Society, 1985), pp. 51–2, 72–3.

18 British ship owner Charles Booth (1840–1916) was born in Liverpool. He moved to London in the 1880s. Active in the Royal Statistical Society, Booth served as its president between 1892 and 1894. His first publication stemmed from a speech to the Society on life and labour in Tower Hamlets. The Booth papers are voluminous and held at the London School of Economics (British Library of Political and Economic Science, London School of Economics). See Charles Booth, *Condition and Occupations of the People of The Tower Hamlets, 1886–1887* (London: Edward Stanford, 1887); *Life and Labour of the People in London: First Results of an Inquiry Based on the 1891 Census* (London: Williams and Norgate, 1891), a rare pamphlet held at London Guildhall Library L[ondon] G[uildhall] L[ibrary]; Charles Booth, *Life and Labour of the People in London* 17 vols. (London: Macmillan and Co., 1902–3). Booth classified the volumes under four headings: Poverty, Work, and Trade, Religious Influences and Miscellaneous. For his analysis of the poor laws see Charles Booth, *Poor Law Reform* (London: Macmillan and Co., 1916).

19 Charles Booth's work provided a prototype for later scientists, planners, urban planners, social engineers and politicians. Mapping, measuring, manipulating the geo-spatial identity of an area frequently reflects the political details as well as geographical and environmental particulars of an area. Edward W. Soja, *Postmodern Geographies: The Reassertion of Space in Critical Social Theory* (London: Verso, 1989), p. 75; Soja relies on Lefebvre to make this argument. For Lefebvre's explanation of this point see Lefebvre, *The Production of Space*, pp. 38–9.

20 Adrian Wilson, ed., *Rethinking Social History: English Society, 1750–1920 and Its Interpretation* (Manchester: Manchester University Press, 1993), pp. 41–2, 293–335. See also Benedict Anderson, *Imagined Communities, Reflections on the Origin and Spread of Nationalism* (London: Verso, 1991); Rob Shields, *Places on the Margin, Alternative Geographies of Modernity* (London: Routledge, 1991), Lefebvre, *The Production of Space*, p. 316; Anthony Giddens, *The Constitution of Society* (Berkeley: University of California Press, 1984), p. 217; and Giddens, *Politics, Sociology and Social Theory: Encounters with Classical and Contemporary Social Thought* (Cambridge: Polity Press, 1995), pp. 265–8.

21 London County Council, *London County Council Lists of the Streets and Places within the Administrative County of London* (London: P. S. King and Son, 1901). Hereafter cited as LCC.

22 See David R. Green, *From Artisans to Paupers: Economic Change and Poverty in London, 1790–1870* (Aldershot, Hants.: Scolar Press, 1995); and David R. Green, *Pauper Capital: London and the Poor Law, 1790–1870* (Farnham: Ashgate, 2010); and Seth Koven, *Slumming: Sexual and Social Politics in Victorian London* (Princeton: Princeton University Press, 2004).

23 Joan W. Scott contends feminist historians lean more toward description than theory and do not address dominant disciplinary ideas. This, Scott argues, marginalizes women's

history because feminists do not challenge the methodological discipline of history sufficiently for their research to alter permanently the way in which historical subjects are researched and reported. Joan W. Scott, 'Gender: A Useful Category of Historical Analysis', *American Historical Review* 91 (1986): 1053–75.

24 Scott, 'Gender: A Useful Category of Historical Analysis', 1055, 1066–9.

25 Nancy J. Chodorow, 'Gender as a Personal and Cultural Construction', *Signs* 20 (1995): 516–43.

26 Chodorow, 'Gender as a Personal and Cultral Construction', 517.

27 Louise A. Tilly, 'Connections (The Legacy of Social Historian E. P. Thompson)', *American Historical Review* 99 (1994): 1–20.

28 E. P. Thompson, *The Making of the English Working Class* (New York: Pantheon Books, 1964), pp. 11. See Paul Johnson's explanation of the evolution of 'class law theory'. Johnson borrows Patrick Atiyah's analysis and refers back to E. P. Thompson's 'moral economy', whereby society was constructed under more paternalistic, protective and customary practices. These historians situate the deepest changes in social structure in the 1770s. Towards the end of the eighteenth century, a new ethos emerged in which individualism, risk-taking, and freedom of choice gained predominance. Johnson argues for a new political and social order that manifested itself in civil laws privileging and protecting trade. The new order provided increased protections for the elite in terms of financial investments. The non-elite lost standing in this powerful transition. The rising economy of the 'elect' did not lift all boats. Rather, the brilliant economy manifested in West London's suburbs sank them in the mud of moral judgments. Johnson wrote: 'A contract economy – one in which all economic actors are treated according to the same free-market rules – was rapidly made subservient to moral prejudice. Economic actions undertaken by people of different social standing became regulated in different ways because of a priori value judgments about the character traits of the different classes.' Paul Johnson, 'Class Law in Victorian England', *Past and Present* 141 (1993): 147–9.

29 F. M. L. Thompson, 'Social Control in Victorian Britain', *Economic History Review* 34 (1981): 189–208.

30 Giddens, *The Constitution of Society*, pp. 3–6, 9, 217, 362-3; and *Politics, Sociology and Social Theory: Encounters with Classical and Contemporary Social Thought*, pp. 265–8.

31 Giddens avoids the use of the word 'structure' which suggests a direct connection to the old sociological debate surrounding structuralism and functionalism. Giddens prefers the word 'structuration' to describe a framework of social relationships. Giddens relies on history, long histories, stretching over several life spans, or the longue durée to prove his theory of 'structuration'. The 'theory of structuration' underpins Giddens' concepts of space, 'locales' and 'modes of regionalization'. Locales refer to the use of space and how it provides opportunities and settings for social interaction between men and women, women and children, etc. Analysis of these locales adds context to our understanding of social interrelatedness. 'Locales' may be defined as the physical properties of the surrounding world, such as manufacturing, slum, financial, cultural, historical and political districts. Locales provide understanding about the 'fixity' of underlying institutions, although there is no clear sense in which they 'determine' such 'fixity', or permanence. It is usually possible to designate locales in terms of their physical properties, such as lying along a river or a main

thoroughfare. If the observer recognizes a structure is a 'dwelling' with a range of other properties specified by the modes of its utilization in human activity, then it is a locale. Anthony Giddens, *New Rules of Sociological Method: A Positive Critique of Interpretative Sociologies* (New York: Basic Books, Inc., 1976), pp.118–26.

32 For a discussion of historical miniatures as case studies see Geoffrey Eley, 'Introduction', *The History of Everyday Life: Reconstructing Historical Experiences and Ways of Life*, ed. Alf Lüdtke, trans. William Templer (Princeton: Princeton University Press, 1995), pp. ix–xi.

33 Henry Longley, *Report to the Local Government Board on Poor Law Administration in London* (London: Local Government Board, 1874); Major P. G. Craigie, 'The English Poor Rate and Recent Statistics of Its Administration and Pressure, Read before the Royal Statistical Society', *Journal of the Royal Statistical Society* (1888): 450–93.

34 The institution admitted the last child in 1953. See R. H. Nichols and F. A. Wray *The History of the Foundling Hospital* (London: Oxford University Press, 1935), p. 64 and Foundling Hospital Finding Guide, LMA.

35 See Rejected Petitions Code Numbers beginning with A/FH/A/08/001/003/, LMA.

36 The 110 year applies to the petitions held by the LMA for the Th]omas Coram Foundation.

Chapter One

1 House of Commons, 'Eighteenth Recommendation, Poor Law Amendment Bill, First Report From the Poor Law Commissioners' *Sessional Papers*, 1835, Poor Laws, vol. 8, p. 196.

2 Thomas Robert Malthus, *An Essay on the Principle of Population* (1798; repr., Ann Arbor: University of Michigan Press, 1959), pp.120–1. Thomas Malthus' (1766–1834) influence in structuring the Poor Law debates is inestimable. Himmelfarb regards Malthus' *Essay* (1798) as a footnote to *An Enquiry into the Wealth of Nations* by Adam Smith, suggesting the later essay *Principles of Political Economy* (1820) served as a supplement to the *Wealth of Nations*. Together, these essays explain the principles of classical political economics. See Gertrude Himmelfarb's thorough discussion of this intellectual development, particularly Chapter 4, 'Malthus: Political Economy De-Moralized', Gertrude Himmelfarb, *The Idea of Poverty: England in the Early Industrial Age* (New York: Alfred A. Knopf, 1983), pp.100–44.

3 Henry Brougham, Lord Chancellor of England, Speech to Parliament, 'Poor Law Amendment Bill', *The Times*, 22 July 1834.

4 Thomas Mackay, *A History of the English Poor Law, from 1834 to the Present Time: Being a Supplementary Volume to 'A History of the English Poor Law' by Sir George Nicholls, K. C. B.*, rev. ed., vol. 3 (1900; repr., New York: Augustus M. Kelley, 1967), pp.145–6.

5 See the remainder of a moving speech offered by MP Scrope in which he details the history of the Poor Laws from Elizabeth I forward. Mr Poulette Scrope, MP, Speech to the House of Commons, 26 May 1834, *Parliamentary Debates*, Commons, 3d ser. vol. 23, col. 1321–2.

6 Scrope, Speech, 26 May 1834, col. 1322; Mackay, *History of the English Poor Law* 3: 125.

7 Scrope, Speech, 26 May 1834, col. 1321–2.

8 Lord Chancellor Brougham, 'Poor Laws Amendment Bill', House of Lords, *The Times*, 22 July 1834.

9 Brougham, 'Poor Laws Amendment Bill', House of Lords, *The Times*, 22 July 1834.

10 Brougham, 'Poor Laws Amendment Bill', House of Lords, *The Times*, 22 July 1834.

11 Brougham, 'Poor Laws Amendment Bill', House of Lords, *The Times*, 22 July 1834.

12 Brougham, 'Poor Laws Amendment Bill', House of Lords, *The Times*, 22 July 1834.

13 Sir George Nicholls, *A History of the English Poor Law*, vol. 2 (London: P. S. King & Son, 1898), pp. 68–9.

14 Lord Chancellor of England, Speech to Parliament, 'Poor Law Amendment Bill', *The Times*, 22 July 1834.

15 Thomas Lacqueur, 'Sexual Desire and the Market Economy during the Industrial Revolution', in Domna Stanton, ed., *Discourses of Sexuality: from Aristotle to AIDS* (Ann Arbor: University of Michigan Press, 1992), pp. 185. As cited by Anna Clark, *Struggle for the Breeches: Gender and the Making of the British Working Class* (Berkeley: University of California Press, 1995), pp. 180.

16 Himmelfarb, *The Idea of Poverty*, pp. 102, 105, 111.

17 Malthus' works were an inspiration to Darwin and anathema to Karl Marx. Robert Woods, 'The Population of Britain in the Nineteenth Century', in *British Population History: from the Black Death to the Present Day*, edited by Michael Anderson (Cambridge: Cambridge University Press, 1996), pp. 293.

18 Statute 11 Geo. 4, c. 30 legislated the first census to enumerate occupations. Commons, 'Comparative Account of the Population of Great Britain, 1831', vol. 8, p. 1.

19 The government established the General Registration Office (GRO) to keep track of inheritances and property rights. Record keeping and abstracting statistical data proved useful as well. By the mid-1830s, the government recognized the GRO's worth, and authorized the office to record occupations, classes of people, marriage and illegitimacy rates, widowing, and health statistics. Edward Higgs, 'The 1891 Census: Continuity and Change', *The Local Historian* (1992): 184–90.

20 Woods, 'The Population of Britain in the Nineteenth Century', Table 4, p. 305.

21 Rates of pauperism and population growth prove more reliable after 1831. Michael Anderson, 'Population Change in North-Western Europe, 1750–1850', in *British Population History: from the Black Death to the Present Day*, ed. Michael Anderson (Cambridge: Cambridge University Press, 1996), pp. 226.

22 Mr Robert Slaney, MP, Speech to House of Commons, 17 April 1828, *Parliamentary Debates*, Commons, 2nd ser., 18, col. 1527.

23 'Poor Laws Commission', *The Times*, 11 April 1832.

24 'Poor Laws Commission', *The Times*, 11 April 1832.

25 The commissioners surveyed nine American states, Latin American countries, and 22 large cities and countries in Europe. Of the 64 questions they raised, 21 specifically related to women, children and the family, while ten investigated the condition of the 'destitute able-bodied'. The 'Foreign Communications' revealed policies contrasting sharply with those in England, with the exception of the examples from the United States where poor law provisions reflected English practices. House of Commons, Foreign Communications with Index, 'Report from His Majesty's Commissioners for Inquiring into the Administration

and Practical Operation of the Poor Laws', *Sessional Papers, 1834, Poor Laws*, vol. 18: appendix F.

26 Brundage, *The Making of the New Poor Laws*, pp. 18–22; Himmelfarb, *The Idea of Poverty*, pp. 154–7.

27 Edwin Chadwick (1800–90), an essential figure in the sanitary movement, laid down precise descriptions for the construction of dwellings and hospitals. In his later years, he became a close friend of the influential Dr Southwood Smith of the London Fever Hospital and an adviser to Florence Nightingale. Geoffrey Rivett, *The Development of the London Hospital System, 1823–1982*, King's Fund Historical Series No. 4 (London: King Edward's Hospital Fund for London, 1986), pp. 17; Himmelfarb, *The Idea of Poverty*, 78–85.

28 William Cobbett (1762–1835), a Radical politician, won the seat from Oldham after passage of the 1832 Reform Bill. Cobbett argued if men could fight in the militia, then they were entitled to rights as citizens. When Cobbett participated in the poor law debates. He brought with him the wisdom of age, as he would have been about 60 years of age at the time. Radical politicians such as William Cobbett generally assumed the English government had a right and duty to provide for the poor, a premise rooted in the history of the relationship between the nobility and local community. In times of need, noblesse oblige would alleviate the distress. Cobbett listed the considerable contributions of the medieval church, and the Elizabethan poor laws. Some nineteenth-century politicians regarded the responsibility of the government to provide for the poor as part of the Constitution. Linda Colley, *Britons: Forging the Nation* (New Haven: Yale University Press, 1992), pp. 318–9. See Clark's fine discussion of the ties between feminism and radicalism as these relate to William Cobbett in *Struggle for the Breeches*, pp. 188–95. *Documents in British History, 1688 to Present*, ed. Brian L. Blakeley and Jacquelin Collins, 2 vols. (New York: McGraw-Hill, 1993), pp. 2, 104.

29 Mr William Cobbett, MP, Speech to the House of Commons, 26 May 1834, *Parliamentary Debates*, Commons, 3d ser., vol. 23, col. 1336–7.

30 Cobbett, Speech, Commons, 26 May 1834, col. 1336–7.

31 Colonel Evans, MP, 'Poor Law Amendment Bill', *The Mirror of Parliament*, 9 May 1834, 2: 1618; Poulette Scrope, MP, Speech to the House of Common, 26 May 1834, *Parliamentary Debates*, Commons, 3d ser., vol. 23, col. 1321.

32 Assistant Overseer of a Parish in Westminster, 'Poor Laws, To the Editor of The Times', *The Times*, 24 April 1832.

33 Assistant Overseer of a Parish in Westminster, 'Poor Laws, To the Editor of The Times', *The Times*, 24 April 1832.

34 House of Commons, 'Answers to Town Queries, Report from His Majesty's Commissioners for Inquiring into the Administration and Practical Operation of the Poor Laws', *Sessional Papers*, 1834, Poor Laws, vol. 17, appendix B.2.

35 Commons, 'Foreign Communications, Poor Laws', vol. 18, appendix F.

36 Commons, 'Answers to Town Queries, Poor Laws', vol. 17, pp. 76.

37 Commons, 'Answers to Town Queries, Poor Laws', vol. 17, appendix B.2.

38 Statement attributed to Lord Althorp, 'Editorial', *The Times*, 12 July 1834. Lord Althorp, Viscount Earl Spencer (1782–1845), educated at Harrow and Cambridge, he represented Northamptonshire and avidly studied 'political economy'. Althorp led the Whig opposition

in 1830, and served as Chancellor of the Exchequer and leader of the House of Commons during passage of the Reform Bill and the Poor Law Amendments. Like Henry Brougham, Lord Althorp retired after passage of the Poor Law Amendments in 1834. Jonathan Parry, *The Rise and Fall of Liberal Government in Victorian Britain* (New Haven: Yale University Press, 1996), p. 319.

39 Henriques, 'Bastardy and the New Poor Law', 110.

40 Henriques, 'Bastardy and the New Poor Law', 211.

41 House of Commons, "Bastardy', First Report from the Poor Law Commissioners, appendix A', *Sessional Papers*, 1834, Poor Laws, vol. 8, p. 113A.

42 'Answers to Town Queries, Report from His Majesty's Commissioners for Inquiring into the Administration and Practical Operation of the Poor Laws', *Sessional Papers*, 1834, Poor Laws, vols. 10–11, p. 98.

43 Commons, "Bastardy', First Report from Poor Law Commissioners', vol. 8, p. 113A.

44 Commons, "Bastardy', First Report from Poor Law Commissioners', vol. 8, p. 113A.

45 Magistrates committed thirty-six women to Cold Baths Fields on charges of 'lewdness' between 1828 and 1832. Commons, "Bastardy', First Report from Poor Law Commissioners', vol. 8, p. 115A.

46 Commons, "Bastardy', First Report from Poor Law Commissioners', vol. 8, p. 115A.

47 Commons, "Bastardy', First Report from Poor Law Commissioners', vol. 8, p. 115A.

48 Commons, "Bastardy', First Report from Poor Law Commissioners', vol. 8, p. 115A.

49 Commons, "Bastardy', First Report from Poor Law Commissioners', vol. 8, p. 114–5A.

50 Commons, "Bastardy', First Report from Poor Law Commissioners', vol. 8, p. 114–5A.

51 Commons, "Bastardy', First Report from Poor Law Commissioners', vol. 8, p. 116A.

52 House of Commons, "Seventeenth Recommendation', Poor Law Amendment Bill, First Report from the Poor Law Commissioners', *Sessional Papers*, 1835, Poor Laws, vol. 8, p. 196.

53 Commons, 'Eighteenth Recommendation, Poor Law Amendment Bill', First Report from the Poor Law Commissioners', *Sessional Papers,* 1835, Poor Laws, vol. 8, p. 196.

54 Commons, 'Eighteenth Recommendation, Poor Law Amendment Bill', vol. 8, p. 196. Ann Higginbotham, '"Sin of the Age": Infanticide and Illegitimacy in Victorian London' *Victorian Studies* 32 (1989): 320–1; Lara Marks, *Model Mothers: Jewish Mothers and Maternity Provision in East London, 1870–1939* (Oxford: Oxford University Press, 1994), pp. 180–1; Jane Lewis, *Women in England, 1870–1950* (Bloomington: Indiana University Press, 1984), p. 64; Joan Perkins, *Women and Marriage in Nineteenth-Century England* (Chicago: Lyceum Books, 1989), pp. 160–1.

55 House of Commons, 'Sixteenth Recommendation', Poor Law Amendment Bill, First Report from the Poor Law Commissioners', *Sessional Papers*, 1835 Poor Laws, vol. 8, p. 195.

56 Commons, "Bastardy', First Report from Poor Law Commissioners', vol. 8, p. 195.

57 Commons, "Bastardy', First Report from Poor Law Commissioners', vol. 8, p. 195.

58 Bishop of Exeter, 'Poor Law Amendment Bill', *The Mirror of Parliament* 4: 3021.

59 Commons, 'Twentieth Recommendation, Poor Law Amendment Bill', First Report from the Poor Law Commissioners', *Sessional Papers*, 1835, Poor Laws, vol. 8, p. 198.

60 The Parliamentary Papers used the capital letters to express the full strength of their opinion. House of Commons, 'Twenty-first Recommendation, Poor Law Amendment Bill, First Report from the Poor Law Commissioners', *Sessional Papers*, 1835, Poor Laws, vol. 8, p. 197.

61 Commons, 'Twenty-first Recommendation, Poor Law Amendment Bill', vol. 8, p. 197.
62 House of Commons, "Fifteenth Recommendation', Poor Law Amendment Bill, First Report from the Poor Law Commissioners', *Sessional Papers*, 1835, Poor Laws, vol. 8, p. 193–4.
63 Commons, 'Sixteenth Recommendation, Poor Law Amendment Bill' First Report from the Poor Law Commissioners', *Sessional Papers*, 1835, Poor Laws, vol. 8, p. 195.
64 Commons, 'Sixteenth Recommendation, Poor Law Amendment Bill', vol. 8, p. 195.
65 Commons, 'Eighteenth Recommendation, Poor Law Amendment Bill', *Sessional Papers*, 1835, Poor Laws, vol. 8, p. 196.
66 Bishop of Exeter, 'Poor Law Amendment Bill', *The Mirror of Parliament* 4: 3021; Commons, 'Seventeenth Recommendation, Poor Law Amendment Bill', vol. 8, p. 195.
67 Commons, 'Twentieth Recommendation, Poor Law Amendment Bill', vol. 8, p. 197.
68 Commons, 'Sixteenth Recommendation, Poor Law Amendment Bill', vol. 8, p. 195.
69 J. H. Baker, *An Introduction to English Legal History*, 3rd edn (London: Butterworth, 1990), pp. 557–9.
70 House of Commons, 'Letter to Sir James Graham, Baronet from George Nicholls, George Cornewall Lewis, and Edmund Walker Head, Commissioners, 31 January 1844, 10th Annual Report of the Poor Law Commissioners, appendix no. 7', *Sessional Papers*, 1845, Poor Laws, vol. 27, p. 141.
71 Himmelfarb discusses the problem in her discussion of the Lords. *The Idea of Poverty*, pp. 156, 175.
72 Mackay, *History of the English Poor Law* 3: 124.
73 Colonel DeLacy Evans, Radical MP, Westminster, Speech to the House of Commons, 9 May 1834, *Parliamentary Debates*, Commons, 3d ser., vol. 23, col. 803. F. W. S. Craig, ed., *The Parliaments of England, 1715–1847* (Chichester: Political Reference Publications, 1973), p. 216.
74 At the time, no special provisions existed for workhouse deliveries; in fact, the first official workhouse infirmary dedicated to gynaecological and obstetrical needs of women opened in Mile End, East London in 1898. Colonel Evans, 'Poor Law Amendment Bill', House of Commons, *The Mirror of Parliament*, 9 May 1834, 2: 1618.
75 Mr Samuel Whalley, MP, speech to the House of Commons, 9 May 1834, *Parliamentary Debates*, Commons, 3d ser., vol. 23, col. 807–8.
76 Whalley, Speech, 9 May 1834, Commons, vol 23, col. 807–8.
77 Whalley, Speech, 9 May 1834, Commons, vol 23, col. 807–8.
78 Whalley, Speech, 9 May 1834, Commons, vol 23, col. 807–8.
79 Whalley, Speech, 9 May 1834, Commons, vol 23, col. 807–8.
80 Mr George Grote, Radical MP, City of London, Speech to the House of Commons, 9 May 1834, *Parliamentary Debates*, Commons, 3d ser., vol. 23, col. 813. Craig, ed. *The Parliaments of England, 1715–1847*, p. 209.
81 Mr Robert Slaney, MP, Speech to the House of Commons, 9 May 1834, *Parliamentary Debates*, Commons, 3d ser., vol. 23, col. 820.
82 Sir Francis Burdett, MP, Westminster, Speech to the House of Commons, 9 May 1834, *Parliamentary Debates*, Commons, 3d ser., vol. 23, col. 823. Craig, *The Parliaments of England*, p. 216.

83 Mr William Cobbett, MP Speech to the House of Commons, 26 May 1834, *Parliamentary Debates*, Commons, 3d. ser., vol. 23, col. 1336.

84 Mr John Walter, MP, Speech to the House of Commons, 9 May 1834, *Parliamentary Debates*, Commons, 3d ser., vol. 23, col. 830–1; Mackay, *History of the English Poor Law* 3: 127.

85 House of Commons, 9 May 1834, *Parliamentary Debates*, Commons, 3d ser., vol. 23, col. 842.

86 Mackay, *History of the English Poor Law* 3: 145–6.

87 Lord Althorp, Speech to the House of Commons, 26 May 1834, *Parliamentary Debates*, Commons, 3d ser., vol. 23, col. 1348–9.

88 William Cobbett, MP, Speech to the House of Commons, *Parliamentary Debates*, 6 June 1834, vol. 24, col. 310–11.

89 Lord Althorp, Speech to the House of Commons, 9 June 1834, *Parliamentary Debates*, Commons, 3d ser., vol. 24, col. 336.

90 Commons, 9 June 1834, *Parliamentary Debates*, vol. 24, col. 337–8.

91 Mr Edward Buller, MP, Speech to the House of Commons, 9 May 1834, *Parliamentary Debates*, Commons, 3d ser., vol. 23, col. 830.

92 Buller, Speech, 9 May 1834, Commons, vol. 23, col. 830.

93 Althorp, Speech, 9 June 1834, Commons, vol. 24, col. 338.

94 Mr Thomas Hodges, MP, Speech to the House of Commons, 9 June 1834, *Parliamentary Debates*, Commons, 3d ser., vol. 24, col. 338–9.

95 Mr John Benett, MP, Speech to the House of Commons, 9 June 1834, *Parliamentary Debates*, Commons, 3d ser., vol. 24, col. 389.

96 Mr Poulette Scrope, MP, Speech to the House of Commons, 9 June 1834, *Parliamentary Debates*, Commons, 3d ser. vol. 24, col. 339–40.

97 Scrope, Speech, 9 June 1834, Commons, vol 24, col. 334–6.

98 Lord Althorp, Speech to the House of Commons, 9 June 1834, *Parliamentary Debates*, Commons, 3d ser., vol. 24, col. 347.

99 Mr William Cobbett, MP, Speech to the House of Commons, 10 June 1834, *Parliamentary Debates*, Commons, 3d ser., vol. 24, col. 347–8, 352.

100 Cobbett, Speech, 10 June 1834, *Parliamentary Debates*, Commons, vol. 24, col. 347–8, 352.

101 M. A. Crowther explained the inequities in the rating system in the following way: The commissioners hoped new policies would make pauperism disappear and rate reform unnecessary. 'The story of the reform of the rating system requires an historian with superhuman patience.' Mary Ann Crowther, *The Workhouse System, 1834–1929: the History of an English Social Institution* (London: Methuen, 1981), pp. 23–4.

102 House of Commons, 10 June 1834, *Parliamentary Debates*, Commons, 3d ser., vol. 24, col. 351.

103 House of Commons, 16 June 1834, *Parliamentary Debates*, Commons, 3d ser., vol. 24, col. 433.

104 Consider this, Charles Dickens worked as a court reporter for the *Mirror of Parliament* during the debates, the language used, such as 'surplus population' and 'surplus labourers' appears in his published works, including *The Christmas Carol*.

105 Mr Wolryche Whitmore, MP, Speech to the House of Commons, 16 June 1834, *Parliamentary Debates*, Commons, 3d ser., vol. 24, col. 451–6.

106 Colonel Robert Torrens, MP, Speech to the House of Commons, 16 June 1834, *Parliamentary Debates*, Commons, 3d ser., vol. 24, col. 456–62.

107 Torrens, Speech, 16 June 1834, Commons, vol. 24, col. 456–62.

108 Lord Althorp, Speech to the House of Commons, 18 June 1834, *Parliamentary Debates*, Commons, 3d ser., vol. 24, col. 523–5.

109 Althorp, Speech, Commons, 18 June 1834, 523–5.

110 Althorp, Speech, 18 June 1834, Commons, vol. 24, col. 523–5.

111 Althorp, Speech, 18 June 1834, Commons, vol. 24, col. 523–5.

112 Mr Charles Buller, MP, Speech to the House of Commons, 18 June 1834, *Parliamentary Debates*, Commons, 3d ser., Speech, vol. 24, col. 529.

113 Mr Wolryche Whitmore, MP, Speech to the House of Commons, 18 June 1834, *Parliamentary Debates*, Commons, 3d ser., vol. 24, col. 529.

114 Mr George Robinson, MP, Speech to the House of Commons, 18 June 1834, *Parliamentary Debates*, Commons, 3d ser., vol. 24, col. 541–2.

115 Mr Robinson, Speech, 18 June 1834, vol. 24, col. 541–2.

116 Robinson, Speech, 18 June 1834, vol. 24, col. 541–2.

117 Mr John Benett, who served as magistrate for 30 years, stated, 'he had never reason to suspect that any woman who had sworn her child before him acting as a Magistrate had perjured herself'. Benett claimed magistrates took account the circumstances of unwed mothers in making awards. In doing so, the magistrates acted against law. Mr John Benett, Speech to the House of Commons, 18 June 1834, *Parliamentary Debates*, Commons, 3d ser., vol. 24, col. 530.

118 Benett, Speech, 18 June 1834, vol. 24, col. 530.

119 Benett, Speech, 18 June 1834, vol. 24, col. 530.

120 Commons, 18 June 1834, *Parliamentary Debates*, vol. 24, col. 520–41.

121 Mackay, *History of the English Poor Law* 3: 150.

122 Mackay, *History of the English Poor Law* 3: 315–7; Beatrice Webb and Sidney Webb, *English Local Government: English Poor Law History: Part II, The Last Hundred Years* (1906; repr., Private Subscription, 67/450 edn, London: Beatrice and Sidney Webb, 1929), p. 98.

123 Mackay, *History of the English Poor Law* 3: 150.

124 Commons, 'Letter to Sir James Graham, Bart., 10th Annual Report, appendix no. 7', vol. 27, p. 141.

125 Mr John Leech, MP, 'Poor Laws' Amendment Bill', *The Times*, 2 July 1834.

126 Mr Thomas Law Hodges, MP, 'Poor Laws' Amendment Bill', *The Times*, 2 July 1834.

127 Mr Thomas Law Hodges, MP, 'Poor Laws' Amendment Bill', *The Times*, 2 July 1834.

128 Lord Althorp, MP, 'Poor Laws' Amendment Bill', *The Times*, 2 July 1834.

129 'Poor Laws' Amendment Bill', *The Times*, 2 July 1834.

130 Mackay, *History of the English Poor Law* 3: 138, 'Poor Laws' Amendment Bill', *The Times*, 2 July 1834.

131 Lord Henry Brougham, 'Poor Laws' Amendment Bill', House of Lords, *The Times*, 22 July 1834.

132 Brougham, 'Poor Laws' Amendment Bill', House of Lords, *The Times*, 22 July 1834.

133 Brougham, 'Poor Laws' Amendment Bill', House of Lords, *The Times*, 22 July 1834.

134 Brougham, 'Poor Laws' Amendment Bill', House of Lords, *The Times*, 22 July 1834.

135 13 Geo. 3, c. 82, The Lying-in Hospitals Act, 1773.

136 Nicholls, *A History of the English Poor Law* 2: 68–9.

137 Bishop of London, House of Lords, *The Mirror of Parliament*, 28 July 1834, 4: 3017.

138 Lord Kenyon, Speech to Lords, 8 August 1834, *Parliamentary Debates*, Lords, 3d ser., vol. 25, col. 1058.

139 Mackay, *History of the English Poor Law* 3: 144. By 1837 the Bishop of London, Charles James Blomfield engaged in real estate development on his large Paddington estate. As a land owner, potential for poor law rate increases concerned him. For this reason alone, Blomfield probably identified with MPs who opposed taking responsibility for illegitimate children and the unwed. Donald Olsen, *The Growth of Victorian London* (London: B.T. Batsford, 1976), p. 154.

140 Lord Wynford, Lords, *The Mirror of Parliament*, 28 July 1834, 4: 3024–5.

141 Bishop of Exeter, Henry Philpotts, 'Poor Law Amendment Bill', *The Mirror of Parliament* 4: 3021.

142 Exeter, 'Poor Law Amendment Bill', *The Mirror of Parliament* 4: 3020.

143 Exeter, 'Poor Law Amendment Bill', *The Mirror of Parliament* 4: 3020–1.

144 Lord Wynford, Lords, *The Mirror of Parliament*, 28 July 1834, 4: 3024–5.

145 Lord Wynford, Lords, *The Mirror of Parliament*, 28 July 1834, 4: 3024–5.

146 Lord Chancellor, Lords, *The Mirror of Parliament*, 28 July 1834, 4: 3026.

147 Bishop of London, Speech to House of Lords, 8 August 1834, *Parliamentary Debates*, Lords, 3d ser., vol. 25, col. 1080.

148 Exeter, Speech, 8 August 1834, Lords, vol. 25, col. 1066–7.

149 18 Eliz. 1 c. 3, Poor Laws.

150 Exeter, Speech, 8 August 1834, Lords, vol. 25, col., 1067–8.

151 Exeter, Speech, 8 August 1834, Lords, vol. 25, col., 1071.

152 Exeter, Speech, 8 August 1834, Lords, vol. 25, col., 1071–2.

153 Mackay, *History of the English Poor Law* 3: 315–7. B. Webb and S. Webb, *English Local Government: Part II*, 98.

154 Poor Laws, *Parliamentary Debates*, 8 August 1834, Lords, 3d ser., vol. 25, col. 1059–62.

155 Poor Laws, *Parliamentary Debates*, 8 August 1834, Lords, 3d ser., vol. 25, col. 1059–62.

156 Poor Laws, *Parliamentary Debates*, 8 August 1834, Lords, 3d ser., vol. 25, col. 1059–62.

157 Duke of Richmond, Speech to House of Lords, 8 August 1834, *Parliamentary Debates*, Lords, 3d ser., vol. 25, col. 1097.

158 Richmond, Speech, 8 August 1834, Lords, vol. 25, col., 1097–1100.

159 George Nicholls, *A History of the English Poor Law: A.D. 1714 to 1853*, vol. 2 (London: P.S. King and Son, 1904), p. 431.

160 Barret-Ducrocq, *Love in the Time of Victoria*, p. 156.

161 William Pinder Eversley, *The Law of Domestic Relations* (London: Stevens and Haynes, 1906), pp. 591–4.

162 Jenny Teichman, *Illegitimacy, An Examination of Bastardy* (Ithaca: Cornell University Press, 1982), p. 65.

163 4 & 5 Wm. 4 c. 76, s. 71; Barret-Ducrocq, *Love in the Time of Victoria*, p. 156.

164 Karl De Schweinitz, *England's Road to Social Security, from the Statute of Laborers in 1349 to the Beveridge Report of 1942* (1943; repr. New York: A.S. Barnes & Co., 1975), pp. 10–11.

165 Henry Longley, *Third Annual Report to the Local Government Board*, 1873–74, as cited by de Scheinwitz, *England's Road to Social Security*, p. 157.

166 10 & 11 Vict. c. 109 , Poor Law Board Act. De Schweinitz, *England's Road to Social Security*, p. 138.

167 Statute 34 & 35 Vict. c. 70, The Local Government Board Act. De Scheinwitz, *England's Road to Social Security*, p. 156.

168 Mary MacKinnon, 'English Poor Law Policy and the Crusade Against Outrelief', 605.

169 Longley, *Third Annual Report to the Local Government Board on Poor Law Administration in London*, p. 5.

170 Mackay, *History of the English Poor Law* 3: 315–7.

171 House of Commons, 'Poor Law Commissioners' Response to Nottinghamshire Magistrates, 10th Annual Report of the Poor Law Commissioners, appendix no. 7', *Sessional Papers*, 1845, Poor Laws, vol. 27, p. 141.

172 Commons, 'Commissioners' Response, 10th Annual Report', vol. 27, p. 140.

173 Commons, 'Commissioners' Response, 10th Annual Report', vol. 27, p. 141.

174 Commons, 'Commissioners' Response, 10th Annual Report', vol. 27, p. 141.

175 Statute 2 & 3 Vict. c. 85, Bastard Children Act, House of Commons, 'Report of Commissioners to Sir James Graham, Bart., 10th Annual Report of the Poor Law Commissioners, appendix no. 7', *Sessional Papers*, 1845, Poor Laws, vol. 27, see 2 & 3 Vict. c. 54, Custody of Infants Act, p. 142.

176 The significance of this problem for Victorian society not only appeared in popular literature, but legal historians generally included a section on 'bastardy' in their discussion of the laws of England. See Arthur Rackham Cleveland, *Woman under the English Law* (1896; repr. Fred B. Rothman: Littleton, CO, 1987), pp. 269–70. Stanley Giffard Hardinge, Earl of Halsbury, *Laws of England: A Complete Statement of the Whole Law of England* (London: Butterworth & Co., 1908), p. 2, pp. 425–51; and William Pinder Eversley, *The Law of The Domestic Relations* (London: Stevens and Haynes, 1906), pp. 589–90.

177 Cleveland, *Woman under the English Law*, pp. 269–70, 275.

178 *O.E.D.*, s. v. 'Summary jurisdiction' the determination of cases expeditiously without reference to the ordinary requirements of the common law.

179 House of Commons, 'Response of Poor Law Commissioners to Nottinghamshire Magistrates, 10th Annual Report of the Poor Law Commissioners, appendix no. 7', *Sessional Papers*, 1845, Poor Laws, vol. 27, p. 143.

180 Parliament framed the 1844 laws in favour of the child, not the mother. Statute 7 & 8 Vict. c. 101, s. 40, 42–4, Poor Law Amendment Act, 1844. B. Webb and S. Webb, *English Poor Law Policy*, p. 16.

181 Statute 7 & 8 Vict. c. 101, s. 40, 42–4. B. Webb and S. Webb, English Poor Law Policy, p. 16.

182 Nicholls, *History of the English Poor Law* 2: 318.

183 T. W. Fowle, *The Poor Law: The English Citizen, His Rights and Responsibilities* (London: Macmillan, 1893), p. 98.

184 Pat Thane, 'Women and the Poor Law in Victorian and Edwardian England', *History Workshop* 6 (1978): 32.

185 Illustrations of the relationship between domestic servants, seduction, illegitimacy, and

infanticide are in the following articles: 'Infanticide', *The Saturday Review* 20 (1865): 161–2; 'Seduction and Infanticide', *The Saturday Review* 22 (1866): 481–2, 545–6. See 'Illegitimacy in England and Wales, 1879', *Annual Reports of the Registrar General*, pp. 394–8. The Royal Statistical Society also investigated the problem of illegitimacy. See William Acton, F. R. C. S., 'Observations on Illegitimacy in the London Parishes of St Marylebone, St Pancras, and St George's Southwark, during the year 1857', *Journal of the Royal Statistical Society* 21 (1859): 491–505; W. G. Lumley, 'Observations upon the Statistics of Illegitimacy', *Journal of the Royal Statistical Society* 25 (1862): 219–63.

186 For an account of the Infant Life Protection Hearings see Margaret L. Arnot, 'Infant Death, Childcare and the State: The Baby-Farming Scandal and the First Infant Life Protection Legislation of 1872', *Continuity and Change* 9 (1994): 271–311.

187 See Ernest Hart, *The Protection of Infant Life: An Inquiry into the Practice of Baby Farming, with Suggestions for the Protection of Infants* (London: British Medical Journal, 1871), pp. 1–36.

188 Hart, *Protection of Infant Life*, pp. 1–36.

189 House of Commons, 'Mr John Brendan Curgenven, Secretary, Secretary Harveian Medical Society', Select Committee on Protection of Infant Life', *Sessional Papers*, 1872, Infant Life Protection, 5 June 1871, vol. 7, par. 1206–17.

190 House of Commons, 'Mr Jacob Bright, MP Select Committee on Protection of Infant Life', *Sessional Papers*, 1872, Infant Life Protection, 5 June 1871, vol. 7, par. 1217.

191 Commons, 'Select Committee on Protection of Infant Life, 1872', vol. 7, par 203, p. 41.

192 See Lionel Rose, *The Massacre of Innocents: Infanticide in Britain, 1800–1939* (London: Routledge, 1986).

193 35 Vict., c. 109, s. 1–10, Bastardy Amendment Act, 1872.

194 35 Vict., c. 109, s. 1–10.

195 See 8 Edw. 7 c. 27 Married Women's Property Act, 1908; 8 Edw. 7 c. 67 Children Act, 1908; and 9 Edw. 7 c. 13 Local Education Authorities, 1909.

196 9 Edw. 7 c. 13.

197 9 Edw. 7 c. 13.

198 Eversley, *The Law of Domestic Relations*, pp. 611–13. Cleveland, *Woman Under the English Law*, pp. 269–70; and Thane, 'Women and the Poor Law in Victorian and Edwardian England', 32. Barring the charge of adultery by the married mother, Talfourd's Act permitted the courts to grant her custody or access to her children under the age of 16. William R. Cornish, and George Norman Clark, *Law and Society in England: 1750–1950* (London: Sweet & Maxwell, 1989), p. 403, and n. 5.

199 Cornish and Clark, *Law and Society in England*, p. 403, and n. 5.

200 12 Car. II. c. 24, Tenures Abolition Act.

201 A Bill to Amend the Law Relating to the Guardianship and Custody of Infants', Statute 47 & 48 Vict. c. 27.

202 'Lords Amendments to the Infants Bill', Statute 47 & 48 Vict. c. 27.

203 Statute 24 & 25 Vict. c. 100, s. 50–1 (1861–62), Offenses against the Person Act.

204 In the case of boys, the law presumed they could exercise discretion at age fourteen. Parents had a right to protect their daughters to age 21, as much right at 15 as at 17, according to Eversley. Eversley, *The Law of Domestic Relations*, pp. 611–3.

205 Longley, *Report to the Local Government Board*, p. 6.
206 Longley, *Report to the Local Government Board*, p. 6.
207 Henriques, *Before the Welfare State*, p. 58; and Henriques, 'Bastardy and the New Poor Law', 103–29.
208 Poor Law Commissioners, *Third Annual Report of the Poor Law Commissioners*, p. 135.
209 According to a male nurse who worked in the Mile End Poor Law Infirmary during the 1880s, the workhouse poor were 'squalid and dirty, starving and dying, they suffered but at least felt they maintained their dignity. Once admitted, it was difficult to get out, and live their lives as they had before. After all, they would go back on to the streets in the same condition as they had gone in: destitute.' Fraser Cleminson, *Beyond Recall: The Making of Mile End Hospital* (London: Tower Hamlets Arts Project, 1983), p. 15.
210 *Association for the Improvement of the London Workhouse Infirmaries: The Condition of the Sick in the London Infirmaries. Report for a Deputation* (London: Association for the Improvement of London Workhouse Infirmaries, 1867), p. 21.
211 Lambeth Guardian, *The New Pauper Infirmaries and Casual Wards* (London: Norgate, 1875), p. 12.
212 Lambeth Guardian, *The New Pauper, Infirmaries and Casual Wards*, p. 12.
213 Lambeth Guardian, *The New Pauper, Infirmaries and Casual Wards*, p. 12.
214 Dora Downright, *Why I Am a Guardian* (Gerritsen Collection. Manchester: Headley Bros., 1888), p. 2.
215 Women married and single relied on Poor Law infirmaries for their confinements. Although this example is taken from an account of a workhouse board in the countryside, we may assume London guardians used a similar plan. Downright, *Why I Am a Guardian*, p. 2.
216 Downright, *Why I Am a Guardian*, p. 2.
217 Downright, *Why I Am a Guardian*, p. 2.
218 Downright, *Why I Am a Guardian*, p. 1.
219 House of Commons, 'Appendix to the Report from the Select Committee on Protection of Infant Life, Answers to Circular Addressed by Mr Corbett, appendix no. 4', *Sessional Papers*, 1871, Select Committee on Protection of Infant Life, vol. 7, pp. 254–71.
220 House of Commons, 'Appendix to the Report from the Select Committee on Protection of Infant Life, Answers to Circular Addressed by Mr Corbett, vol. 7, pp. 254–71.
221 The problem of foundlings rose to new heights in the nineteenth century. Poor Law registers showing lists of foundlings include: St Mary Abbot's Baptismal Register, Kensington (West London) H17/SMA/G1/1, 1877–1884, 'Register of Deserted Women and Children', Chelsea Board of Guardians, ChBG 197/1, LMA; St Andrews Hospital, formerly Poplar and Stepney Sick Asylum Registers, 1881, 1891, 1901, SA/M/1/8, LMA. Lady Georgiana Fullerton, 'Letter to the Editor of *The Times*', 14 January 1877; and Father Seddon's poor law correspondence, folios 1–22, Westminster Diocesan Archives W[estminster] D[iocesan] A[rchives]. Although the Sisters of Charity had not kept a list of foundlings, they reported they had received many on their doorstep. 'Awful Mortality in a Convent', *The Catholic Times and Catholic Opinion*, 2 February 1877.
222 Charles Dickens, 'A Walk in a Workhouse', *Household Words* 1 (1850): 203–4.
223 Mr Daniel Cooper, Secretary to the Society for the Rescue of Women and Young Children,

House of Commons, 'Select Committee on Protection of Infant Life', *Sessional Papers*, 1872, Infant Life, 15 June 1871, vol. 7, par. 2633, p. 123.

224 St Mary Abbot's Baptismal Registers, H17/SMA/G1/01-03, LMA.

225 'The Mortality in an Orphanage', *The Globe*, 17 January 1877.

226 'Alleged Murder of an Infant – A Sad Case', *Evening Standard*, 18 September 1889; 'Alleged Child Murder', *Evening Standard*, 25 September 1889; 'Marlborough Street Police Log', *The Times*, 19 September 1889.

227 Great Portland Street is located in the Oxford Street area of Marylebone on the south side of Regent's Park. *LCC, List of the Streets and Places in the Administrative County of London*, p. 222.

228 'Alleged Murder of An Infant – A Sad Case' *The Evening Standard*, 18 September 1889.

229 Judith Walkowitz discusses the role of the press as an observer of social dangers posed by 'sexual dangers.' Judith R. Walkowitz, 'Urban Spectatorship', *City of Dreadful Delight: Narratives of Sexual Danger in Late-Victorian London* (London: Virago, 1992), pp. 15–41.

230 The most thorough account of infant abandonment can be found in Valerie Fildes, *Women as Mothers in Pre-industrial England: Essays in Memory of Dorothy McLaren* (New York: Routledge, 1990), pp. 139–78.

231 'Police, Marlborough Street', *The Times*, 19 September 1889; 'Alleged Murder of an Infant – A Sad Case', *Evening Standard*, 18 September 1889.

232 'Central Criminal Court, Mary Griffiths, indicted for the willful murder of John Griffiths', *The Times*, 24 October 1889.

233 'Alleged Murder of An Infant – A Sad Case', *The Evening Standard*, 18 September 1889.

234 'Central Criminal Court, Mary Griffiths, indicted for the willful murder of John Griffiths', *The Times*, 24 October 1889.

235 'Police, Marlborough Street', *The Times*, 19 September 1889; 'Alleged Murder of an Infant – A Sad Case', *Evening Standard*, 18 September 1889.

236 'Alleged Murder of an Infant – A Sad Case', *Evening Standard*, 18 September 1889.

237 'Alleged Child Murder – A Sad Case', *Evening Standard*, 25 September 1889.

238 'Central Criminal Court, 'Mary Griffiths indicted for the willful murder of John Griffiths', *The Times*, 24 October 1889.

239 'Naming Pauper Children', *The Times*, 5 January 1867.

240 See 36 & 37 Vict. c. 12, Custody of Infants Act, and 49 & 50 Vict. c. 27 Guardianship and Custody of Infants Act, 1886.

241 Register of Deserted Children, pursuant to Poor Law Act, 1889, 52 & 53 Vict. c. 56., November 11, 1889 to June 29, 1924, St. BG/L/147, LMA.

242 Baptismal Register, St Mary Abbot's H17/SMA/G1/01, LMA.

243 Baptismal Register, St Mary Abbot's H17/SMA/G1/01, LMA.

244 Register of Deserted Women and Children', Chelsea Board of Guardians, Ch. B.G. 197/01, 1885, LMA.

245 Whitfield Street is situated between Bloomsbury Square and Regent's Park Crescent and runs parallel with Tottenham Court Road. It is in the parliamentary registration district of St Pancras, LCC, *List of the Streets and Places*, p. 555.

Chapter Two

1 Foundling Hospital Petition Form, A/FH/A/08/1, 1813, LMA.
2 Lord Brougham, 'Poor Laws' Amendment Bill', House of Lords, *The Times*, 22 July 1834.
3 Charles Dickens (1812–70) elaborates on his concerns for the poor in his journal *Household Words*, first published in 1850. His objective was to familiarize the public with important social issues. Dickens borrowed a line from Shakespeare, 'Familiar in their Mouths as Household Words', and had drawn on the legitimating authority of the Elizabethan bard for his journal. Several articles combine Dickens's literary style with 'investigative reporting', a genre similar to one employed by Henry Mayhew. In addition to Charles Dickens, 'Received, a Blank Child', *Household Words*, 1850: 49–53. See also Dickens, 'Home for Homeless Women', *Household Words* 7 (1853): 169–75.
4 McClure, *Coram's Children*, p. 76.
5 Nichols and Wray, *The History of the Foundling Hospital*, pp. 19; McClure, *Coram's Children*, pp. 42, 49, 63.
6 Wilson, 'Illegitimacy and Its Implications in Mid-Eighteenth-Century London: The Evidence of the Foundling Hospital', 103.
7 Dickens, 'Received, a Blank Child', 50.
8 Dickens, 'Received, a Blank Child', 50.
9 McClure, *Coram's Children*, p. 49.
10 Nichols and Wray, *The History of the Foundling Hospital*, p. 45.
11 Interestingly Dickens called the approach, admission by ballot, in his review of the Foundling Hospital admission policies in 'Received, a Blank Child', 49–53.
12 Foundling Hospital Admissions Register, vols. 1, 25 March 1741–28 February 1757, A/FH/A/09/2/1, LMA.
13 Nichols and Wray, *The History of the Foundling Hospital*, p. 62.
14 This table represents the yearly admissions totals. Foundling Hospital Admissions Registers as listed in vols. 1–2: vol. 1, 25 March 1741–28 February 1757, vol. 2. 1 March 1757–30 June 1758, A/FH/A/09/2/1–2, LMA.
15 McClure, *Coram's Children*, pp. 121–2.
16 McClure, *Coram's Children*, p. 121.
17 Wilson, 'Illegitimacy and Its Implications', 107; McClure, *Coram's Children*, pp. 80–114; Nichols and Wray, *The History of the Foundling Hospital*, pp. 56–65.
18 McClure, *Coram's Children*, p. 96.
19 *Journals of the House of Commons*, vol. 28, 571; Gen. Com. 7:57–8, McClure, *Coram's Children*, pp. 284 n. 58, p. 96.
20 'Lloyd's Speech in Parliament', Sir Richard Lloyd Speech, Resolutions of the Commons Respecting the State of the Poor and of the Poor Laws, 30 May 1759, *Parliamentary History*, Commons, 15: col. 941–3.
21 'The Foundling Hospital, A Useless Burden', *Gentleman's Magazine* 30 (1760): 54–5.
22 'The Foundling Hospital, A Useless Burden', *Gentleman's Magazine* 30 (1760): 54–5; and Table appearing under 'D', *Gentleman's Magazine* 30 (1760): 201.
23 Table appearing under 'D', *Gentleman's Magazine* 30 (1760): 201.
24 Researcher David Allin re-tallied the counts from the official Foundling Hospital registers,

which do not agree with the figures reported in *Gentleman's Magazine*. Allin finds 23 more children received before 21 June 1756. While the magazine reported 13,633 children were received during the general reception, Allin's count indicates 14,934 had been received. Allin's count likewise shows 2,535 more children had died. The discrepancy suggests the magazine had not received a full accounting of the Foundling Hospital registers. Allin, A/FH/A/09/2/1, vol. 1, 25 March 1741–28 February 1757, and vol. 2, 1 March 1757–30 June 1758, LMA.

25 Nichols and Wray, *The History of the Foundling Hospital*, p. 62.
26 'The Foundling Hospital, A Useless Burden', *The Gentleman's Magazine* 30 (1759): 55.
27 McClure, *Coram's Children*, pp. 114–5, 120.
28 McClure, *Coram's Children*, p. 45.
29 John Orr's List of Present and Missing Foundling Hospital Petitions, Thomas Coram Foundation.
30 Wilson makes this point in 'Illegitimacy in Its Implications', 137.
31 Foundling Hospital Admission Registers, A/FH/A/09/2–4, 1761–77, LMA.
32 For an overview of admission policies after the general reception, see Nichols and Wray, *The History of the Foundling Hospital*, pp. 81–97.
33 Foundling Hospital Admission Registers, A/FH/A/09/2–4, 1759–1771, LMA.
34 The principles for Hanway Acts are found under the following laws: Statute 2 Geo. 3, c. 22; Statute 7 Geo. 3, c. 39, Nicholls, *A History of the English Poor Law* 2: 62–4.
35 Statute 7 Geo. 3, c. 39; McClure, *Coram's Children*, pp. 80–1, 87.
36 Statute 7 Geo. 3, c. 39, Nicholls, *A History of the English Poor Law* 2: 62–4.
37 Statute 7 Geo. 3, c. 39, McClure, *Coram's Children*, pp. 144–7. B. Webb and S. Webb, *English Local Government: English Poor Law History*, Part I. The Old Poor Law (1906; repr., Private Subscription, 67/450 edn, London: Beatrice and Sidney Webb, 1929), p. 196.
38 Foundling Hospital Register, vol. 4, 13 May 1759–3 Dec. 1777, A/FH/A/09/2/4, LMA.
39 See Jonas Hanway, *Plan for a Magdalen-House for Repentant Prostitutes* (London, 1759), 17.
40 The concept of pleading a case grew out of English constitutional traditions and has a long history dating from the seventeenth century. Ellis Sandoz, ed., *The Roots of Liberty: Magna Carta, Ancient Constitution, and the Anglo-American Tradition of Rule of Law* (Columbia: University of Missouri Press, 1993), pp. 137–46. The use of petitions to influence policy became a general parliamentary procedure by the end of the eighteenth century. Examples include the Roman Catholic Relief Bill (1780), the movement for the abolition of slavery (1782), and parliamentary reform (1782). In the nineteenth century, the People's Charter stands out as one of the most significant petitions. H. St Clair Feilden, *A Short Constitutional History of England* (Littleton, CO: Fred B. Rothman and Co., 1986), pp. 246–7; McClure, *Coram's Children*, p. 141.
41 Sir William Holdsworth, *A History of English Law: The Centuries of Settlement and Reform* (1936; repr., London: Methuen and Co., Ltd, Sweet and Maxwell, 1966), 10: 696–701.
42 Petitions from 1768–1800 were flattened and placed into bound volumes; those after 1800 were folded into bundles, and in 1813 the bundles were folded into the application form. From 1820, the 'registry number' appears on most petitions and an inscription as to whether the committee accepted or rejected the petition. LMA, Archivist Notes, 6 June 1992.

43 Foundling Hospital Petition Form, A/FH/A/08/1, 1813, LMA.

44 Foundling Hospital Revised Petition Form, 1856, A/FH/A/06/15/7, 1856, LMA.

45 David Owen, *English Philanthropy, 1660–1960* (Cambridge: Belknap Press, 1964), pp. 14–5.

46 Archivist Notes on Foundling Hospital Records, LMA Finding Guide, LMA.

47 James Augustus Hessey, 'The Tenderness of Christ Towards Sinners', Sermon delivered to the Governors of the Foundling Hospital Pamphlet # 6155, 9–10, LGL.

48 For more information on the development of laws of evidence and standards for proof, see Mark Jackson, *New-Born Child Murder: Women, Illegitimacy and the Courts in Eighteenth-Century England* (Manchester: Manchester University Press, 1996), pp. 145–51.

49 Dickens, 'Home for Homeless Women', 170.

50 Lord Wynford, House of Lords, 28 July 1834, *The Mirror of Parliament* 4: 3025.

51 Lord Wynford, House of Lords, 28 July 1834, *The Mirror of Parliament* 4: 3025.

52 Commons, 'Select Committee on Protection of Infant Life, 1871', vol. 7: par. 1815, 1759.

53 Nichols and Wray, *The History of the Foundling Hospital*, p. 278.

54 Nichols and Wray, *The History of the Foundling Hospital*, p. 277–8.

55 Foundling Hospital Petition Form Instructions, A/FH/A/08/1-1856, LMA.

56 Foundling Hospital Petition Form Instructions, A/FH/A/06/15/7, 1856, LMA.

57 Dickens, 'Received, a Blank Child', 51.

58 Foundling Hospital Petition Form Instructions, A/FH/A/06/15/7, LMA.

59 Hessey, 'The Tenderness of Christ towards Sinners', Pamphlet # 6155, 9–10, 12, LGL.

60 Hessey, 'The Tenderness of Christ towards Sinners', Pamphlet # 6155, 9–10, 12, LGL.

61 Hessey, 'The Tenderness of Christ towards Sinners', Pamphlet # 6155, 9–10, 12, LGL.

62 Hessey, 'The Tenderness of Christ towards Sinners', Pamphlet # 6155, 9–10, 12, LGL.

63 Hessey, 'The Tenderness of Christ towards Sinners', Pamphlet # 6155, 12, LGL.

64 For a discussion of the teachings of the Church fathers on 'guilt' beginning with Tertullian (AD 160-225) see Gerda Lerner, *The Creation of Feminist Consciousness: from the Middle Ages to Eighteen-Seventy* (New York: Oxford University Press, 1993), pp. 140-1.

65 Foundling Hospital Petitions, A/FH/A/08/1, 1842–1892, LMA.

66 Barristers resorted to the 'crim. con. suit' to prove adulterous behaviour. As late as 1857, the 'injured husband in his heartbroken agonies' was required to prove such was the case before he could file for divorce. 'The Last of Crim. Con.', *The Saturday Review* 3 (1857): 590–1. *Oxford English Dictionary*, s. v. 'Criminal conversation.' A husband filed legal charges against his wife's suitor for trespassing on his property.

67 Commons, 'Protection of Infant Life, 1871', vol. 7, par. 1810.

68 Commons, 'Protection of Infant Life, 1871', vol. 7, par. 1759.

69 Commons, 'Protection of Infant Life, 1871', vol. 7, par. 1759.

70 Dickens, 'Received, a Blank Child', 49.

71 Although the original building was destroyed, the Thomas Coram Foundation reconstructed the centre offices and essential public rooms of the Foundling Hospital on Brunswick Square. When the Thomas Coram returned its offices to London in 1937, it reconstructed the second floor of the building to replicate the demolished office centre; this image appears in the 1935 *History of the Foundling Hospital*. This setting includes

a large, long room, with tall windows, and deep windowsills wrapped with dark wood molding. In the centre of the room was a long oblong table. Perhaps this was the same table, or very similar to the one in front of which petitioners stood before committee men during the hearing process. Nichols and Wray placed a picture of 'The Courtroom' in their 1935 history. Nichols and Wray, *History of the Foundling Hospital*, facing p. 70.

72 Gregory testimony, 'Protection of Infant Life', vol. 7, par. 1736.

73 Barret-Ducrocq relied on Michel Foucault to explain this view. 'It is also a ritual that unfolds within a power relationship, for one does not confess without the presence (or virtual presence) of a partner who is not simply the interlocutor but the authority who requires the confession, prescribes and appreciates it, and intervenes in order to judge, punish, forgive, console, and reconcile; a ritual in which the truth is corroborated by the obstacles and resistance it has had to surmount in order to be formulated.' Michel Foucault, *The History of Sexuality, the Use of Pleasure* (London: Penguin Press, 1990), pp. 61–2 as cited in Barret-Ducrocq, *Love in the Time of Victoria*, p. 42.

74 Foundling Hospital Petition Form, A/FH/A/08/1, 1813, LMA.

75 Mr Twiddy reported he held an interview with 'Pet' after her examination by the committee. She recapitulated her former statements accurately. Foundling Hospital Fifty-Year Survey, A/FH/A/08/1, 1853, LMA.

76 Commons, 'Protection of Infant Life, 1871', vol. 7, par. 1844–8.

77 Charles Dickens, *Little Dorrit*, John Holloway ed. (1857; repr., London: Penguin Books, 1967). pp. 54–7.

78 Barret-Ducrocq implies the women wrote the petitions themselves. This was not the case. The secretary working as a transcriber attended the meetings and recorded the petitioner's statements as a court reporter, so to speak. Barret-Ducrocq, *Love in the Time of Victoria*, pp. 42.

79 Commons, 'Select Committee on Protection of Infant Life, 1871', vol. 7, par. 1806.

80 Questions about money, drugs, and alcohol relate directly to the following pieces of legislation: 1844 Bastardy Amendment Act, Statute 7 & 8 Vict. c. 101, s. 40; 1872 Bastardy Amendment Act, Statute 35 Vict., c. 109, s. 1–10; Bill to Amend the law relating to the Guardianship and Custody of Infants – Statute 47 & 48 Vict., c. 308, s. 1–8; Lords Amendments to the Infants Bill, Statute 47 & 48 Vict., c. 308, s. 1–8. Commons, 'Select Committee on Protection of Infant Life, 1871', vol. 7, par. 1806. Foundling Hospital Petitions, Fifty-Year Survey, 1842–92, A/FH/A/08/1, 1842–1892, LMA.

81 Foundling Hospital Petitions, Fifty-Year Survey, 1842–92, A/FH/A/08/1, 1842–1892, LMA.

82 Foundling Hospital Petition Form Instructions, A/FH/A/06/15/7, LMA.

83 Barret-Ducrocq, *Love in the Time of Victoria*, p. 42.

84 Commons, 'Protection of Infant Life, 1871', vol. 7, par. 1736.

85 Commons, 'Protection of Infant Life, 1871', vol. 7, par. 1736.

Chapter Three

1 Edward Walford, *Old and New London: A Narrative of Its Places*, vols. 3 and 5 (London: Cassell, Petter, and Galpin, 1868–77), 3: 394.

2 The following works, Andrew Mearns, *The Bitter Cry of Outcast London* (London: J. Clark, 1883), William Booth, *In Darkest England and the Way Out* (Chicago: Charles H. Sergel & Co., 1890), and Charles Booth, *Life and Labour of the People in London* (1889–1902) surveyed London poverty between 1885 and 1902 and represent this trend.

3 Foundling Hospital petitions frequently included first-hand accounts of the sleeping arrangements for domestics, A/FH/A/08/1, 1842–1892, LMA.

4 Walter Thornbury, 'London Parks, St James's Park-Hyde Park', *Belgravia* 3 (1867): 410–20; 'London Parks, Hyde Park', *Belgravia* 4 (1868): 68–79; 'London Palaces, St James's Palace–Carlton House–Buckingham Palace', *Belgravia* 5 (1868): 184–92.

5 Roy Porter, *London, a Social History*, 211; (London: Hamish Hamilton, 1994), p. 211. Ben Weinreb and Christopher Hibbert, *The London Encyclopaedia* (Bethesda, MD: Adler and Adler Publishers, Inc., 1986), pp. 104–6.

6 For a discussion of the place of 'country homes' in English society, see F.M.L. Thompson, *The Rise of Respectable Society* (Cambridge: Harvard University Press, 1988), pp. 152–62.

7 Charles Booth, *Life and Labour of the People in London*, First Series, Poverty, vol. 3 (London: Macmillan and Co., 1902–3), pp. 96–7.

8 *Building News* 3 (1857): 635 as cited in Olsen, *The Growth of Victorian*, pp. 164–5.

9 Walter Thornbury, 'London Squares, Bloomsbury and Bedford Squares', *Belgravia* 2 (1867): 325–37.

10 Lefebvre, *The Production of Space*, p. 33.

11 Walford, *Old and New London* 5: 360.

12 McClure, *Coram's Children*, p. 65.

13 The Marquis of Tavistock was the Duke of Bedford's grandson.

14 The Foundling Hospital, LMA Print Collection; Registration Districts of London, 1845, #645 FN 1843, LMA; London County Council Map, 1913 #6, LMA.

15 'Bernard Street' is situated directly across the street from the Russell Square Underground Station. Nichols and Wray, *A History of the Foundling Hospital*, p. 79.

16 P. J. Atkins, 'How the West End was Won: the Struggle to Remove Street Barriers in Victorian London,' *Journal of Historical Geography* 19 (1993): 266.

17 Walford, *Old and New London* 5: 363–4.

18 Thomas H. Shepherd, *London and Its Environs in the Nineteenth Century* (1829; repr., New York: Benjamin Blom, 1968), pp. 135–6.

19 John Brownlow, *Memoranda: or Chronicles of The Foundling Hospital, Including Memoirs of Captain Coram* (London: Sampson Low, 1847), pp. 223–5.

20 John Timbs, *Curiosities of London: Exhibiting the Most Rare and Remarkable Objects of Interest in the Metropolis; with Nearly Sixty Years' Personal Recollections*, New Edition (1867; repr., Detroit: Singing Tree Press, 1968), p. 210. David Owen, *English Philanthropy, 1660–1960* (Cambridge: Belknap Press, 1964), p. 56.

21 Owen, *English Philanthropy, 1660-1960*, pp. 53–7. McClure, *Coram's Children*, pp. 61–5.

22 Marquis de Levis, *England at the Beginning of the Nineteenth Century*. Trans. by M. De Levis (London: D. Jacques, 1851), pp. 103–4.

23 'Chapel of the Foundling Hospital', *The Penny Magazine* 14 (1845): 345.

24 Lithograph, 'Interior of the Chapel of the Foundling Hospital', Walford, *Old and New London* 5: 360.

25 Lithograph, 'Interior of the Chapel of the Foundling Hospital', Walford, *Old and New London* 5: 360.

26 'Chapel of the Foundling Hospital', *The Penny Magazine* 14 (1845): 345.

27 Seating Plan of Pews at the Foundling Hospital Chapel, 1840–64, A/FH/A14/8–49, LMA.

28 Timbs, *Curiosities of London*, p. 210.

29 Of course, St Joseph was not as popular a figure in the Protestant tradition as in the Roman Catholic Church, and would have been considered secondary.

30 Frederick Hunt reported that Surrey's mortality rates were lowest in the metropolitan area; the area in closest proximity to Westminster with low mortality, good water, a wide and clean street was found in St George Hanover Square. Frederick Hunt, 'The Registrar-General on "Life" in London', *Household Words* 14 (1850): 330–3.

31 Nicholas Draper, *The Price of Emancipation: Slave Ownership, Compensation and British Society at the End of Slavery* (Cambridge: Cambridge University Press, 2010), appendix: Geographic Distribution of Mercantile Awards over Five Hundred Pounds, Table 7.1.

32 John, *Aristocratic Century*, (Cambridge: Cambridge University Press, 1987), pp. 76–7.

33 Steen Eiler Rasmussen, *London: The Unique City* (Cambridge, MA: Massachusetts Institute of Technology Press, 1967), pp. 190–2; Atkins, 'How the West End was Won', 273–5.

34 Rasmussen, *London: The Unique City*, 190–2; Atkins, 'How the West End was Won', 273–5.

35 Mrs Main's testimony, Commons, 'Infant Life Protection Bill', vol. 13, par. 4648–51, 4683–9.

36 Thornbury, 'London Squares, Bloomsbury and Bedford Squares', *Belgravia* 2 (1867): 325–37.

37 Walter Thornbury, *London: Old and New: Its History, Its People, and Its Places* (London: Cassell, Petter, Galpin, and Co., 1881), pp. 553–6.

38 'The Registration Districts of the Metropolis, 1843', G43/FN/1843, LMA Map Collection.

39 Dickens, 'Received, a Blank Child', 50.

40 Foundling Hospital Petition Form Instructions, A/FH/A/06/15/7, 1856, LMA.

41 Foundling Hospital Petition Form Instructions, A/FH/A/06/15/7, 1856, LMA.

42 Foundling Hospital Petition Form Instructions, A/FH/A/06/15/7, 1856, LMA.

43 John Brownlow, *Memoranda; or Chronicles of The London Foundling Hospital, Including Memoirs of Captain Coram* (London: Sampson Low, 1847), p. 190.

44 The Foundling Hospital data sample surveys 'accepted' and 'rejected' petitions. It is most safe to say that the data collected and analyzed here represents the petitioner population. The degree to which the fifty-year Foundling Hospital survey reflects the larger population will require more research. See the introduction for further explanation. Whether the individual petition was accepted or rejected will be noted accordingly in the footnote.

45 The 'three year rule' for residency parallels the three-year residency requirement for voting in municipal elections established under the 1835 Municipal Corporations Act. David R. Green, *From Artisans to Paupers: Economic Change and Poverty in London, 1790–1870* (Aldershot, Hants: Scolar Press, 1995), appendix 1.1.

46 Green, *Artisans to Paupers*, appendix 1.1.

47 N = the database number for accepted and rejected petitions. Foundling Hospital Survey, A/FH/A/08/1 1842–1892, LMA.

48 Barret-Ducrocq surveyed Foundling Hospital petitions between 1850 and 1880. Her study may not have included extra-metropolitan petitions. This may partially account for significant differences in interpretation of the Foundling Hospital petitions, *Love in the Time of Victoria*, p. 205.

49 Geoffrey Rivett, Table 1, *The Development of the London Hospital System, 1823–1982* (London: King Edward's Hospital Fund for London, 1986), p. 21.

50 Registration Districts of the Metropolis, 1843, G45/FN/1843, LMA Map Collection. Hippolyte Taine, *Notes on England* (London: Holt & Williams, 1872), p. 36.

51 N = database figures for accepted and rejected petitions. Foundling Hospital Survey, A/FH/A/08/1 1842–1859, LMA.

52 Rivett, Table 1, *The Development of the London Hospital System*, p. 21.

53 N = accepted and rejected petitions, 1842–9. A/FH/A/08/1-1842-1849, LMA.

54 Rivett, Table 1, *The Development of the London Hospital System*, p. 21.

55 Accepted Foundling Hospital Petition, A/FH/A/08/1-1874, LMA.

56 N = accepted and rejected petitions. Foundling Hospital Survey, A/FH/A/08/1 1850–59, LMA.

57 See the account of 'Norah the Irish Maid' in Henry and Augustus Mayhew, *The Greatest Plague of Life: or The Adventures of a Lady in Search of a Good Servant* (Philadelphia: Carey and Hart, 1847).

58 'Alleged Murder of an Infant – A Sad Case' *Evening Standard*, 18 September 1889; 'Alleged Child Murder', *Evening Standard*, 25 September 1889; 'Marlborough Street Police Log', *The Times*, 19 September 1889.

59 Gareth Stedman Jones, *Outcast London: A Study of the Relationship between Classes in Victorian Society* (1971; repr., London: Penguin Books, 1984), p. 138.

60 Charles Booth, *Life and Labour of the People in London*, Second Series, Industry, vol. 4 (London: Macmillan and Co., 1902–3), p. 388.

61 The P-value for the mothers' address tables is P < 05; that is, the percentages of accepted and rejected petitions compared by decade and geographical regions changed significantly. For an explanation of the P- value, the probability factor, see appendix 1

62 N = number of Accepted Petitions by Division, 1860–92. A/FH/A/08/1-1860-92.

63 Commons, 'Protection of Infant Life, 1871', vol. 7, par. 1736. Foundling Hospital Survey, A/FH/A/08/1 1842–1892, LMA.

64 Brougham, 'Poor Laws' Amendment Bill', House of Lords, *The Times*, 22 July 1834.

65 Foundling Hospital Survey, 1842–1892, A/FH/A/08/1 1842–1892, LMA.

66 Accepted Foundling Hospital Petition, A/FH/A/08/1-1841, LMA.

67 Accepted Foundling Hospital Petition, A/FH/A/08/1-1841, LMA.

68 Accepted Foundling Hospital Petition, A/FH/A/08/1-1841, LMA.

69 Accepted Foundling Hospital Petition, A/FH/A/08/1-1841, LMA.

70 Accepted Foundling Hospital Petition, A/FH/A/08/1-1841, LMA.

Chapter Four

1 Foundling Hospital Petition Form, A/FH/A/06/15/7, 1856, LMA.
2 Foundling Hospital Petition Form, A/FH/A/06/15/7, 1856, LMA.
3 Royal London Hospital Maternity Register Case Book, LH/M/118/1901, R[oyal] L[ondon] H[ospital] A[rchives].
4 Royal London Hospital Maternity Register Case Book, LH/M/118/1901, RLHA.
5 Royal London Hospital Maternity Register Case Book, LH/M/118/1901, RLHA.
6 Royal London Hospital Maternity Register Case Book, LH/M/118/1901 and Royal London Hospital Maternity Register, LH/M/5/3-RLHA.
7 The data is based on a 10 per cent survey of all cases served at the institution. Mile End Infirmary Obstetrical Register, St BG/ME/1-1-1899/8-8-1915, LMA.
8 Mrs Ranyard's Bible women visited unwed mothers in London workhouses. They assessed their character, and could feasibly recommend a woman whom they thought capable of reform to the Foundling Hospital.
9 Foundling Hospital Mothers' Letters, A/FH/A/09/19/1-16, 1861–68, 1857–73, LMA.
10 Foundling Hospital Mothers' Letters, A/FH/A/09/19/1-16, 1861–68, 1857–73, LMA.
11 Rev Mr Claxton to Secretary John Brownlow, London, 2 July 1859. Secretary's Correspondence, A/FH/A/06/1, 116/3, LMA.
12 Claxton to Brownlow, A/FH/A/06/1, 116/3, LMA.
13 Claxton to Brownlow, A/FH/A/06/1, 116/3, LMA.
14 Secretary's Correspondence, A/FH/A/06/1, 116/18, LMA.
15 Ellen Davenport to John Brownlow, 8 February 1859, Foundling Hospital Correspondence, A/FH/A/06/1, 116/1-B, LMA.
16 Ann E. to Secretary John Brownlow, Secretary's Correspondence, A/FH/A/06/1, 116/18, LMA.
17 Dickens, 'Received, a Blank Child', 51.
18 Dickens, 'Received, a Blank Child', 50.
19 Walford, *Old and New London* 5: 358.
20 The Foundling Hospital data sample surveys 10 per cent of 'accepted' and 'rejected' petitions submitted between 1842 and 1860, and 10 per cent of all accepted petitions for the years 1861 to 1892. Whether the committee accepted or rejected is noted accordingly in the endnote.
21 Jean Robin, 'Prenuptial Pregnancy in a Rural Area of Devonshire in the Mid-Nineteenth Century: Colyton, 1851–1881', *Continuity and Change* (1986): 113–24; and Jean Robin, 'Illegitimacy in Colyton, 1851–1881', *Continuity and Change* 2 (1987): 311.
22 Foundling Hospital Survey, A/FH/A/08/1 1842–1892, LMA.
23 N= database number. Foundling Hospital Survey, A/FH/A/08/1 1850–1879, LMA.
24 The Foundling Hospital cases may also reflect the transition from the 'family wage economy' to the 'family consumer economy'. Mothers prescribed the work of their daughters, but little of this appears in the petitions. Rather most petitioners presented themselves as independent wage earners. Louise Tilly and Joan Scott, *Women, Work, and Family* (New York: Routledge, 1978), pp. 176–7.
25 N = database number for accepted and rejected petitions. Foundling Hospital Survey, A/FH/A/08/1 1842–1892, LMA.

26 N = database number for accepted and rejected petitions. Foundling Hospital Survey, A/FH/A/08/1 1842–1892, LMA.

27 House of Commons, 'Census England and Wales, 1881–1891', *Sessional Papers*, 1892, Census 1891, vol. 26, p. 348.

28 Commons, 'Census England and Wales, 1881–1891', vol. 26, p. 332.

29 See Sonya Rose, *Limited Livelihoods: Gender and Class in Nineteenth Century England* (Berkeley: University of California Press, 1992).

30 Commons, 'Census England and Wales, 1881–1891', vol. 26, p. 348.

31 Commons, 'Census England and Wales, 1881–1891', vol. 26, p. 348.

32 Clara Collet, 'Wages of Domestic Servants. A Report on the Money Wages of Indoor Domestic Servants', *Sessional Papers,* 1899, Board of Trade, vol. 112; Clara Collet, 'Women's Work', in *Life and Labour of the People in London*, First Series, Poverty. 4 vols (London: Macmillan and Co., 1902), Poverty 4: 256–327. In addition, see Simon R. S. Szreter, 'The Genesis of the Registrar-General's Social Classification of Occupations', *The British Journal of Sociology* 35 (1984): 522–46.

33 Collet, 'Women's Work', *Life and Labour of the People in London*, Poverty 4: 256–327.

34 St Patrick's Wapping 1893 Westminster Diocesan Census, WDA; Dr John James Rygate, *Annual Report to the Vestry of Saint George in the East* (London: J. and B. Dodsworth, 1883), p. 50.

35 Collet, 'Women's Work', *Life and Labour of the People in London*, Poverty 4: 314.

36 Collet, 'Women's Work', *Life and Labour of the People in London*, Poverty 4: 314.

37 Collet, *On the Money Wages of Indoor Domestic Servants*, pp. 3–5.

38 Collet, *On the Money Wages of Indoor Domestic Servants*, pp. 3–5.

39 Detailed accounts of elite social life are provided by Richard Davey, *The Pageant of London, 1500 to 1900 AD.* vol. 2 (London: Methuen & Co., 1906), pp. 612–5; Porter, 'Culture Under the Georges', London: *A Social History*, pp. 160–83; Giles Waterfield, 'The Town House as Gallery of Art', *The London Journal* 20 (1995): 47–66; F. M. L. Thompson, 'Moving Frontiers and the Fortunes of the Aristocratic Town House 1830–1930', *The London Journal* 27 (1995): 67–78; and Sheppard, 'London and the Nation in the Nineteenth Century', 67.

40 See M. Jeanne Peterson, 'The Victorian Governess: Status Incongruence in Family and Society', *Suffer and Be Still: Women in the Victorian Age*, ed. Martha Vincinus (Bloomington: Indiana University Press, 1973), p. 8.

41 Collet, *On the Money Wages of Indoor Domestic Servants*, pp. 16–23.

42 Foundling Hospital Survey, A/FH/A/08/1 1842–1892, LMA.

43 The word 'class' is retained to reflect the language used by the Registrar General to describe male occupations. If such a study or survey other than Clara Collet's had been done for women's occupations, the compilers would probably have retained the same language, using the term 'class' as a categorizing function.

44 In the 1970s and 1980s, historical demographers studied the relationship between fertility and occupation, illegitimacy and marriage patterns to produce insight into 'normative values'. Many demographers believe that legitimate fertility and the age at marriage is related to the phenomena of prenuptial pregnancy and illegitimacy. The methodological underpinnings for this part of the study were drawn from Michael Anderson's studies

and more importantly R. I. Woods. Michael Anderson was the first to analyze marriage patterns by applying statistical techniques to 1861 census data from parliamentary registration districts in England and Wales. In 1985, Robert I. Woods and P. R. A. Hinde built on Anderson's technique and developed a 'collective biography' approach to data drawn from local areas in order to consider variations among individuals. The 'collective biography' measures and compares data on age, occupation, location and fertility rates within and between populations. Woods and Hinde based their thesis on Anderson's research from the 1970s in which he suggests that employment influenced both male and female marriage patterns. Woods and Hinde examined statistics for marriage ages, occupation (particularly female employment outside the home), sex ratios and changes in agricultural production; drawing a distinction between urban and rural locales (based on parliamentary registration districts or RDs).

According to Woods and Hinde, marriage patterns may be associated with or caused by the geography of employment structures. Changing employment structures shifted the marriage age downward. Employment opportunities were higher in urban areas for women than men. Employment opportunities in agriculture were higher for men than women in rural areas. Geographic dislocation served to push age at marriage downward because the young women were separated from their families, who would have served as protectors. What appeared to be significant in their study was not that women worked outside the home, but rather that types of employment held the greatest influence over age at marriage, and whether a pre-nuptial pregnancy occurred. Their study demonstrates differences between prenuptial pregnancy rates for women who were employed as domestics and women who were employed in some sort of millwork. Woods and Hinde focus more on the age at marriage and fertility for women employed in northern industrial cities. They observe, however, that being 'in service' for female domestics represented an important stage in the female life cycle. R. I. Woods and P. R. A. Hinde, 'Nuptiality and Age at Marriage in Nineteenth Century England', *Journal of Family History* 9 (1985): 119–40. See also Michael Anderson, 'Marriage Patterns in Victorian Britain: An Analysis Based on Registration District Data for England and Wales, 1861', *Journal of Family History* 1 (1976): 55–78.

The most extensive historiographical analysis of the relationship between fertility, illegitimacy and occupation can be found in Simon Szreter's chapter on fertility decline in *Fertility Class, and Gender in Britain, 1860–1940*. Szreter notes past methodological oversights and proposes a new form of fertility analysis that takes into account the political and ideological aspects of historical change, as well as, local and cultural variations as these relate to changing employment opportunities. Szreter suggests that 'labour historians' have 'contributed to a fundamental distortion of the investigative process and a gross limitation upon the forms of explanation which can be attained. This kind of model has sent those seeking explanations down a cul-de-sac where only highly general, nationally applicable, sweeping causal mechanisms are attended to.' Szreter, 'The Study of the Fertility Decline', in *Fertility, Class and Gender in Britain, 1860–1940*, pp. 9–66. John Gillis' study on the Foundling Hospital women relates specifically to domestic service and age at marriage. Gillis, 'Servants, Sexual Relations, and the Risks of Illegitimacy in London, 1801–1900', 142–73.

45 N = database figures for accepted and rejected petitions. See appendix 8, Foundling Hospital Petitioners' Occupations, 1842–1892. Foundling Hospital Survey, A/FH/A/08/1 1842–1892, LMA.
46 Charles Booth, *Life and Labour of the People in London* First Series, Poverty, vol. 4 (London: Macmillan and Co., 1902–3), p. 322.
47 N = database figures for accepted and rejected petitions. Foundling Hospital Survey, A/FH/A8/0/1-1842–92, LMA.
48 Woods and Hinde show that women's occupations, especially in domestic service delayed marriage and reduced the proportion of married couples. Woods and Hinde, 'Nuptiality and Age at Marriage in Nineteenth Century England', 120.
49 Foundling Hospital Survey, A/FH/A/08/1 1842–1892, LMA.
50 Foundling Hospital Survey, A/FH/A/08/1 1842–1892, LMA.
51 Foundling Hospital Survey, A/FH/A/08/1 1842–1892, LMA.
52 Accepted Foundling Hospital Petitions, A/FH/A/08/1- 1858–60, LMA.
53 The Foundling Hospital transcriber did not begin keeping the ages of the fathers until John Brownlow took office in 1848. Foundling Hospital Survey, A/FH/A/08/1 1842–1892, LMA.
54 Foundling Hospital Survey, A/FH/A/08/1 1842–1892, LMA. The study relies on socio-economic census categories as modified and condensed into six categories in 1950. Gareth Stedman Jones cited and incorporated these occupational categories in *Outcast London*, appendix 2, Table 15. For a treatment of London's occupation structures by socio-economic categories, see Green, *From Artisans to Paupers.*
55 Foundling Hospital Survey, A/FH/A/08/1 1842–1892, LMA.
56 For contemporary assessments of this problem see Jill Matus, *Unstable Bodies: Victorian Representations of Sexuality and Maternity* (Manchester: Manchester University Press, 1995), pp. 1–3.
57 Sheppard, 'London and the Nation in the Nineteenth Century', 69.
58 Foundling Hospital Survey, A/FH/A/08/1 1842–1892, LMA.
59 Foundling Hospital Survey, A/FH/A/08/1 1842–1892, LMA.
60 Foundling Hospital Survey, A/FH/A/08/1 1842–1892, LMA.
61 Commons, 'Protection of Infant Life, 1871', vol. 7, par. 1758.
62 Commons, 'Protection of Infant Life, 1871', vol. 7, par. 1758.
63 Commons, 'Protection of Infant Life, 1871', vol. 7, par. 1758.
64 Commons, 'Protection of Infant Life, 1871', vol. 7, par. 1758.
65 Foundling Hospital Petitions A/FH/A/08/1 1842–1892, LMA.
66 Scott, 'Gender: A Useful Category of Historical Analysis', 1066–9.

Chapter Five

1 'Servants' Characters', *The Saturday Review*, 10 January 1863, 48: 47–9.
2 Sarah F. to John Brownlow, 23 April 1853, Foundling Hospital Correspondence, A/FH/A/06/1-116/1-B, LMA.
3 Stefan Collini, *Public Moralists: Political Thought and Intellectual Life in Britain, 1850–1930* (Oxford: Clarendon Press, 1993), p. 91.

4 Dickens, 'Home for Homeless Women', 170.

5 Martin Wiener, *Reconstructing the Criminal: Culture, Law, and Policy in England, 1830–1914* (Cambridge: Cambridge University Press, 1994), p. 39.

6 Steven Mintz argues that nineteenth-century responsibility for enculturation and socialization shifted from the larger kin group (parents, aunts, uncles, grandparents, cousins), church, and state to the nuclear family in Great Britain and the United States. Family values were a mirror image of the changing values of the larger society. Simultaneously new emotional, economic and legal pressures placed on the institution of the family created 'a prison of expectations'. Steven Mintz, *A Prison of Expectations: The Family in Victorian Culture* (New York: New York University Press, 1983).

7 John Brownlow as cited by Nichols and Wray, *History and Objects of the Foundling Hospital*, p. 3.

8 Barret-Ducrocq, *Love in the Time of Victoria*, pp. 54–5.

9 Barret-Ducrocq, *Love in the Time of Victoria*, pp. 3–4.

10 Barret-Ducrocq, *Love in the Time of Victoria*, Table of Contents.

11 Clark, *The Struggle for the Breeches*, pp. 43–4; Robin, 'Prenuptial Pregnancy in Devon, 1851–1881', 117.

12 Peter Laslett, '*The Bastardy Prone Sub-Society*', In *Bastardy and its Comparative History*, edited by Peter Laslett and Richard M. Smith (Cambridge: Harvard University Press, 1980), p. 8.

13 Thompson, *The Making of the English Working Class*, p. 11.

14 Tables 5.1 and 5.2 are drawn from the Foundling Hospital Survey, A/FH/A/08/1 1842–1892, LMA.

15 Foundling Hospital Survey, A/FH/A/08/1 1860–1892, LMA.

16 Foundling Hospital Survey, A/FH/A/08/1 1842–1859, LMA.

17 'Alleged Murder of an Infant – A Sad Case', *Evening Standard*, 18 September 1889; 'Alleged Child Murder', *Evening Standard*, 25 September 1889; 'Marlborough Street Police Log', *The Times*, 19 September 1889.

18 Sarah F. to John Brownlow, March 1853, Foundling Hospital Correspondence, A/FH/A/06/1-116/1-B, LMA.

19 Sarah F. to John Brownlow, March 1853, Foundling Hospital Correspondence, A/FH/A/06/1-116/1-B, LMA.

20 Peterson, 'The Victorian Governess: Status Incongruence, pp. 3–4.

21 Sarah F. to John Brownlow, March 1853, Foundling Hospital Correspondence, A/FH/A/06/1-116/1-B, LMA.

22 Sarah F. to Brownlow, A/FH/A/06/1-116/1-B, LMA.

23 Sarah F. to Brownlow, A/FH/A/06/1-116/1-B, LMA.

24 Sarah F. to Brownlow, A/FH/A/06/1-116/1-B, LMA.

25 Sarah F. to John Brownlow, 23 March 1853. Foundling Hospital Correspondence, A/FH/A/06/1-116/1-B, LMA.

26 Sarah F. to John Brownlow, 23 March 1853. Foundling Hospital Correspondence, A/FH/A/06/1-116/1-B, LMA.

27 Sarah F. to Brownlow, 23 March 1853, A/FH/A/06/1-116/1-B, LMA.

28 Sarah F. to Brownlow, 23 March 1853, A/FH/A/06/1-116/1-B, LMA.

29 Sarah F. to Brownlow, 23 March 1853, A/FH/A/06/1-116/1-B, LMA.
30 Sarah F. to Brownlow, 23 March 1853, A/FH/A/06/1-116/1-B, LMA.
31 Sarah F. to Brownlow, 23 March 1853, A/FH/A/06/1-116/1-B, LMA.
32 Sarah F. to Brownlow, 23 March 1853, A/FH/A/06/1-116/1-B, LMA.
33 Sarah F. to Brownlow, 23 March 1853, A/FH/A/06/1-116/1-B, LMA.
34 Accepted Foundling Hospital Petition, A/FH/A/08/1-1841, LMA.
35 Foundling Hospital Survey, A/FH/A/08/1-1843, LMA.
36 Foundling Hospital Survey, A/FH/A/08/1-1843, LMA.
37 Accepted Foundling Hospital Petition, A/FH/A/08/1-1846, LMA.
38 This petition was drawn from among the earlier survey years. Until 1848, the transcripts had a formulaic quality; that is no longer the case after John Brownlow becomes secretary. Noticeably more details surrounding the primary event are provided. Accepted Foundling Hospital Petition, A/FH/A/08/1-1846, LMA.
39 Accepted Foundling Hospital Petition, A/FH/A/08/1-1846, LMA.
40 Accepted Foundling Hospital Petition, A/FH/A/08/1-1846, LMA.
41 Accepted Foundling Hospital Petition, A/FH/A/08/1-1846, LMA.
42 Accepted Foundling Hospital Petition, A/FH/A/08/1, 1865, LMA.
43 Accepted Foundling Hospital Petition, A/FH/A/08/1, 1865, LMA.
44 'The Highgate and Hampstead Mystery, The Cook's Body Found', *The Evening Standard*, 25 July 1889.
45 N = the database number for accepted and rejected petitions. Foundling Hospital Survey, A/FH/A/08/1 1842–1892, LMA. See appendix 5, Foundling Hospital Consent & Promise to Marry Codes, 1842–92, and appendix 6, Promise to Marry Codes, 1842–92.
46 N = the database number for accepted. Foundling Hospital Survey, A/FH/A/08/1 1842–1892, LMA.
47 N = the database number for accepted petitions. Rejected Foundling Hospital Petitions, A/FH/A/08/1, 1842-1856, LMA.
48 N = the database number for accepted and rejected petitions. Foundling Hospital Survey, A/FH/A/08/1 1842-1892, LMA.
49 Foundling Hospital Survey, A/FH/A/08/1-1853, LMA.
50 Foundling Hospital Survey, A/FH/A/08/1-1855, LMA.
51 Accepted Foundling Hospital Survey, A/FH/A/08/1-1891, LMA.
52 Accepted Foundling Hospital Petition, A/FH/A/08/1-1891, LMA.
53 N = the database number for accepted and rejected petitions. Foundling Hospital Survey, A/FH/A/08/1 1842–1892, LMA; rejected petitions, Foundling Hospital Survey, A/FH/A/08-1842-59.
54 Accepted Foundling Hospital Petition, A/FH/A/08/1-1891, LMA.
55 Scott, 'Gender: A Useful Category of History Analysis', 1066–9. For an historical overview of sexual abuse appearing in the early Foundling Hospital petitions, see Clark, *Women's Silence, Men's Violence: Sexual Assault in England, 1770–1845.*
56 Foundling Hospital Survey, A/FH/A/08/1 1842-1892, LMA.
57 N = the database number for accepted and rejected petitions. Foundling Hospital Survey, A/FH/A/08/1 1842–92, LMA.
58 Accepted Foundling Hospital Petition, A/FH/A/08/1-1842, LMA.

59 Accepted Foundling Hospital Petition, A/FH/A/08/1-1842, LMA.
60 Accepted Foundling Hospital Petition, A/FH/A/08/1-1842, LMA.
61 Accepted Foundling Hospital Petition, A/FH/A/08/1-1842, LMA.
62 Accepted Foundling Hospital Petition, A/FH/A/08/1-1851, LMA.
63 Accepted Foundling Hospital Petition, A/FH/A/08/1-1851, LMA.
64 Accepted Foundling Hospital Petition, A/FH/A/08/1-1858, LMA.
65 Accepted Foundling Hospital Petition, A/FH/A/08/1-1858, LMA.
66 Accepted Foundling Hospital Petition, A/FH/A/08/1-1858, LMA.
67 Accepted Foundling Hospital Petition, A/FH/A/08/1-1858, LMA.
68 For a description of Notting Hill Gate, and the development of large estates in Haverstock Hill, see Olsen, *The Growth of Victorian London*, pp. 169–70, 247–64.
69 Accepted Foundling Hospital Petition, A/FH/A/08/1-1881, LMA.
70 Accepted Foundling Hospital Petition, A/FH/A/08/1-1881, LMA.
71 Accepted Foundling Hospital Petition, A/FH/A/08/1-1861, LMA.
72 Accepted Foundling Hospital Petition, A/FH/A/08/1-1861, LMA.
73 Foundling Hospital Survey, A/FH/A/08/1 1842–1892, LMA.
74 Accepted Foundling Hospital Petition, A/FH/A/08/1-1888, LMA.
75 Accepted Foundling Hospital Petition, A/FH/A/08/1-1888, LMA.
76 Accepted Foundling Hospital Petition, A/FH/A/08/1-1890, LMA.
77 Accepted Foundling Hospital Petition, A/FH/A/08/1-1890, LMA.
78 N = number for all petitions. Foundling Hospital Survey, A/FH/A/08/1 1842–92, LMA.
79 In the survey, there were one or two other cases of reported incest; and one case from a small town outside London was accepted. Foundling Hospital Accepted Petition, A/FH/A/08/1-1854, LMA.
80 Rejected Foundling Hospital Petition, A/FH/A/08/1-1851, LMA.
81 Rejected Foundling Hospital Petition, A/FH/A/08/1-1851, LMA.
82 Rejected Foundling Hospital Petition, A/FH/A/08/1-1851, LMA.
83 Rejected Foundling Hospital Petition, A/FH/A/08/1-1851, LMA.
84 Foundling Hospital Survey, A/FH/A/08/1-1842, LMA.
85 Foundling Hospital Survey, A/FH/A/08/1-1842, LMA.
86 Rejected Foundling Hospital Petition, A/FH/A/08/1-1851, LMA.
87 Accepted Foundling Hospital Petition, A/FH/A/08/1-1843, LMA.
88 Accepted Foundling Hospital Petition, A/FH/A/08/1-1851, LMA.
89 Accepted Foundling Hospital Petition, A/FH/A/08/1-1851, LMA.
90 Accepted Foundling Hospital Petition, A/FH/A/08/1-1857, LMA.
91 Rejected Foundling Hospital Petition, A/FH/A/08/1-1853, LMA.
92 Accepted Foundling Hospital Petition, A/FH/A/08/1-1841, LMA.
93 Accepted Foundling Hospital Petition, A/FH/A/08/1-1841, LMA.
94 Barret-Ducrocq argues that in a society invested in the principle of sexual inequality, which made constant allowance for the strength of sexual desire in men while questioning its very existence in women, drunkenness as a supplementary cause of violence would have passed more or less unnoticed. The Foundling Hospital committee men did not ignore such mitigating factors. Barret-Ducrocq, *Love in the Time of Victoria*, p. 47.
95 Accepted Foundling Hospital Petition, A/FH/A/08/1-1881, LMA.

96 Accepted Foundling Hospital Petition, A/FH/A/08/1-1881, LMA.
97 Rejected Foundling Hospital Petition, A/FH/A/08/1-1850, LMA.
98 Rejected Foundling Hospital Petition, A/FH/A/08/1-1850, LMA.
99 Rejected Foundling Hospital Petition, A/FH/A/08/1-1850, LMA.
100 Rejected Foundling Hospital Petition, A/FH/A/08/1-1856, LMA.
101 Rejected Foundling Hospital Petition, A/FH/A/08/1-1856, LMA.
102 Rejected Foundling Hospital Petition, A/FH/A/08/1-1854, LMA.
103 N = the number petitions in database with these specific characteristics. Foundling Hospital Survey, A/FH/A8/1-1850-59, LMA. The committee accepted 412 infants between 1850 and 1859 and reviewed about 700 or more petitions.
104 Rejected Foundling Hospital Petition, A/FH/A/08/1-1843, LMA.
105 Rejected Foundling Hospital Petition, A/FH/A/08/1-1851, LMA.
106 Rejected Foundling Hospital Petition, A/FH/A/08/1-1852, LMA.
107 Rejected Foundling Hospital Petition, A/FH/A/08/1-1851, LMA.
108 Rejected Foundling Hospital Petition, A/FH/A/08/1-1851, LMA.
109 Rejected Foundling Hospital Petition, A/FH/A/08/1-1851, LMA.
110 Rejected Foundling Hospital Petition, A/FH/A/08/1-1851, LMA.
111 Rejected Foundling Hospital Petition, A/FH/A/08/1-1851, LMA.
112 For a legal history of breach of promise, including the ramifications of bigamy see Ginger S. Frost, *Promises Broken: Courtship, Class, and Gender in Victorian England* (Charlottesville: University of Virginia Press, 1995), pp. 13–24.
113 Accepted Foundling Hospital Petition, A/FH/A/08/1-1859, LMA.
114 Research coupling Foundling Hospital petitions with magistrate court records would prove fruitful. Foundling Hospital Survey, A/FH/A/08/1-1842–1892, LMA.
115 Rejected Foundling Hospital Petition, A/FH/A/08/1-1853, LMA.
116 Rejected Foundling Hospital Petition, A/FH/A/08/1-1853, LMA.
117 Accepted Foundling Hospital Petition, A/FH/A/08/1-1881–1992, LMA.
118 Accepted Foundling Hospital Petitions, A/FH/A/08/1-1858, LMA.
119 Accepted Foundling Hospital Petitions, A/FH/A/08/1-1861, LMA.
120 Rejected Foundling Hospital Petition, A/FH/A/08/1-1848, LMA.
121 Rejected Foundling Hospital Petition, A/FH/A/08/1-1848, LMA.
122 Rejected Foundling Hospital Petition, A/FH/A/08/1-1848, LMA.
123 Accepted Foundling Hospital Petition, A/FH/A/08/1-1875, LMA.
124 Accepted Foundling Hospital Petition, A/FH/A/08/1-1891, LMA.
125 Accepted Foundling Hospital Petition, A/FH/A/08/1-1891, LMA.
126 Accepted Foundling Hospital Petition, A/FH/A/08/1-1881, LMA.
127 Accepted Foundling Hospital Petition, A/FH/A/08/1-1881, LMA.
128 Accepted Foundling Hospital Petition, A/FH/A/08/1-1891, LMA.
129 Accepted Foundling Hospital Petition, A/FH/A/08/1-1891, LMA.
130 Accepted Foundling Hospital Petition, A/FH/A/08/1-1891, LMA.
131 Accepted Foundling Hospital Petition, A/FH/A/08/1-1891, LMA.
132 Accepted Foundling Hospital Petition, A/FH/A/08/1-1888, LMA.
133 Legally, the 1872 Bastardy Amendment Act, section three of Statute 35 Vict., c. 109, s. 110 added new supports to unwed mothers. If she could prove the father had given her money

for support before the birth of the child, she could start filiation proceedings at once, appear in petty sessions, and testify to this.

134 1872 Bastardy Amendment Act, Statute 35 Vict., c. 109, s. 1–10.
135 Accepted Foundling Hospital Petition, A/FH/A/08/1-1871, LMA.
136 'Parliamentary Bills of Importance, The Saint Pancras Petition in Reference to the Maintenance of Deserted Women Bill', *The Metropolitan*, 7 April 1886.
137 9 Edw. 7 c. 13., Local Education Authorities (Medical Treatment Act), 1909.
138 Foundling Hospital Petitions Survey, A/FH/A/08/1-1842–1892, LMA.
139 Rejected Foundling Hospital Petition, A/FH/A8/1-1849, LMA; Timbs, *Curiosities of London*, p. 749.
140 Rejected Foundling Hospital Petition, A/FH/A/08/1-1849, LMA.
141 Accepted Foundling Hospital Petition, A/FH/A/08/1-1851, LMA.
142 The emphasis in the petition on the young man's return from India suggested its foreign and corrupted nature; and upon returning home, he may have spread 'cultural degeneration' or contamination. See Antoinette Burton, *Burdens of Empire: British Feminists, Indian Women, and Imperial Culture, 1865–1915* (Chapel Hill: University of North Carolina Press, 1994), pp. 47–9.
143 Accepted Foundling Hospital Petition, A/FH/A/08/1-1851, LMA.
144 Accepted Foundling Hospital Petition, A/FH/A/08/1-1851, LMA.
145 Accepted Foundling Hospital Petition, A/FH/A/08/1-1871, LMA.
146 Accepted Foundling Hospital Petition, A/FH/A/08/1-1871, LMA.
147 Sarah F. to Brownlow, 23 March 1853, A/FH/A/06/1-116/1-B, LMA.
148 Foundling Hospital Survey, A/FH/A/08/1, 1842–1892, LMA.
149 N = figures extrapolated from manuscript register. 'Applications, 1879–1907', A/FH/A/06/7, LMA.

Chapter Six

1 Accepted Foundling Hospital Petition, A/FH/A/08/1-1856, LMA.
2 'Servants' Characters', *The Saturday Review*, 10 January 1863, 49.
3 'Servants' Characters', *The Saturday Review*, 10 January 1863, 49.
4 Foundling Hospital Petition Form, 1856, A/FH/A/06/15/7, LMA.
5 See appendix 7: Foundling Hospital Recommenders, 1842–92.
6 N = the database number for accepted petitions. Foundling Hospital Survey, A/FH/A/08/1-1842–1892, LMA.
7 N = the database number for accepted petitions. Foundling Hospital Survey, A/FH/A/08/1-1842–1892, LMA.
8 Barret-Ducrocq, *Love in the Time of Victoria*, pp. 31, 48–9, 68.
9 Walford, *Old and New London* 5: 358.
10 Accepted Foundling Hospital Petition, A/FH/A/08/1-1851, LMA.
11 Accepted Foundling Hospital Petition, A/FH/A/08/1-1851, LMA.
12 Accepted Foundling Hospital Petition, A/FH/A/08/1-1850, LMA.
13 Accepted Foundling Hospital Petition, A/FH/A/08/1-1850, LMA.

14 Accepted Foundling Hospital Petition, A/FH/A/08/1-1850, LMA.
15 Accepted Foundling Hospital Petition, A/FH/A/08/1-1865, LMA.
16 Accepted Foundling Hospital Petition, A/FH/A/08/1-1865, LMA.
17 Accepted Foundling Hospital Petition, A/FH/A/08/1-1865, LMA.
18 Accepted Foundling Hospital Petition, A/FH/A/08/1-1865, LMA.
19 Tripe is a foodstuff made from the stomach lining of cattle, usually pickled in brine. Accepted Foundling Hospital Petition, A/FH/A/08/1-1841, LMA.
20 Accepted Foundling Hospital Petition, A/FH/A/08/1-1841, LMA.
21 Accepted Foundling Hospital Petition, A/FH/A/08/1-1841, LMA.
22 Accepted Foundling Hospital Petition, A/FH/A/08/1-1841, LMA.
23 Accepted Foundling Hospital Petition, A/FH/A/08/1-1880, LMA.
24 Accepted Foundling Hospital Petition, A/FH/A/08/1-1880, LMA.
25 Accepted Foundling Hospital Petition, A/FH/A/08/1-1880, LMA.
26 Accepted Foundling Hospital Petition, A/FH/A/08/1-1880, LMA.
27 Montague House was described by John Timbs as 'the elegant detached mansion' situated on the northwest angle of Portman Square and built for Mrs Elizabeth Montague. The owner was known for holding an annual party for the chimney sweeps of London on her front lawn. Timbs, *Curiosities of London*, p. 554. The area had declined by 1902 when Charles Booth described it in the following way: 'The great majority of these people are of the artisan and labouring classes. Houses are fairly large and in some cases much sublet. Rough lot in some of the Mews. Some decent shopkeepers and well-to-do people.' Charles Booth, 'Appendix, Table 1 – Classification and Description of the Population of London, 1887–1889 by School Board Blocks and Districts', *Life and Labour of the People in London*, First Series, Poverty, vol. 2 (London: Macmillan and Co., 1902), p. 11.
28 Accepted Foundling Hospital Petition, A/FH/A/08/1-1851, LMA.
29 Accepted Foundling Hospital Petition, A/FH/A/08/1-1851, LMA.
30 Accepted Foundling Hospital Petition, A/FH/A/08/1-1858, LMA.
31 Accepted Foundling Hospital Petition, A/FH/A/08/1-1859, LMA.
32 Accepted Foundling Hospital Petition, A/FH/A/08/1-1859, LMA.
33 Accepted Foundling Hospital Petition, A/FH/A/08/1-1859, LMA.
34 Foundling Hospital Survey, A/FH/A/08/1, 1842–1892, LMA.
35 Accepted Foundling Hospital Petition, A/FH/A/08/1-1859, LMA.
36 Foundling Hospital Survey, A/FH/A/08/1, 1842–1892, LMA.
37 Occasionally medical conditions prevented wealthy women from nursing their own infants, or they were part of a group of women who found it more convenient to employ a wet-nurse rather than nursing their infant themselves. Hiring a wet-nurse was regarded as a controversial practice, and whether the mothers did this in anticipation of the advancements of infant formula, not a reliable substitute for breast milk at the time, or as a matter of social convention warrants more research.
38 Accepted Foundling Hospital Petition, A/FH/A/08/1-1891, LMA.
39 Brixton, Peckham, Dulwich, and Walworth were situated south of the Thames. In the nineteenth century, each neighbourhood had its own shopping area, or high street. Real estate was depressed in these areas because of a glut in the building markets. The town of Brixton was fashionable, but not as prestigious as Norwood situated further to the

south in Surrey, or Lancaster Gate in Central London situated just off Hyde Park. Some people characterized London as a city of small towns, each little town with their own town centre, high street, churches and pubs. Today London retains this characteristic. Many nineteenth- and early twentieth-century neighbourhoods grew up with their own 'town centres'. These town centres retain many of these features, including a 'high street' where the shops, bank, post office, local public library, lottery shop, wine shop and laundry are located. Olsen, *The Growth of Victorian London*, pp. 199, 207.

40 Margaret B. earned about seven shillings a week in addition to her room and board. Accepted Foundling Hospital Petition in which infant had died before admission, A/FH/A/08/1-1863, LMA.

41 Accepted Foundling Hospital Petition, A/FH/A/08/1-1863, LMA.

42 Accepted Foundling Hospital Petition, A/FH/A/08/1-1863, LMA. See James Greenwood, *The Seven Curses of London* (Boston: Fields, Osgood & Co., 1869), pp. 22–43.

43 Accepted Foundling Hospital Petition, A/FH/A/08/1-1871, LMA.

44 Accepted Foundling Hospital Petition, A/FH/A/08/1-1888, LMA.

45 Foundling Hospital Survey, A/FH/A/08/1-1842–1892 LMA.

46 Accepted Foundling Hospital Petition, A/FH/A/08/1-1881, LMA.

47 Accepted Foundling Hospital Petition, A/FH/A/08/1-1881, LMA.

48 Accepted Foundling Hospital Petition, A/FH/A/08/1-1881, LMA.

49 Accepted Foundling Hospital Petition, A/FH/A/08/1-1881, LMA.

50 Accepted Foundling Hospital Petition, A/FH/A/08/1-1891, LMA.

51 Accepted Foundling Hospital Petition, A/FH/A/08/1-1891, LMA.

52 Accepted Petition, Foundling Hospital Survey, A/FH/A/08/1-1861, LMA.

53 Accepted Foundling Hospital Petition, A/FH/A/08/1-1851, LMA.

54 In a similar 1862 case, the banns of marriage had been read at St James Piccadilly but the father died of typhus before their marriage. Foundling Hospital Survey, A/FH/A/08/1-1860, LMA; A/FH/A/08/1-1863, LMA.

55 Accepted Foundling Hospital Petition, A/FH/A/08/1-1880, LMA.

56 Accepted Foundling Hospital Petition, A/FH/A/08/1-1880, LMA.

57 Accepted Foundling Hospital Petition, A/FH/A/08/1-1880, LMA.

58 Accepted Foundling Hospital Petition, A/FH/A/08/1-1881 LMA.

59 Rejected Foundling Hospital Petition, A/FH/A/08/1-1854, LMA.

60 Rejected Foundling Hospital Petition, A/FH/A/08/1-1854, LMA.

61 Richard Croft, Curate, St Matthew's Westminster to Foundling Hospital Secretary John Brownlow, 24 October 1855, Rejected Foundling Hospital Petition, A/FH/A/08/1-1855.

62 Croft to Brownlow, 24 October 1855, Rejected Foundling Hospital Petition, A/FH/A/08/1-1855, LMA.

63 Rejected Foundling Hospital Petition, A/FH/A/08/1-1862, LMA.

64 Rejected Foundling Hospital Petition, A/FH/A/08/1-1862, LMA.

65 Rejected Foundling Hospital Petition, A/FH/A/08/1-1862, LMA.

66 Robert Archey Woods, *English Social Movements* (New York: Charles Scribner Sons, 1891), p. 192 and Herbert Fry, *Royal Guide to the Principal London and Other Charities* (London: Churchman Publishing Col, Ltd., 1939).

67 N = database figures. Foundling Hospital Survey, A/FH/A/08/1-1842–1892, LMA.

68 Magdalen House, *The Rules, Orders and Regulations of the Magdalen House* (London, 1759), 19–23.

69 Anglican sisterhoods opened their first institution in 1845, five years after the Roman Catholic Congregation of the Good Shepherds, a French order of nuns began similar work in Hammersmith. 'English Sisterhoods', *The Saturday Review*, 223–4. See Susan Mumm, '"Not Worse Than Other Girls", The Convent-Based Rehabilitation of Fallen Women in Victorian Britain,' *Journal of Social History* 29 (1996): 527–46.

70 *Ninth Annual Report of the Committee of the Westminster and North-West London Female Asylum, est. 1837*. Annual report presented at the yearly meeting held at the institution on Weston Street, St Pancras, 25 January 1847. Pamphlet no. 5493, 9–13, LGL.

71 *Ninth Annual Report of the Committee of the Westminster and North-West London Female Asylum*, 1837, 9–13, LGL.

72 'Rescue Work', *The Women's Herald*, 11 May 1893.

73 N = database figures. Foundling Hospital Survey, A/FH/A/08/1-1842-1892, LMA.

74 Foundling Hospital Survey, A/FH/A/08/1-1842–1892, LMA. 'Home for Gentlewomen,' *The Times*, 17 January 1861; 'Home of Hope', *The Times*, 17 January 1861.

75 Commons, 'Select Committee on Protection of Infant Life, 1871', vol. 7, par. 4631–44, par. 4715–21.

76 Foundling Hospital Survey, A/FH/A/08/1-1842–1892, LMA.

77 Weymouth Street is situated near Portland Place in Marylebone, just south of the Royal Academy of Music on Marylebone Road. LCC, *List of the Streets and Places*, p. 552.

78 John Dewhurst, *Queen Charlotte's The Story of a Hospital* (London: Queen Charlotte's Hospital), p. 85.

79 Records of the Ranyard Mission and Ranyard Nurses in the LMA, finding guide to documents A/RYN, LMA.

80 Records show the women working across London, from offices in Holborn to the East End. A/RYN, LMA.

81 Foundling Hospital Survey, A/FH/A/08/1-1842–1892, LMA.

82 N = database figures. Foundling Hospital Survey, A/FH/A/08/1-1842–1892, LMA.

83 Foundling Hospital Survey, A/FH/A/08/1-1842–1892, LMA.

84 Foundling Hospital Survey, A/FH/A/08/1-1842–1892, LMA.

85 Accepted Foundling Hospital Petition, A/FH/A/08/1-1861, LMA.

86 Further evidence is provided in letters to Mr Brownlow. Foundling Hospital Accepted Petition, A/FH/A/08/1-1861, LMA.

87 N = database figures. Foundling Hospital Survey, A/FH/A/08/1-1842–1892, LMA.

88 Accepted Foundling Hospital Petition, A/FH/A/08/1-1849, LMA.

89 Accepted Foundling Hospital Petition, A/FH/A/08/1-1849, LMA.

90 Accepted Foundling Hospital Petition, A/FH/A/08/1-1881 LMA.

91 Accepted Foundling Hospital Petition, A/FH/A/08/1-1881 LMA.

92 Mayhew commented at length on the question of 'juvenile and general prostitution' and those who lived in 'low-lodging houses' in 'cantons' such as St George in the East. Henry Mayhew, *The Morning Chronicle Survey of Labour and the Poor*, 6 vols. Edited by P. Razzell. (1850–52; repr., Firle, Sussex: Caliban Books, 1980), pp. 1:6; 4:56, 67.

93 Foundling Hospital Survey, A/FH/A/08/1-1842–1892, LMA.

94 Gillis, 'Servants, Sexual Relations, and the Risks of Illegitimacy in London, 1801-1900', 142–3. Foundling Hospital Survey, A/FH/A/08/1-1842–1892, LMA.
95 Rejected Foundling Hospital Petition, A/FH/A/08/1-1851, LMA.
96 Foundling Hospital Survey, A/FH/A/08/1-1842–1892, LMA.
97 Foundling Hospital Survey, A/FH/A/08/1-1842–1892, LMA.
98 N = number of petitions accepted at Queen Charlotte's by decade. Foundling Hospital Survey, A/FH/A/08/1-1842–1892, LMA.
99 Accepted Foundling Hospital Petition, A/FH/A/08/1-1861, LMA.
100 Queen Charlotte's Lying-in Hospital Mothers' Profiles, A/FH/A/08/1-1842-92, LMA.
101 Rejected Foundling Hospital Petition, A/FH/A/08/1-1854, LMA
102 Rejected Foundling Hospital Petition, A/FH/A/08/1-1854, LMA
103 Rejected Foundling Hospital Petition, A/FH/A/08/1-1854, LMA
104 Rejected Foundling Hospital Petition, A/FH/A/08/1-1854, LMA
105 House of Commons, *Sessional Papers*, Poor Law Report, vol. 15, 1862.
106 Institutions such as the Foundling Hospital were not permitted to house more than one infant over a 24-hour period. The legislation proposed to prevent women from leaving their infants with baby-farmers. Commons, 'Select Committee on the Infant Life Protection Bill, 1890', vol. 13, par. 965, 48.
107 Commons, 'Select Committee on the Infant Life Protection Bill, 1890', vol. 13, 841–6, 43.
108 Commons, 'Select Committee on the Infant Life Protection Bill, 1890', vol. 13, 841–6, 43.
109 Commons, 'Select Committee on the Infant Life Protection Bill, 1890', vol. 13, 841–6, 43.
110 Commons, 'Select Committee on the Infant Life Protection Bill, 1890', vol. 13, 952, 47.
111 See appendix 7 for a list of Foundling Hospital Recommenders, 1842–92.
112 Commons, 'Select Committee on Protection of Infant Life, 1871', vol. 7: par. 1759.
113 Foundling Hospital Survey, A/FH/A/08/1, 1842–1892, LMA.
114 N = database number for accepted and rejected petitions. Foundling Hospital Survey, A/FH/A/08/1, 1842–1892, LMA.
115 Any of these factors would lend support to Nancy Chodorow's argument that gender and power relationships are influenced by larger social forces, but rather there is a strong element of personal 'construction: of one's place in society', lending support to the 'constrained agency' theory. Women make choices that we may not always understand, but they make them for their own reasons, and as Giddens argued, they can explain the why and wherefore without difficulty. Chodorow, 'Gender as a Personal and Cultural Construction', 517; Giddens, *The Constitution of Society*, p. 217.
116 N = rejected petitions. Foundling Hospital Petitions Survey, A/FH/A/08/1, 1842–1860, LMA.
117 Steven Marcus, 'Who is Fagin?' *Oliver Twist*, ed. Fred Kaplan, Norton Critical Edition (New York: W.W. Norton, 1993), pp. 480–2; Dickens, 'Received, a Blank Child', 49.
118 Charles Dickens, *Oliver Twist*, ed. Fred Kaplan, Norton Critical Editions (New York: W. W. Norton, 1993), p. 343. All subsequent citations refer to this edition.
119 Graham Greene, 'The Young Dickens', *Oliver Twist*, ed. Fred Kaplan, Norton Critical Edition (New York: W.W. Norton, 1993), pp. 426–32. Keith Hollingsworth, 'The Newgate Novel and the Moral Argument, 1837–1840, or The 'Real' World of Oliver Twist', as cited in Fred Kaplan, ed., *Oliver Twist*, Norton Critical Edition (New York: W. W. Norton, 1993), pp. 469–77.

120 Commons, 'Protection of Infant Life, 1871,' vol. 7, appendix no. 6, p. 274.

121 Dickens, *Oliver Twist*, p. 343.

122 Charles Dickens to John Brownlow, 26 February 1840, *Charles Dickens, The Letters of Charles Dickens*, eds. Graham, Storey, Kathleen Tillotson and Angus Easson, Pilgrim Edition (Oxford: Clarendon Press, 1993), 2:33–4.

123 Unpublished letter, Charles Dickens at Tavistock House to John Brownlow, 14 February 1859, A/FH/A/06/1 116/3, LMA.

124 Chapel Seating Plans, Christmas 1852, Box 43, A/FH/A/14/0; Plans of Pews, 1860–64, A/FH/A14/8–49, LMA. See also Valerie L. Gager, 'Our Pew at Church: Another Interpretation by Way of Shakespeare', *Dickensian* 89 (1993): 25–31.

125 Unpublished letter, Charles Dickens to John Brownlow, n.d., Secretary's Correspondence, A/FH/A6/1, 116/17, LMA.

126 Dickens, 'Received, a Blank Child', 51.

127 Dickens, 'Received, a Blank Child', 51.

128 Dickens, 'Home for Homeless Women', 169–75.

129 Great Marlboro Street intersects Regent Street, and is one block south of Oxford Street, and Oxford Circus. Great Marlboro Street was situated in St James Parish, the City of Westminster, and the Strand parliamentary registration district. Mayne's petition was among the rejected petitions from Central London. LCC, *List of the Streets and Places*, p. 222. Rejected Foundling Hospital Petition, Susan M., aged 21, A/FH/A/08/1-1855, LMA.

130 Secretary Twiddy's interview with Great Marlboro Street gaoler, Rejected Foundling Hospital Petitions, A/FH/A/08/1-1855, LMA. Charles Dickens to John Hardwick, 8 February 1855, *The Letters of Charles Dickens* 7: 527.

131 *Oxford Dictionary of National Biography*, s. v. 'Mayne, Sir Richard (1796–1868), London police commissioner.'

132 Rejected Foundling Hospital Petition, A/FH/A/08/1-1855, LMA.

133 Rejected Foundling Hospital Petition, A/FH/A/08/1-1855, LMA.

134 The baroness was the second wealthiest woman in Britain. Only Queen Victoria was wealthier. *Oxford Dictionary of National Biography*, s. v. 'Burdett-Coutts, Baroness.'

135 For more information on Urania Cottage see Michael Mason, *The Making of Victorian Sexual Attitudes* (Oxford: Oxford University Press, 1994), pp. 87–8, 99.

136 Charles Dickens to Miss Burdett-Coutts, 21 January 1855, *The Letters of Charles Dickens* 7: 507–8.

137 Dickens, 'Home for Homeless Women', 161, 169.

138 Dickens, 'Home for Homeless Women', 161, 169.

139 Charles Dickens to Miss Burdett-Coutts, 21 January 1855, *The Letters of Charles Dickens* 7: 507–8.

140 Charles Dickens to Miss Burdett-Coutts, 21 January 1855, *The Letters of Charles Dickens* 7: 507–8.

141 In his position as magistrate, Mr Hardwick distributed funds placed in the 'Poor Box' at the Great Marlborough Street Police Station. Contributors and amounts received were acknowledged in *The Times* on a weekly basis in the column headed 'Police Log.' Charles Dickens to John Hardwick, 8 February 1855, *The Letters of Charles Dickens* 7: 527.

142 Charles Dickens to John Hardwick, 8 February 1855, *The Letters of Charles Dickens* 7: 527.
143 Rejected Foundling Hospital Petition, A/FH/A/08/1-1855, LMA.
144 Charles Dickens to John Hardwick, 8 February 1855, *The Letters of Charles Dickens* 7: 527.
145 Mrs Marchmont, Superintendent of the Burdett-Coutts Home for Destitute Females, Shepherds Bush to Mr Twiddy, Foundling Hospital Enquirer, n. d., Rejected Foundling Hospital Petition, A/FH/A/08/1-1855, LMA.
146 Mrs Marchmont to Mr Twiddy, Foundling Hospital Enquirer, n. d., Rejected Foundling Hospital Petition, A/FH/A/08/1-1855, LMA.
147 Owen, *English Philanthropy: 1660–1960*, p. 416.
148 Mrs Marchmont sent a note from Charles Dickens to Mr Twiddy as evidence of support. Charles Dickens, Folkestone, Kent, to Mrs Marchmont, Urania Cottage, 3 October 1855, unpublished letter. Rejected Foundling Hospital Petition, A/FH/A/08/1-1855, LMA.
149 Queen Charlotte's Lying-in Hospital matron interview with Mr Twiddy, Foundling Hospital enquirer, Rejected Foundling Hospital Petition, A/FH/A/08/1-1855, LMA.
150 Hospital matron interview with Foundling Hospital enquirer, Rejected Foundling Hospital Petition, A/FH/A/08/1-1855, LMA.
151 Rejected Foundling Hospital Petition, A/FH/A/08/1-1855, LMA.
152 Rejected Foundling Hospital Petition, A/FH/A/08/1-1855, LMA.
153 For further discussion on rational choice making see Regenia Gagnier, *Subjectivities: A History of Self-Representation in Britain*, 1832–1920 (New York: Oxford University Press, 1991), pp. 59–62; Dina Copelman, 'Victorian Subjects', *Journal of British Studies* 34 (1995): 414.
154 Sarah F. to John Brownlow, 23 April 1853. Foundling Hospital Correspondence, A/FH/A/06/1-116/1-B, LMA.

Chapter Seven

1 Dickens, *Little Dorrit*, p. 56.
2 Charles Dickens and Wilkie Collins, 'No Thoroughfare' in *The Christmas Stories from All the Year Round* (London: Chapman and Hall, 1868).
3 Dickens and Collins, 'No Thoroughfare'.
4 See John Burnett, ed. *Destiny Obscure: Autobiographies of Childhood, Education, and Family from the 1820s to the 1920s* (London: A. Lane, 1982).
5 N = the database number for accepted and rejected petitions. Foundling Hospital Survey, A/FH/A/08/1-1842–1892, LMA. See coding sheet, appendix 9, Foundling Hospital Mothers' Literacy, 1842–92.
6 See appendix 2, Foundling Hospital Petition Form and appendix 3, Foundling Hospital Petition Form – insert.
7 Foundling Hospital Survey, A/FH/A/08/1, 1860–1892, LMA.
8 N = database figures. Foundling Hospital Survey, A/FH/A/08/1-1842–1892, LMA.
9 1820–1911 Foundling Hospital Reclamation and Inquiry Form, A/FH/A/01/3/1, LMA.
10 Foundling Hospital Parchments – A/FH/A/01/3/1, – LMA. Although eighteenth-century courts had not officially developed the legalities of adoption, and adoption cases would

not become an issue until the nineteenth century in England, the Foundling Hospital governors had legally adopted the accepted infants. McClure, *Coram's Children*, p. 48.

11 Walford, *Old and New London* 5:361; Commons, 'Select Committee on the Infant Life Protection Bill, 1890', vol. 13, par. 806–17, p. 41.
12 Foundling Hospital Bye laws and Regulations, A/FH/A/06/15/7, 1856, LMA.
13 N = database figures. Foundling Hospital Survey, A/FH/A8/1, 1842–1892, LMA.
14 See Table 4.4 FH Mothers' Occupations by Class, 1842–92.
15 Accepted Foundling Hospital Petition, A/FH/A/08/1-1842, LMA.
16 Accepted Foundling Hospital Petition, A/FH/A/08/1-1842, LMA.
17 Accepted Foundling Hospital Petition, A/FH/A/08/1-1852, LMA.
18 Sister Maria at St Mary Magdalene's Home to John Brownlow, Infant Died, Accepted Foundling Hospital Petition, A/FH/A/08/1-1866, LMA.
19 Sarah F. to John Brownlow, 6 April 1854, A/FH/A/06/1/115/1-B, LMA.
20 Anne H. to John Brownlow, n.d. A/FH/A/06/128, LMA.
21 Letters to Secretary, A/FH/A/06/1/116/67, 1861, LMA.
22 Foundling Hospital Mothers' Letters, A/FH/A/09/19/1-16/217, 1858, LMA.
23 Walford, *Old and New London* 5:360.
24 Foundling Hospital Mothers' Letters, A/FH/A/09/19/1-16/74, 76, 78, 87, c. 1861, LMA.
25 Foundling Hospital Mothers' Letters, A/FH/A/09/19/1-16/73, 1857, LMA.
26 Foundling Hospital Mothers' Letters, A/FH/A/09/19/1-16/8, 1873, LMA.
27 Foundling Hospital Mothers' Letters, A/FH/A/09/19/1-16/29, c. 1859, LMA.
28 Foundling Hospital Mothers' Letters, A/FH/A/09/19/1/158, 1861, LMA.
29 Foundling Hospital Mothers' Letters, A/FH/A/09/19/1-135, LMA.
30 Foundling Hospital Mothers' Letters, A/FH/A/09/19/1-16/61, LMA.
31 Foundling Hospital Mothers' Letters, A/FH/A/09/19/1-16/322, LMA; Accepted Foundling Hospital Petition, A/FH/A/08/1-1858, LMA.
32 Foundling Hospital Mothers' Letters, A/FH/A/09/19/1-16/403, LMA.
33 Foundling Hospital Mothers' Letters, A/FH/A/09/19/1-16/344, LMA.
34 Letters to Secretary, A/FH/A/06/1/116/411, 1859, LMA.
35 Letters to Secretary, A/FH/A/06/1/116/98, 1859, LMA.
36 Foundling Hospital Mothers' Letters, A/FH/A/09/19/1-16/61, LMA.
37 Letters to Secretary, A/FH/A/06/1/116/218, 1858, LMA.
38 Foundling Hospital Mothers' Letters, A/FH/A/09/19/1-16/208, LMA.
39 Foundling Hospital Mothers' Letters, A/FH/A/09/19/1-16/ 39, LMA.
40 Amelia H. to Secretary Brownlow, A/FH/A/06/1/116/10, 1858, LMA.
41 Amelia H. to Secretary Brownlow, A/FH/A/06/1/116/10, 1858, LMA.
42 Foundling Hospital Mothers' Letters, A/FH/A/09/19/1-16/237, LMA.
43 Letters to Secretary, A/FH/A/06/1/116/4, c. 1858, LMA.
44 Letters to Secretary, A/FH/A/06/1/116/11, 1859, LMA.
45 Dickens, *Household Words*, 51.
46 Foundling Hospital Registers, A/FH/A/09/2/1-4, LMA; Dickens, *Household Words*, 51.
47 Foundling Hospital Registers, A/FH/A/09/2/1-4, LMA; Dickens, *Household Words*, 51.
48 Morris Lievesley, 'Instruction to Medical Officers and Inspectors of the Infant Children in the Country', 14 April 1838, A/FH/A/01/8, 1838, LMA.

49 McClure, *Coram's Children*, pp. 80–1, 87.
50 Lievesley, 'Instruction to Medical Officers', A/FH/A.01/8, 1838, LMA.
51 Lievesley, 'Instruction to Medical Officers', A/FH/A.01/8, 1838, LMA.
52 Lievesley, 'Instruction to Medical Officers', A/FH/A.01/8, 1838, LMA.
53 Commons, 'Select Committee on Protection of Infant Life, 1871', vol. 7, par. 1746, p. 84.
54 The St George Hanover Square Board of Guardians charged the Sisters of Charity with neglect of the infants received at Carlisle Place in 1876. See 'Morality in a London Orphanage', *The Times*, 11 January 1877.
55 See Medical Officer of Health reports: J. J. Rygate, *Report to the Vestry of St George in the East, 1877* (London: J. and B. Dodsworth, 1881); Brougham Rygate, *Report to the Vestry of Saint George in the East, 1888* (London: J. and B. Dodson, 1891).
56 N = register figures. Foundling Hospital Admission Register, A/FH/A/09/3/2, 1842–1893, LMA.
57 Commons, 'Protection of Infant Life, 1871', vol. 7, par. 1746, p. 84.
58 Commons, 'Protection of Infant Life, 1871', vol. 7, par. 1899, p. 91.
59 N = register counts. Foundling Hospital Admission Register, A/FH/A/09/3/2, 1794–1893, LMA; and Commons, 'Protection of Infant Life', appendix, no. 3.
60 N = register counts. Foundling Hospital Admission Register, A/FH/A/09/3/2, 1794–1893, LMA; and Commons, 'Protection of Infant Life', appendix, no. 3.
61 Jonas, *Sentiments of an English Country Gentleman* (London, 1759), 33.
62 Although McClure does not provide a date marking the end of public exhibitions of children, it is probable Jonas Hanway stopped this practice when he took office in 1768. McClure, *Coram's Children*, p. 72.
63 McClure, *Coram's Children*, p. 148.
64 Thomas Bernard, *An Account of the Foundling Hospital in London, for the Maintenance and Education of Exposed and Deserted Young Children*, 2nd edn (London, 1799) as cited in McClure, *Coram's Children*, p. 148.
65 Walford, *Old and New London* 5: 361.
66 Walford, *Old and New London* 5: 361.
67 Nichols and Wray, *The History of the Foundling Hospital*, p. 155.
68 Nichols and Wray, *The History of the Foundling Hospital*, pp. 318–9.
69 Training in needlework for girls was discontinued ten years later than training for boys. Nichols and Wray, *The History of the Foundling Hospital*, pp. 318–21.
70 Commons, 'Brownlow, 'Analysis of the Expenditure, & c., 1863 (1869)', vol. 7, appendix no. 3, p. 241.
71 Commons, 'Brownlow, 'Analysis of the Expenditure, & c., 1863 (1869)', vol. 7 appendix, no. 3, p. 241, and appendix no. 4, p. 242
72 'The services of the Foundling Chapel commence as follows: Morning at 11.00, Afternoon at 1.00', *The Times*, 2 September 1871.
73 Foundling Hospital Secretary, W. M. Wintle, M. A., 'Charities & etc.', *The Times*, 6 July 1886.
74 'The services of the Foundling Chapel commence as follows: Morning at 11.00, Afternoon at 1.00', *The Times*, 2 September 1871.
75 Walford, *Old and New London* 5: 360.

76 Walford, *Old and New London* 5: 361.

77 One guinea equaled 21 shillings, five guineas equalled £5 5 s. Dickens, 'Received a Blank Child', 52.

78 In many respects, the history of the Foundling Hospital raises questions about the biological, legal and social understanding of 'parents'. Who and what determined the status of parent? Parenting is more than procreation, and entails taking responsibility for care of the child. Dickens, 'Received a Blank Child', 52.

79 Foundling House Admissions Register, A/FH/A/09/3/2, LMA.

80 Foundling Hospital Admissions Registers, 28 January 1784 – 12 December 1893, A/FH/A/09/3/2, LMA.

81 Foundling Hospital Mothers' Letters, A/FH/A/09/19/1-16/237, 1858, LMA.

82 Foundling Hospital Admission Register, A/FH/A/09/3/2, 1842–64, LMA.

83 Foundling Hospital Admissions Register, A/FH/A/09/3/2, LMA.

84 E. N. Fentiman to John Brownlow, Secretary's Correspondence, A/FH/A/06/1-116/4, 1859, LMA.

85 E. N. Fentiman to John Brownlow, Secretary's Correspondence, A/FH/A/06/1-116/4, 1859, LMA.

86 Dickens and Wills, 'Received a Blank Child', 49.

Appendices

1 Derek Rowntree, 'The Significance of Significance', *Statistics Without Tears: A Primer for Non-mathematicians* (London: Penguin Books, 1981), pp. 116; R. Lyman Ott, 'The Level of Significance of a Statistical Test', *An Introduction to Statistical Methods and Data Analysis*, 4th edn (Belmont, CA: Duxbury Press, 1993), pp. 230–4.

2 1856 Petition Form, A/FH/A/06/15/7, LMA.

3 1856 Petition Form, A/FH/A/06/15/7, LMA.

Bibliography

Unpublished Sources

London Metropolitan Archives, Clerkenwell

Chelsea Board of Guardians Deserted Women and Children Register, 1882–1891, Ch. B.G. 197/001.

Queen Charlotte's Lying-in Hospital, 1854 Annual Report, H27/QC/A/27.

Poplar and Stepney Sick Asylum Registers, 1881, 1891, 1901, SA/M/1/8.

St Mary Abbot's Baptismal Register, Kensington (West London) H17/SMA/G1/01–3, 1877– 1901.

Foundling Hospital Papers

Foundling Hospital Registers, A/FH/A/09/2/1–4.

Vol. 1 – 25 March 1741 – 28 February 1757.

Vol. 2 – 1 March 1757 – 30 June 1758.

Vol. 3 – 1 July 1758 – 12 May 1759.

Vol. 4 – 13 May 1759 – 3 Dec. 1777.

Foundling Hospital Admission Register, A/FH/A/09/3/2, 1794–1893.

Foundling Hospital Apprenticeship Register A/FH/A/12/3/3, 1851–1891.

Foundling Hospital Bye-Laws and Regulations, A/FH/A/06/015/7, 1856.

Foundling Hospital Chapel Seating Plan, 1840–1864, A/FH/A/14/8–49.

Foundling Hospital Chapel Seating Plan, Christmas 1852, A/FH/A/14/1.

Foundling Hospital Correspondence, Mothers' Letters, A/FH/A/09/12, 1857–1873.

Foundling Hospital Parchments, A/FH/A/01/3/1.

Foundling Hospital Petition Form, A/FH/A/08/1, 1813.

Foundling Hospital Petitions, A/FH/A/08–1, 1842–1892.

Foundling Hospital Secretary Morris Lievesley, 'Instruction to Medical Officers and Inspectors of Infant Children in the Country', 14 April 1838, A/FH/A/01/8, 1838.

Foundling Hospital Secretary's Correspondence, A/FH/A/06/1/116/1–16.

Foundling Hospital State of Children Daily A/FH/A/09/011/1–6, 1818–1905.

Foundling Hospital Table of Applications, A/FH/A/06/007, 1879–1906, uncatalogued.

Royal London Hospital Archives, Whitechapel

London Hospital Obstetrical and Gynaecological Case Book, LH/M/5/3.
Mile End Infirmary Obstetrical Register, St BG/ME/1-1-1899/8-8-1915.
Royal London Hospital Obstetric and Gynaecological Case Book, LH/M/118/1901.

Westminster Diocesan Archives, Kensington

Father Seddon's Poor Law Correspondence, Folios 1–22.
Saint Patrick's Wapping, 1893 Westminster Diocesan Census.

Eighteenth- and Nineteenth-Century Published Sources

Newspaper and Journals

Belgravia, 1866–99.
Household Words, 1850–59.
The Catholic Times and Opinion, 1877.
The Gentleman's Magazine, 1736–39, 1744–83.
The Globe, 1877.
The Mirror of Parliament, 1834.
The Penny Magazine, 1831–35.
The Saturday Review, 1855–1901.
The Times (London), 1788–1901.

Government Documents

Board of Trade. Clara Collet. 'Wages of Domestic Servants Servants. A Report on the Money Wages of Indoor Domestic Servants', *Sessional Papers*, 1899, Board of Trade, vol. 112.

House of Commons. 'Sir Richard Lloyd Speech, Resolutions of the Commons Respecting the State of the Poor and of the Poor Laws, 30 May 1759'. *Parliamentary History*, Commons, vol. 15, cols 941–3.

House of Commons. 'Population: Comparative Account of the Population of Great Britain in the Years 1801, 1911, 1821 and 1831: with the annual value of Real property in the year 1815: also, A Statement of Progress in the Inquiry regarding the Occupations of Families and Persons, and the Duration of Life'. *Sessional Papers*, 1831, Census, vol. 8.

House of Commons. 'Answers to Town Queries, Report from His Majesty's Commissioners for Inquiring into the Administration and Practical Operation of the Poor Laws', *Sessional Papers*, 1834, Poor Laws, vols 10–11.

House of Commons. 'Bastardy', First Report from the Poor Law Commissioners, Appendix A', *Sessional Papers*, 1834, Poor Laws, vol. 8.

House of Commons. 'Sixteenth Recommendation', Poor Law Amendment Bill, First Report from the Poor Law Commissioners', *Sessional Papers*, 1835 Poor Laws, vol. 8.

House of Commons. 'Seventeenth Recommendation', Poor Law Amendment Bill, First Report from the Poor Law Commissioners', *Sessional Papers*, 1835, Poor Laws, vol. 8.

House of Commons. 'Eighteenth Recommendation', Poor Law Amendment Bill, First Report from the Poor Law Commissioners', *Sessional Papers*, 1835, Poor Laws, vol. 8.

House of Commons, 'Twentieth Recommendation', Poor Law Amendment Bill, First Report from the Poor Law Commissioners', *Sessional Papers*, 1835, Poor Laws, vol. 8.

House of Commons. 'Report from the Select Committee on Poor Relief, Minutes of Evidence', *Sessional Papers*, 1862, Poor Laws, vol. 26.

House of Commons. 'Report from the Select Committee on Poor Relief, Minutes of Evidence', *Sessional Papers*, 1864, Poor Laws, vol. 9.

House of Commons. 'Select Committee on Protection of Infant Life', *Sessional Papers*, 1872, Protection of Infant Life Hearings, vol. 7.

House of Commons. 'Select Committee on Protection of Infant Life', *Sessional Papers*, 1890, Protection of Infant Life Hearings, vol. 13.

Parliament. Report of the Royal Commission on the Poor Laws and Relief of Distress. Cd.4499, 1909.

Poor Law Commission. *Extracts from the Information Received by His Majesty's Commissioners, as to the Administration and Operation of the Poor Laws.* (London: B. Fellowes, 1833).

Eighteenth- and Nineteenth-Century Books, Pamphlets and Journal Articles

Acton, William. 'Observations on Illegitimacy in the London Parishes of St Marylebone, St Pancras, and St George's, Southward during the Year 1857', *Journal of the Statistical Society of London* 21 (1859): 491–505.

Booth, Charles. *Conditions and Occupations of the People of The Tower Hamlets, 1886–1887.* (London: Edward Stanford, 1887).

—'Life and Labour of the People in London: First Results of an Inquiry

Based on the 1891 Census'. In *Opening Address Delivered Before the Royal Statistical Society, 1893*. (London: Charles Booth, 1893).

—*Life and Labour of the People in London*. First Series: Poverty, 4 vols. (London: Macmillan and Co., 1902).

—*Life and Labour of the People in London*. Third Series: Religious Influences, 7 vols. (London: Macmillan, 1902).

—*Life and Labour of the People in London*. Second Series: Industry, 5 vols. (London: Macmillan and Co., 1903).

—*Life and Labour of the People in London*. Concluding volume. (London: Macmillan and Co., 1903).

—*Poor Law Reform*. (London: Macmillan and Co., 1916).

Booth, William. *In Darkest England and the Way Out*. (Chicago: Charles H. Sergel & Co., 1890).

Brownlow, John. *Memoranda: Or Chronicles of the Foundling Hospital, Including Memoirs of Captain Coram*. (London: Sampson Low, 1847).

—*The History and Objects of the Foundling Hospital with a Memoir of the Founder*. In *The History of the Foundling Hospital* by R. H. Nichols and F. A. Wray. (London, 1881; repr. Oxford University Press, 1935).

Collet, Clara. 'Women's Work', in *Life and Labor of the People in London*, First Series: Poverty. 4 vols. (London: Macmillan and Co., 1902).

—*Report on the Money Wages of indoor Domestic Servants. Presented to Parliament by Command of Her Majesty*. (London: H. M. Stationery Office, 1899).

Cleveland, Arthur Rackham. *Woman under the English Law*. (London, 1896; repr. Littleton, CO: Fred B. Rothman, 1987).

Craigie, Major P. G. 'The English Poor Rate and Recent Statistics of its Administration and Pressure, Read before the Royal Statistical Society'. *Journal of the Royal Statistical Society* (1888): 450–93.

Davey, Richard. *The Pageant of London, 1500 to 1900 AD*. vol. 2. (London: Methuen & Co., 1906).

Dickens, Charles. *Oliver Twist*. Norton Critical Edition, edited by Fred Kaplan. (London, 1838; repr. New York: W. W. Norton, 1993).

—'Received a Blank Child'. *Household Words* 1 (1850): 49–53.

—'A Walk in a Workhouse'. *Household Words* 1 (1850): 330–2.

—'Home for Homeless Women'. *Household Words* 7 (1853): 169–75.

—*Little Dorrit*. Edited by John Holloway. (London, 1857; repr. London: Penguin Books, 1967).

—*Our Mutual Friend*. (London, 1865; repr. New York: Signet Classic, 1964).

—and W. H. Wills. 'Received a Blank Child'. *Household Words* 7 (1853): 49–53.

—and Wilkie Collins. *No Thoroughfare: A Drama in Five Acts*. (London: Chapman, 1868).

Dickens, Charles. Madeline House, and Graham Storey, eds. *Letters of Charles Dickens*. 7 vols. (Oxford: Clarendon Press, 1965–2002).

Downright, Dora. *Why I Am a Guardian*. Gerritsen Collection. (Manchester: Headley Bros., 1888).

Eversley, William Pinder. *The Law of Domestic Relations*. (London: Stevens and Haynes, 1906).

Fowle, T. W. *The Poor Law: The English Citizen, His Rights and Responsibilities*. (London: Macmillan, 1893).

Greenwood, James. *The Seven Curses of London*. (Boston: Fields, Osgood & Co., 1869).

Hanway, Jonas. 'The Genuine Sentiments of an English Country Gentleman upon the Present Plan of the Foundling Hospital'. (London, 1759).

—'The Rules, Orders, and Regulations of the Magdalene House for the General Reception of Prostitutes'. (London, 1759).

—'Thoughts on the Plan for A Magdalen-House for Repentant Prostitutes'. (London, 1759).

Hardinge, Stanley Giffard, Earl of Halsbury. *Laws of England: A Complete Statement of the Whole Law of England*. vol. 2 (London: Butterworth and Co., 1908).

Hart, Ernest. *The Protection of Infant Life: An Inquiry into the Practice of Baby Farming, With Suggestions for the Protection of Infants*. (London: British Medical Association, 1871).

Hessey, James Augustus. 'Sermon to the Governors of the Foundling Hospital. The Tenderness of Christ towards Sinners'. London, 1862. (London Guildhall pamphlet, #6155).

Hunt, Frederick Knight. 'The Registrar-General on "Life" in London'. *Household Words* 1 (1850): 330–2.

Levis, Marquis de. *England at the Beginning of the Nineteenth Century*. Trans. by M. De Levis. (London: D. Jacques, 1851).

Lumley, W. G. 'Observations upon the Statistics of Illegitimacy'. *Journal of the Statistical Society of London* 25 (1862): 219–63.

Longley, Henry. *Report to the Local Government Board on Poor Law Administration in London*. (London: Local Government Board, 1874).

London County Council. *County Council Lists of the Streets and Places Within the Administrative County of London*. (London: P. S. King and Son, 1901).

Mackay, Thomas. *A History of the English Poor Law, from 1834 to the Present Time: Being a Supplementary Volume to 'A History of the English Poor Law' by Sir George Nicholls, K. C. B.*, rev. ed., 3 vols. (London, 1900; repr. New York, Augustus M. Kelley, 1967).

Malthus, Thomas Robert. *An Essay on the Principle of Population*. (London, 1799; repr. Ann Arbor: University of Michigan Press, 1959).

Mayhew, Henry. *The Morning Chronicle Survey of Labour and the Poor, 1850–52*. 6 vols. Edited by P. Razzell. (Firle, Sussex: Caliban Books, 1980).

Mayhew, Henry and Augustus. *The Greatest Plague of Life: Or The Adventures of a Lady in Search of a Good Servant*. (Philadelphia: Carey and Hart, 1847).

Mearns, Andrew. *The Bitter Cry of Outcast London*. (London: J. Clarke, 1883).

Mill, John Stuart. *Principles of Political Economy: With Some of Their Applications to Social Philosophy*. 2 vols. (New York: B. Appleton and Company, 1890).

—'The Subjection of Women'. In *Feminism: The Essential Historical Writings*. Edited by Miriam Schneir. (New York: Vintage Books, 1994).

Nicholls, Sir George. *A History of the English Poor Laws*. 2 vols. (London, 1854–56; repr. New York: Augustus M. Kelley, 1967).

Nicholls, George, et. al., *A History of the English Poor Law: A. D. 1714 to 1853*, vol. 2 (London: P. S. King and Son, 1904).

Rygate, Brougham. *Report to the Vestry of Saint George in the East, 1888* (London: J. and B. Dodson, 1891).

Rygate, John James. *Annual Report to the Vestry of Saint George in the East*. (London: J. and B. Dodsworth, 1883).

Shepherd, Thomas H. *London and Its Environs in the Nineteenth Century*. (London, 1829; repr. New York: Benjamin Blom, 1968).

Smith, Adam. *An Enquiry into the Nature and Causes of the Wealth of Nations*. (London, 1776; repr. New York: Modern Library, 1937).

Taine, Hippolyte. *Notes on England*. (London: Holt & Williams, 1872).

Thornbury, Walter. 'London Squares, Bloomsbury, and Bedford Squares'. *Belgravia* 2 (1867): 325–37.

—'London Parks, St James's Park Hyde Park'. *Belgravia* 3 (1867): 410–20.

—'London Palaces, St James's Palace-Carlton House-Buckingham Palace'. *Belgravia* 5 (1868): 184–92.

Timbs, John. *Curiosities of London: Exhibiting the Most Rare and Remarkable Objects of Interest in the Metropolis; with Nearly Sixty Years' Personal Recollections*. (London, 1867; repr. Detroit, Michigan: Singing Tree Press, 1968).

Walford, Edward. *London: Old and New: A Narrative of Its History, Its People, and Its Places*. 6 vols. (London: Cassell Petter and Galpin, 1868–77).

Webb, Sidney, and Beatrice Webb. *English Poor Law Policy*. (London: Longmans, Green, 1913).

—*English Local Government: English Poor Law History: Part I: The Old Poor Laws*. 1906, reprint. Private Subscription, Limited Edition, #67 edn. (London: Beatrice and Sidney Webb, 1929).

—*English Local Government: English Poor Law History: Part II, The Last*

Hundred Years. Private Subscription, 67/450 edn. (1906; repr. London: Beatrice and Sidney Webb, 1929).

Woods, Robert Archey. *English Social Movements*. (New York: Charles Scribner's Sons, 1891).

Contemporary Monographs, Edited Collections and Journal Articles

Anderson, Benedict. *Imagined Communities, Reflections on the Origin and Spread of Nationalism*. (London: Verso, 1991).

Anderson, Michael. 'Population Change in North-Western Europe, 1750–*1850*'. In *British Population History: From the Black Death to the Present Day*. Edited by Michael Anderson. (Cambridge: Cambridge University Press, 1996).

Baker, J. H. *An Introduction to English Legal History*. 3rd edn (London: Butterworths, 1990).

Barret-Ducrocq, Françoise. *Love in the Time of Victoria: Sexuality and Desire Among Working-Class Men and Women in Nineteenth-Century London*. Translated by John Howe. 2nd edn (London: Penguin Books, 1991).

Brundage, Anthony. *The Making of the New Poor Laws: The Politics of Inquiry, Enactment, and Implementation, 1832–1839*. (New Brunswick, NJ: Rutgers University Press, 1978).

Burton, Antoinette. *Burdens of Empire: British Feminists, Indian Women, and Imperial Culture, 1865–1915*. (Chapel Hill: University of North Carolina Press, 1994).

Cannon, John. *Aristocratic Century: The Peerage of Eighteenth-Century England*, Wiles Lecture Series. (New York: Cambridge University Press, 1987).

Clark, Anna. *Women's Silence, Men's Violence: Sexual Assault in England, 1770–1845*. (London: Pandora Press, 1987).

—*The Struggle for the Breeches: Gender and the Making of the English Working Class*. (Berkeley: University of California Press, 1995).

Cleminson, Fraser. *Beyond Recall: The Making of Mile End Hospital*. (London: Tower Hamlets Arts Project, 1983).

Colley, Linda. *Britons: The Forging of the Nation, 1707–1837*. (New Haven: Yale University Press, 1992).

Collini, Stefan. *Public Moralists: Political Thought and Intellectual Life in Britain, 1850–1930*. (Oxford: Clarendon Press, 1993).

Copelman, Dina. 'Victorian Subjects'. *The Rise of Popular Literacy in Victorian England: The Influence of Private Choice and Public Policy. Journal of British Studies* 34 (1995): 412–22.

Cornish, William R. and George Norman Clark. *Law and Society in England, 1750–1950*. (London: Sweet & Maxwell, 1989).

Craig, F. W. S. ed. *The Parliaments of England, 1715–1847*. (Chichester: Political Reference Publishing, 1973).

Crowther, Mary Ann. *The Workhouse System, 1834–1929: The History of an English Social Institution*. (London: Methuen, 1981).

Dewhurst, Sir John. *Queen Charlotte's, The Story of a Hospital*. (London: Queen Charlotte's Hospital, 1989).

Draper, Nicholas. *The Price of Emancipation: Slave Ownership, Compensation and British Society at the End of Slavery*. (Cambridge: Cambridge University Press, 2010).

Dunkley, Peter. *The Crisis of the Old Poor Law in England, 1795–1834: An Interpretive Essay*. (New York: Garland, 1982).

Edsall, Nicholas C. *The Anti-Poor Law Movement, 1834–1844*. (Totowa, NJ: Rowan and Littlefield, Inc., 1971).

Eley, Geoffrey. 'Introduction'. In *The History of Everyday Life: Reconstructing Historical Experiences and Ways of Life*. Edited by Alf Lüdtke and translated by William Templer. (Princeton: Princeton University Press, 1995).

Foucault, Michel. *The History of Sexuality, the Use of Pleasure*. (London: Penguin Books, 1990).

Fraser, Derek. 'Introduction'. In *The New Poor Law in the Nineteenth Century*. (New York: St Martin's Press, 1976).

Frost, Ginger S. *Promises Broken: Courtship, Class and Gender in Victorian England*. (Charlottesville: University of Virginia Press, 1995).

Fry, Herbert. *Royal Guide to the Principal London and Other Charities*. (London: Churchman Publishing Col, Ltd., 1939).

Gagnier, Regenia. *Subjectivities: A History of Self-Representation in Britain, 1832–1920*. (New York: Oxford University Press, 1991).

Giddens, Anthony. *New Rules of Sociological Method: A Positive Critique of Interpretative Sociologies*. (New York: Basic Books, Inc., 1976).

—*The Constitution of Society*. (Berkeley: University of California Press, 1984).

—*Politics, Sociology, and Social Theory: Encounters with Classical and Contemporary Social Thought*. (Cambridge: Polity Press, 1995).

Gillis, John. 'Servants, Sexual Relations and the Risks of Illegitimacy in London, 1801–1900'. In *Sex and Class in Women's History*. Edited by Judith Newton, Mary P. Ryan and Judith Walkowitz. (London: Routledge and Kegan Paul, 1983).

Green, David R. *From Artisans to Paupers: Economic Change and Poverty in London, 1790–1870*. (Aldershot, Hants.: Scolar Press, 1995).

—*Pauper Capital: London and the Poor Law, 1790–1870* (Farnham: Ashgate, 2010).

Hall, Catherine, and Leonore Davidoff. *Family Fortunes: Men and Women of the English Middle Class, 1780–1850*. (Chicago: University of Chicago Press, 1987).

Henriques, Ursula R. Q. *Before the Welfare State: Social Administration in Early Industrial Britain*. (London: Longman, 1979).

Himmelfarb, Gertrude. *The Idea of Poverty: England in the Early Industrial Age*. (New York: Alfred A. Knopf, 1983).

—*Marriage and Morals Among the Victorian and Other Essays*. (London: I. B. Tauris, 1989).

—*Poverty and Compassion: The Moral Imagination of the Late Victorians*. (New York: Vintage Books, 1992).

Holdsworth, Sir William. *A History of English Law: The Centuries of Settlement and Reform*. vol. 10. (London, 1936; repr. London: Methuen & Co Ltd, Sweet and Maxwell, 1966).

Jackson, Mark. *New-Born Child Murder: Women, Illegitimacy, and the Courts in Eighteenth-Century England*. (Manchester: Manchester University Press, 1996).

Knott, John. *Popular Opposition to the 1834 Poor Law*. (New York: St Martin's Press, 1986).

Koven, Seth. *Slumming: Sexual and Social Politics in Victorian London*. (Princeton, NJ: Princeton University Press, 2004, 2006).

Laqueur, Thomas. *Making Sex: Body and Gender from the Greeks to Freud*. (Cambridge: Harvard University Press, 1990).

—'Sexual Desire and the Market Economy during the Industrial Revolution'. In *Discourses of Sexuality: From Aristotle to Aids*. Edited by D. Stanton. (Ann Arbor, MI: University of Michigan Press, 1992).

Laslett, Peter. 'Introduction'. In *Bastardy and Its Comparative History*. Edited by Peter Laslett and Richard M. Smith. (Cambridge: Harvard University Press, 1980).

—'*The Bastardy Prone Sub-Society*'. In *Bastardy and its Comparative History*. Edited by Peter Laslett and Richard M. Smith. (Cambridge: Harvard University Press, 1980).

Lefebvre, Henri. *The Production of Space*. Translated by Donald Nicholson-Smith. (Oxford: Blackwell, 1991).

Lerner, Gerda. *The Creation of Feminist Consciousness: from the Middle Ages to Eighteen-Seventy*. (Oxford: Oxford University Press, 1993).

Levene, Alysa. *Childcare, Health, and Mortality at the London Foundling Hospital*. (New York: Manchester University Press, 2007).

Lewis, Jane. *Women in England, 1870–1950*. (Bloomington: Indiana University Press, 1984).

McClure, Ruth. *Coram's Children: The London Hospital in the Eighteenth Century*. (New Haven: Yale University Press, 1981).

Mandler, Peter, ed. *The Uses of Charity: The Poor on Relief in the Nineteenth-Century Metropolis*. (Philadelphia: University of Pennsylvania Press, 1990).

Marks, Lara V. 'Irish and Jewish Women's Experience of Childbirth and Infant Care in East London, 1870–1939: The Responses of Host Society and Immigrant Communities to Medical Welfare Needs'. D. Phil. (Oxford: Oxford University, 1990).

—*Mothers, Babies and Hospitals: 'The London' and the Provision of Maternity Care in East London, 1870–1939*. In *Women and Children First: International Maternal and Infant Welfare, 1870–1945*. Edited by Valerie Fildes, Lara Marks and Hilary Marland. (London: Routledge, 1992).

—*Model Mothers: Jewish Mothers and Maternity Provision in East London, 1870–1939*. (Oxford: Clarendon Press, 1994).

Massey, Doreen. *Space, Place and Gender*. (Cambridge: Polity Press, 1994).

Matus, Jill L. *Unstable Bodies: Victorian Representations of Sexuality and Maternity*. (Manchester: Manchester University Press, 1995).

Mintz, Steven. *A Prison of Expectations: The Family in Victorian Culture*. (New York: New York University Press, 1983).

Nichols, R. H., and F. A. Wray. *The History of the Foundling Hospital*. (London: Oxford University Press, 1935).

Olsen, Donald. *The Growth of Victorian London*. (London: B. T. Batsford, 1976).

Owen, David. *English Philanthropy, 1660–1960*. (Cambridge, MA: Belknap Press, 1964).

Parry, Jonathan. *The Rise and Fall of Liberal Government in Victorian Britain*. (New Haven: Yale University Press, 1996).

Perkin, Joan. *Women and Marriage in Nineteenth-Century England*. (Chicago: Lyceum Books, 1989).

Peterson, M. Jeanne. 'The Victorian Governess: Status Incongruence in Family and Society'. *Suffer and Be Still: Women in the Victorian Age*. Edited by Martha Vicinus. (Bloomington: Indiana University Press, 1973).

Poovey, Mary. *Making a Social Body: British Cultural Formation, 1830–1864*. (Chicago: Chicago University Press, 1995).

Porter, Roy. *London: a Social History*. (London: Hamish Hamilton, 1994).

Pugh, Gillian. *London's Forgotten Children: Thomas Coram and the Foundling Hospital*. (London: The History Press, 2007).

Rasmussen, Steen Eiler. *London: The Unique City*. (Cambridge, MA: Massachusetts Institute of Technology Press, 1967).

Rivett, Geoffrey. *The Development of the London Hospital System, 1823–1982*. King's Fund Historical Series No. 4. (London: King Edward's Hospital Fund for London, 1986).

Rose, Lionel. *The Massacre of the Innocents: Infanticide in Britain, 1800–1939*. (London: Routledge, 1986).

Rose, Michael E. *The English Poor Law, 1780–1930*. (New York: Barnes & Noble, Inc., 1971).

Rose, Sonya. *Limited Livelihoods: Gender and Class in Nineteenth-Century England.* (Berkeley and Los Angeles: University of California Press, 1992).

Ross, Ellen. *Love and Toil: Motherhood in Outcast London, 1870–1918.* (New York: Oxford University Press, 1993).

Said, Edward W. *Orientalism.* 1st edn (New York: Pantheon, 1978).

—*Culture and Imperialism.* 1st edn (New York: Knopf, 1993).

Sandoz, Ellis, ed. *The Roots of Liberty: Magna Carta, Ancient Constitution and the Anglo-American Tradition of Rule of Law.* (Columbia: University of Missouri Press, 1993).

Sheppard, Francis W. *London, 1808–1870: The Infernal Wen.* (Berkeley: University of California Press, 1971).

Shields, Rob. *Places on the Margin, Alternative Geographies of Modernity.* (London: Routledge, 1991).

Soja, Edward W. *Postmodern Geographies: The Reassertion of Space in Critical Social Theory.* (London: Verso, 1989).

Spain, Daphne. *Gendered Spaces.* (Chapel Hill: University of North Carolina Press, 1992).

Stedman Jones, Gareth. *Outcast London: A Study of the Relationship between Classes in Victorian Society.* (Oxford, 1971; repr. London: Penguin Books, 1984).

—and David Feldman (eds), *Metropolis London: Histories and Representations since 1800.* (London: Routledge, 1989).

Stone, Lawrence. *The Family, Sex and Marriage in England, 1500–1800.* (New York: Harper and Row, 1977).

Szreter, Simon R. S. *Fertility, Class and Gender in Britain, 1860–1940.* (Cambridge: Cambridge University Press, 1996).

Teichman, Jenny. *Illegitimacy: An Examination of Bastardy.* (Ithaca: Cornell University Press, 1982).

Thane, Pat. *The Origins of British Social Policy.* (London: Croom and Helm, 1978).

Thompson, E. P. *The Making of the English Working Class.* (New York: Pantheon Books, 1964).

Thompson, F. M. L. *The Rise of Respectable Society: A Social History of Victorian Britain, 1830–1900.* (Cambridge: Harvard University Press, 1988).

Tilly, Louise A. and Joan Wallach Scott. *Women, Work and Family.* (New York: Routledge, 1989).

Tosh, John. 'The Strengths and Weaknesses of Analytical History'. *The Pursuit of History.* 4th edn (Harlow: Pearson Longman, 2006).

Walkowitz, Judith R. *Prostitution and Victorian Society: Women, Class and the State.* (Cambridge: Cambridge University Press, 1980).

—*City of Dreadful Delight: Narratives of Sexual Danger in Late-Victorian London.* (London: Virago, 1992).

Watkins, Susan Cotts. *From Provinces into Nations: Demographic Integration in Western Europe, 1870–1960.* (Princeton: Princeton University Press, 1991).

Weinreb, Ben and Christopher Hibbert. *The London Encyclopaedia.* (Bethesda, MD: Adler and Adler Publishers, Inc., 1986).

Wiener, Martin J. *Reconstructing the Criminal: Culture, Law, and Policy in England, 1830–1914.* (Cambridge: Cambridge University Press, 1990).

Wilson, Adrian, ed. *Rethinking Social History: English Society, 1570–1920 and Its Interpretation.* (Manchester: Manchester University Press, 1993).

Woods, Robert I. 'The Population of Britain in the Nineteenth Century'. In *British Population History: From the Black Death to the Present* Day. Edited by Michael Anderson. (Cambridge: Cambridge University Press, 1996).

Journal Articles

Anderson, Michael. 'Marriage Patterns in Victorian Britain: An Analysis Based on Registration District Data for England and Wales, 1861'. *Journal of Family History* 1 (1976): 55–78.

Arnot, Margaret L. 'Infant Death, Childcare, and the State: The Baby-farming Scandal and the First Infant Life Protection Legislation of 1872'. *Continuity and Change* 9 (1994): 271–311.

Atkins, P. J. 'How the West Was Won: The Struggle to Remove Street Barriers in Victorian London'. *Journal of Historical Geography* 19 (1993): 265–77.

Barkan, Elazar. 'Post-anti-colonial Histories: Representing the Other'. *Journal of British Studies* 33 (1994): 180–203.

Bourne Taylor, Jenny. '"Received a Blank Child": John Brownlow, Charles Dickens, and the London Foundling Hospital – Archives and Fictions'. *Nineteenth Century Literature* 56 (2001): 293–363.

Chodorow, Nancy J. 'Gender as a Personal and Cultural Construction'. *Signs* 20 (1995): 516–44.

Finnane, Antonia. 'The Origins of Prejudice: The Malintegration of Subei in Late Imperial China'. *Comparative Studies in Society and History* 35 (1993): 211–48.

Gillis, John. 'Servants, Sexual Relations, and the Risks of Illegitimacy in London, 1801–1900'. *Feminist Studies* 5 (1979): 142–73.

Gregson, Mary Eschelbach. 'Population Dynamics in Rural Missouri, 1860–1880'. *Social Science History* 21 (1997): 85–110.

Harris, Jose. 'Enterprise and Welfare States: A Comparative Perspective'. *Transactions of the Royal Historical Society* (1990): 175–95.

Henriques, Ursula R. Q. 'Bastardy and the New Poor Law'. *Past and Present* 37 (1967): 103–29.

Higginbotham, Ann. 'Sin of the Age: Infanticide and Illegitimacy in Victorian London'. *Victorian Studies* 32 (1989): 319–37.

MacKinnon, Mary. 'English Poor Law Policy and the Crusade Against Outrelief'. *The Journal of Economic History* 63 (1987): 603–25.

Mumm, Susan. '"Not Worse Than Other Girls": The Convent-Based Rehabilitation of Fallen Women in Victorian Britain'. *Journal of Social History* 29 (1996): 527–46.

Prasch, Thomas J. 'Orientalism's Other, Other Otherientalism: Women in the Scheme of Empire'. *Journal of Women's History* 7 (1995): 174–190.

Robin, Jean. 'Prenuptial Pregnancy in a Rural Area of Devonshire in the Mid-Nineteenth Century: Colyton, 1851–1881'. *Continuity and Change* 1 (1986): 113–24.

—'Illegitimacy in Colyton, 1851–1881'. *Continuity and Change* 2 (1987): 307–42.

Ross, Ellen. 'Survival Networks: Women's Neighbourhood Sharing in London Before World War I'. *History Workshop* 15 (1983): 4–27.

Scott, Joan. 'Gender: A Useful Category of Historical Analysis'. *American Historical Review* 91 (1986): 1053–75.

Sheppard, Francis. 'London and the Nation in the Nineteenth Century'. *Transactions of the Royal Historical Society*. 35 (1985): 51–74.

Szreter, Simon R. S. 'The Genesis of the Registrar-General's Social Classification of Occupations'. *The British Journal of Sociology* 35 (1984): 522–46.

Thane, Pat. 'Women and the Poor Law in Victorian and Edwardian England'. *History Workshop* 6 (1978): 29+ 31–51.

Thompson, F. M. L. 'Social Control in Victorian Britain'. *Economic History Review* 34 (1981): 189–208.

—'Moving Frontiers and the Fortunes of the Aristocratic Town House 1830–1930'. *The London Journal* 17 (1995): 67–78.

Tilly, Louise A. 'Connections (The Legacy of Social Historian E. P. Thompson)'. *American Historical Review* 99 (1994): 1–20.

Waterfield, Giles. 'The Town House as Gallery of Art'. *The London Journal* 20 (1995): 47–66.

Wilson, Adrian, 'Illegitimacy and Its Implications in Mid-Eighteenth-Century London: the Evidence of the Foundling Hospital'. *Continuity and Change* 4 (1988): 103–64.

Woods, R. I. and P. R. A. Hinde. 'Nuptiality and Age at Marriage in Nineteenth Century England', *Journal of Family History* 9 (1985): 119–44.

Index